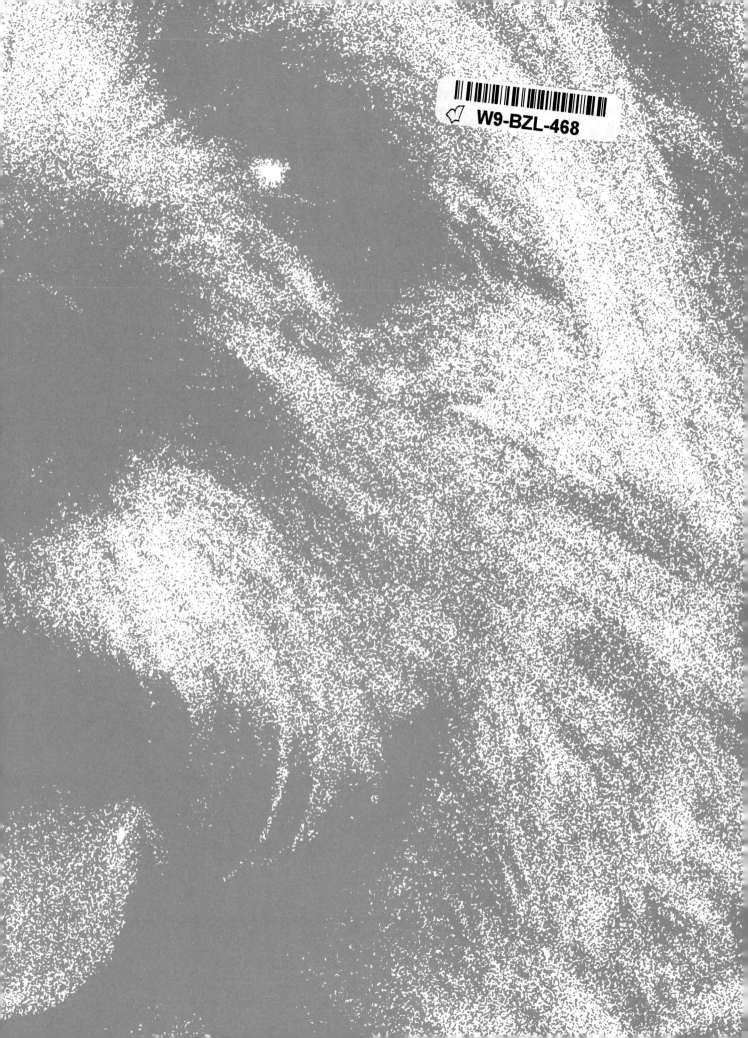

COMPLETE ILLUSTRATED
Guide to
DOG
CARE

COMPLETE ILLUSTRATED
guide to
DOG
CARE

THUNDER BAY
P·R·E·S·S

San Diego, California

ThunderBay
P·R·E·S·S

Thunder Bay Press
An imprint of the Advantage Publishers Group
5880 Oberlin Drive
San Diego, CA 92121-4794
www.thunderbaybooks.com

SECTION ONE

Project Editor Candida Ross-Macdonald
Art Editor Nigel Hazle
Production Manager Maryann Rogers
U.S. Editor Mary Ann Lynch

SECTION TWO

Project Editors Alison Melvin, Lynn Parr
Art Editors Hazel Taylor, Nigel Hazle
Computer page make-up Patrizio Semproni
Production Controller Antony Heller
U.S. Editor Mary Ann Lynch

The ASPCA and Dog Care by Roger Caras, President, ASPCA

3   4   5   6   7   06   05   04   03   02

Library of Congress Cataloging-in-Publication Data

Fogle, Bruce
    [ASPCA complete dog care manual]
    The complete illustrated guide to dog care and behavior / Bruce
Fogle: foreword by Roger Caras.
        p.   cm.
    Originally published: ASPCA complete dog care manual. 1st American
ed. London: Dorling Kindersley, 1993. And Know your dog: an owner's guide
to dog behavior 1st American ed. 1991
        Includes index.
        ISBN 1-57145-185-4
        1. Dogs. 2. Dogs--Behavior. I. Title.
SF427.F615 1993b
    636.7'0887--dc21   99-12151
                                                              CIP

CONTENTS

THE WOLF AT THE DOOR

I T COMES AS no surprise to those of us who share our homes with dogs that their species, *Canis familiaris*, is in many ways much like ours. We are both predators, surviving by preying upon other animals. Both of us are social animals that enjoy the companionship of others of our own species, and pack animals to the very depths of our being. We work well together and, for better or worse, are most contented either when we have leaders to follow and respect, or when we become leaders ourselves. Our two species have a diverse range of emotions and can feel jealousy, affection, anger, or tolerance toward others of their kind. Our needs are so similar that, of all the animal species that ever evolved, the dog was the first to be invited into our homes. It is due to its behavioral characteristics, as well as its usefulness, that the dog has become "man's best friend."

One of a crowd
Although their appearances and temperaments vary, all of these dogs are pack animals, needing social contact to thrive.

Appealing
We have created some breeds that particularly appeal to us, like the Australian Silky Terrier.

Dogs accompanied us from primitive campsites to agricultural settlements and even to the massive cities in which we live today. They made these transitions so successfully because they are highly effective at adapting to changing conditions. A dramatically wide range of shapes and sizes helped them through these transitions, but it is their varied natures that have made dogs the most popular pet in the world today.

We sometimes confuse what suits us in a dog's behavior with what is naturally best for the dog itself, making the mistake of thinking that the more trainable a dog is, the more intelligent it is. In fact, the intractable stray dog that survives by its own wits might be more intelligent than the dog who jumps through hoops at its owner's command. My retrievers, lying on the floor by my side, are not the result of natural survival of the fittest. Although they are large and strong, they would be too gentle to survive for long in the wild.

In order to know your dog completely, it is vital to understand that, just as we sometimes think of our canine companions as humans in strange disguises, they think of us as rather odd dogs. We might be bigger than them, we certainly smell different, and we are able to do awesome things like use can openers, but they can still only think of us as other dogs and treat us accordingly. Their relationships with us are all based on this fact.

Born fighting
Some dogs have been bred as fighting dogs for sport. If we keep these breeds, we must understand what motivates them.

KNOW YOUR DOG

A GUIDE TO DOG BEHAVIOR

THE PACK INSTINCT

THE PACK MENTALITY of hunting, resting, eating, and sleeping together is what has made dogs so successful as a species. This mentality comes from their wolf forebears. Throughout the Northern Hemisphere, wolves radiated out after the last Ice Age, following the herds of large, hoofed animals that were their prey. We humans did the same, the only other social species to migrate north at that time. Young wolves were captured, raised, and played with by our ancestors, who selected which individuals they would eat, and which they would allow to breed.

Just as in the wild, superior size and mental acuity decided who would lead in the pack hierarchy of the dogs that evolved as a result of this human selection. In both situations, males usually dominate because of physical strength. Ritual threats, such as growling and showing the teeth,

Paying respect
This West Highland White Terrier shows submissive behavior by jumping up to lick the Italian Spinone's mouth. Dogs show similar submissive feelings when they try to lick our faces.

Choosing a leader
These Yorkshire Terriers gather around someone they have never met, knowing from experience that humans are excellent pack leaders.

Two's company
Having sensed something, these two Miniature Schnauzers concentrate intently. A natural pack contains a leader and several followers, but it only takes two to make a dog pack.

Team practice
These Norwegian Buhunds naturally coordinate their activities, like the packs of wolves from which they evolved. Resting, waking, and being active together enables them to work as a team.

prevent serious fights and maintain rank and hierarchy. Dogs first learn these rituals and find their place in the pack during play as puppies. Rough-and-tumbles become rougher as the puppies mature, leading to disputes that are won by the strongest in body and spirit. Eventually the most dominant dog emerges, asserting his authority through his body language. Other pack members are usually content to submit to their leader, and indicate this through their own gestures and expressions, although eventually a spirited younger male will challenge the leader's authority.

Other behavior patterns that we see in our domestic dogs are also remnants of this wolf-pack mentality. A canine pack needs a territory in which to hunt and rest. It marks out this territory with body wastes, especially urine, or sometimes with visible markers, made by kicking up earth after defecating. The pack defends its territory, preventing others who are not pack members, be they dogs or humans, from entering it. And our dogs still hunt. Their predatory instinct makes anything that moves, from a mouse to a car, fair game.

Picking places
Using size as a weapon, this Samoyed tries to dominate the Pekingese. In return, the Pekingese asserts himself by biting the larger dog. Dogs learn their place in the pack through encounters such as this.

What's yours is mine...
Two French Bulldogs play a game with a toy. While dominant dogs guard their possessions, most other dogs will use them in play.

The Origins of the Dog

Northern giant
The Kenai wolf of Alaska, commonly weighing 135 lb (60 kg), was hunted to extinction by 1915. It probably evolved from Asian wolves, and may have been a forebear of the Alaskan Malamute dog.

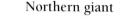

Interbreeding of Asian wolf and North American timber wolf

Bounty victim
The Newfoundland white wolf was one of the 20 strains of wolf that once existed in North America. The last of these elegant, narrow-headed, white and ivory animals was shot in 1911. Just under 6 ft (2 meters) long, they weighed up to100 lbs (45 kg).

North American timber wolf

King of the forest
Timber wolves once ranged over all of North America. Native Americans tamed them and created local breeds of dogs long before the Europeans reached the continent. Today, wolves survive only in Canada and in small enclaves in the United States.

Southern migrants
No true wolves inhabit South America. The species ventured no farther than Mexico, where a small, dark subspecies (Canis lupus baileyi) survives today. The Chihuahua and Mexican Hairless Dog are probably descended from this wolf.

REGARDLESS OF SIZE, all dogs are directly descended from wolves. It is the range of colors, sizes, and temperaments among breeds of wolves that allowed for the dramatic variety of dogs today. That original natural variety is today sadly depleted in the wild. Wolves are intensely social animals with keen senses, who work together to catch animals larger than themselves. Their highly articulate communication and the pack behavior that they use to protect themselves are echoed today in the behavior of even the smallest of dogs.

Lone hunters

European gray wolves, the breeding stock from which many local dogs, such as the spitzes, evolved, are more independent than other subspecies. Only a few wolves survive today, living in the most remote, mountainous regions of Europe.

Intercontinental travelers

Differing forms of the gray wolf ranged across Europe and Asia to Siberia, and into North America, following their prey. Humans followed the same pattern, and the close relationship between the two species was forged.

Asian wolf

European wolf

The smallest wolf

The ash-gray Japanese wolf, or Shamanu, was less than 33 in (85 cm) long, and stood under 14 in (40 cm) high. The probable progenitor of many Japanese breeds of dog, such as the Shiba Inu, it had a short coat and a thick, doglike tail.

Indian wolf

Intrepid voyager

The small Indian wolf – southern subspecies tend to be smaller than their northern cousins – spread throughout Arabia and into Africa. Its genes are probably carried in breeds as diverse as the African Basenji, the Arabian Saluki, the Pekingese from China, and the dingo in Australia.

From Forest to Fireside

WE FIND THE young of most species captivating, but it was the wolf cub's open willingness to become part of the human community that led our ancestors to see the value of incorporating these animals into their settlements. Wolves naturally protected their adopted human pack, alerted it to danger, and helped in the hunt. Eventually, through breeding from the tamest and most reliable stock, dogs for guarding, protecting, hunting, or simple companionship were developed. Early dogs looked much like the wolves from which they were bred, but selective breeding for specific traits has led to the variety that exists today.

Ancient companion
This Pekingese, bred over thousands of years for companionship, might seem far removed from the wolf, but it still retains bedrock wolf traits.

Built for speed
An ancient breed, this fleet-footed Pharaoh Hound is a descendant of the small wolves that once lived in the Middle East. These hounds were bred to sight and chase game.

Family features (LEFT)
Bred from the large and powerful northern timber wolf, this Samoyed retains many of the wolf's physical features. Samoyeds are good guards, growling at the sight of intruders.

Dog in sheep's clothing
(RIGHT AND FAR RIGHT)
The longhaired Briard (right) resembles the sheep it was bred to protect, the likeness acting as a camouflage to fool wolves. By the time the Belgian Sheepdog (far right) had evolved, wolves were no longer a threat, so there was no need for camouflage.

Emergency rations (LEFT)
*These Chow Chows are
descendants of guard dogs bred in
China. Their ancestors would also
have been a source of food in
times of famine.*

Dogs of war (ABOVE)
*Robust, powerful dogs like this Mastiff
were selectively bred both for defense
and for active aggression.*

Working to the gun (ABOVE)
*This German Shorthaired Pointer
happily retrieves a game bird. Even
today, we continue to use selective
breeding to create dogs with
accentuated characteristics that
fulfill our own changing needs.*

Coordinating Activity

PACK INSTINCT evolved to help wolves capture prey larger than themselves. To be successful in the hunt, wolves must coordinate their activities, alerting one another to scents, sights, and sounds. Cooperative behavior is still powerful in all dogs and is one reason why they make good companions. Dogs coordinate their activities not only with each other, but also with our schedules. They sleep and wake together, run and chase one another, eat collectively, and join together in greeting their leader.

Dinner party (*ABOVE*)
This pack of Beagles eats and drinks communally from one bowl. Because they are a true pack and know each other well, there is no competition over who eats first.

Outnumbered
Although they are far smaller than the Rhodesian Ridgeback, these dominant Chihuahuas, who know each other and form a pack of two, eat first. The larger outsider simply watches.

Mother love
These Longhaired Dachshunds look up expectantly at their owner, hoping for food or attention. They respond as they did to their mother when they were puppies. Now they coordinate their behavior to the activities of their human leader.

Working as a team

Sleeping together gives the members of a wolf pack mutual security and warmth. They all arise equally fit to work as a team. Having just awakened, these wolves become alert to a scent, sight, or sound and turn toward it. When one member of the pack finds a scent or hears a noise, his body language alerts the others. By coordinating their activities and working together, they are more alert to danger and better equipped to capture animals larger than themselves than individual wolves would be.

Unblinking stare is held

Leg is raised in anticipation

Pack members keep close together

Teamwork

WHEN GIVEN THE opportunity, dogs readily follow the pack instinct that they have inherited from wolves. The most dominant dog plays "team captain," and the rest willingly obeys its commands. The difference between a Husky team and a wolf pack is that the dogs have two team captains – the top dog and the human pack leader. True pack behavior only occurs in dogs that have lived together long enough to form relationships. Strays might travel together, but they do not coordinate their activity as closely as a sled team.

Relaxing together
The team relaxes as a group, a habit that started when, as puppies, they would huddle with their littermates for warmth. Although these dogs are not littermates, they have learned to behave in the same way with each other.

Leading from behind
The Huskies willingly follow the instructions shouted by their owner and surge ahead pulling the sled. The dogs' pack instinct inhibits disputes while they are working.

Now is no time to argue. Pull!

Pulling together
The Huskies concentrate on working together as a team. Due to a combination of instinct and early learning, they are eager to start running as soon as they feel the harness.

The tail is raised in excitement

Bodies touch as dogs strain to pull sled

Eyes are kept fixed on the trail ahead

I'm powerful, but not as powerful as you.

Paying homage to the leader (LEFT)
The top dog in the Husky pack leaps up to greet the real team leader. In all our relationships with dogs, the human must play the part of "top dog."

Taking the biscuit (ABOVE)
The pack leader leaps in the air to catch a tidbit thrown to the pack, while the rest of her team holds back. She has been chosen to be leader by her owner, but the decision was influenced by her natural authority over the other dogs.

The ears perk forward, showing anticipation

Let's get going!

Team coordinates its effort

Dogs leap forwards with excitement

Going on Appearances

A DOG'S BEHAVIOR IS influenced by its sex and genetic background. The male puppy is masculine from birth because the development of his brain is affected by the sex hormone testosterone, which he produces while still in the womb. Under this hormonal influence he grows bigger, stronger, and more assertive than his female littermates. The female does not experience hormonal influence on behavior until her first season, usually when she is six or seven months old. Mutations in color are also related to variations in behavior in many canine species, including foxes and wolves. Selective breeding has exaggerated these, and the color of a dog's coat can partly predict its behavior.

Male has
muscular body

Typical male

*This male dog is more active than a female, demands more time
for play, and will leave more scent markers on his territory.
He is also more aggressive and destructive, and more
likely to stray from home or to snap at strangers.*

Typical female

*This female dog demands more affection and is
more companionable than the typical male
dog. She is also more willing to learn
obedience and easier to house train.*

Overweight due to
both neutering and
overfeeding

Dangerous colors

Although these Cocker Spaniels are both of the same breed and sex, the golden one is more likely to develop a condition called "avalanche of rage syndrome." This causes fits of aggression, which appear with no warning and vanish just as suddenly. Cocker Spaniels of mixed colors hardly ever develop this problem.

Tail docked unnecessarily for cosmetic reasons

Nature and selection (BELOW)

Because he is male, the darker Golden Retriever is larger than the female. Selective breeding has diminished many of his dominant, aggressive male behavioral traits; neutering could reduce them still further. If the female is also neutered, she might become more dominantly aggressive.

The male has a larger head as well as a larger body

Female's body is smaller than male's

Showing Who's Boss

JUST LIKE US, dogs have a rigid social order, consisting of top dogs, challengers, dogs contented with their position, and underdogs. A wild pack of canine hunters must act as a team and kill to survive. Maintaining this "pecking order" or hierarchy is vital if fights to the death within the pack are to be avoided. The hierarchy is established through ritual displays that reveal the mental and physical strengths and weaknesses of the participants. Once dogs have learned their rank, most are content to behave within the bounds that it dictates.

Signs of appeasement (ABOVE)
Cowering and pursing her lips, this Dalmatian tells the higher-ranking German Shepherd Dog that she offers no challenge.

Show of power
A Greyhound stares intently and places his paw on a Boxer's shoulder, while she turns her head away and tries to avoid any eye contact. This ritual display reaffirms that the Greyhound is top dog and will accept no challenges.

The less dominant dog avoids eye contact

Leg rests firmly on dog's back

All right, you're in charge.

Dog turns to make escape

Puppy concentrates on toy

I might be small, but I'm more confident than you are.

Size is not everything (ABOVE)
Although much smaller than the Afghan Hound, this Yorkshire Terrier stands his ground and uses assertive body language to force the larger dog to back away.

Respect your elders
This Golden Retriever puppy watches while an older Labrador Retriever takes away his toy. The puppy understands that, for the time being, the mature dog has seniority of rank and can do as he likes.

Raised tail shows dominance

I bet I can outstare you.

Eye to eye
Meeting for the first time, a Pyrenean Mountain Dog and a Beagle stare at each other and sniff each other's scent. The dog that maintains eye contact the longest will exert rank seniority.

Stance shows confidence

Ancient ritual
Two wolves bare their teeth and engage in a ritualized tussle. The top wolf in a pack will meet any potential challenge to his authority by physically or psychologically asserting himself. Rank hierarchies are more complex in wolf packs than among dogs.

Playing a Part

THE PRIMARY WAY that dogs learn about their relationships with each other is through play. By playing, dogs discover one another's weak points, and learn to manipulate and hone their social skills. Play activity neutralizes the potentially dangerous situations created by dominance disputes and helps dogs to cement their pack relationships in a ritual manner. Just like us, dogs retain a lifelong enjoyment of playing and for many play is an end in itself, carried out for the fun of it.

1 Scent to investigate
First meetings are always potentially dangerous. Both of these dogs are restrained by their leashes while they scent each other. Neither dog shows aggression, but the Fox Terrier is innately superior due to his gender and greater age.

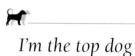

I'm the top dog around here.

2 Teasing moment (ABOVE)
The Cocker Spaniel rolls over in a manner that forestalls any possibility of aggression from the Fox Terrier. All the while, she is careful to maintain eye contact with the terrier to tell him that she is not merely being cowardly.

Leg is raised, ready to restrain the terrier

3 Playful barking
Sensing that there is no danger and still maintaining her direct eye contact, the spaniel playfully barks and bounces up toward the face of the Fox Terrier. In simple play, dogs try to mouth each other or gently chew the head region.

Let's box to see who wins.

4 Head-to-head
Both dogs are now on equal terms and, using their forelimbs, box with each other. They growl, but like most play activity, the growl is slightly "theatrical," just different enough from true growling to indicate that it is not meant in earnest.

Direct eye contact is constantly maintained

The ears flatten back to signal no serious aggressive intent

Now I know you're tougher than you look.

5 Vicious circle (LEFT)
Running in tight circles, the dogs continue their play behavior. Both try to chew at their playmate's neck. Although they met only minutes before, these two dogs have learned instantly about each other's strong and weak points.

Standing allows the dog to play from a position of strength

The Top Dog

TO ENSURE THAT the pack successfully coordinates activity, one individual must exert authority and become leader. Due to hormonal influence on behavior, the dominant dog is often male. He asserts his leadership through displays of dominance – ritualized activities that tell other dogs that a top dog is present. Although helpful, size is not the most important factor in determining who will be top dog. Dobermans and Rottweilers are naturally dominant large breeds, but many small breeds, especially terriers and dachshunds, are more dominant than breeds several times their size.

1 First sniff
A Longhaired Miniature Dachshund makes a dominant investigation of a Pekingese by sniffing her ears and mouth. His tail is raised, and his ears, which are as erect as they can become, signal the assurance of his actions.

2 Head-on-neck dominance
Placing the neck on the other dog's shoulder displays the most common form of dominant body language. Direct eye contact shows the dachshund's confidence.

3 Last things last
Having completed his investigation of the front of the Pekingese, the dachshund, still controlling the meeting, turns his attentions to the posterior region of his subject.

Lowered tail shows lack of confidence

1 Cocksure encounter
The body language of the authoritative dachshund includes a variety of dominant gestures. Unable to sniff the anal region of the larger dog, an Italian Spinone, he scents the prepuce (foreskin) instead. Despite his small size, the dachshund conveys his dominance by taking the lead in these investigations.

2 Problem of size
Having approached the larger spinone with great self-confidence, the dachshund has a problem actually exerting his authority. Although he is too small to dominate the spinone physically, he still actively tries to sniff his mouth.

I'll show him who's boss.

Ears are fully raised

That's better. Now I can show my higher status.

3 Exerting authority
When the spinone eventually lies down, the dominant dachshund can finally show authority. He sniffs his opponent's head region, raises the hair on his back as best he can, and dominantly stares at the eyes of the much larger, but less dominant, dog.

Meeting as Equals

ALTHOUGH ONE DOG always assumes the leadership role within a pack, this does not mean that all the other dogs in the pack will behave in a meek and passive manner. Most dogs are confident and assertive – although in a less provocative way than the top dog – and are called "subdominant" dogs. The ritual displays when they meet are subtle and often brief, allowing almost instant social activity. When two subdominant dogs first come together there is little tension, and the encounter results in either immediate play or relaxed indifference. This situation usually occurs when a puppy comes across an unfamiliar adult dog.

Loose skin protects the dog's neck

2 Rough play
The younger dog yanks a mouthful of skin and pulls. If the adult Mastiff does not repel him, the puppy learns that two dogs can meet and play without having to show overt dominance.

1 Initial encounter
This young Bloodhound trots up to a Mastiff in an unthreatening way and, forgoing ritual introductions (see pages 26–27), starts to play. Despite the fact that she knows that she is stronger, the Mastiff does not exert her dominance and allows the Bloodhound to continue his playful behavior.

Raised tail shows excitement

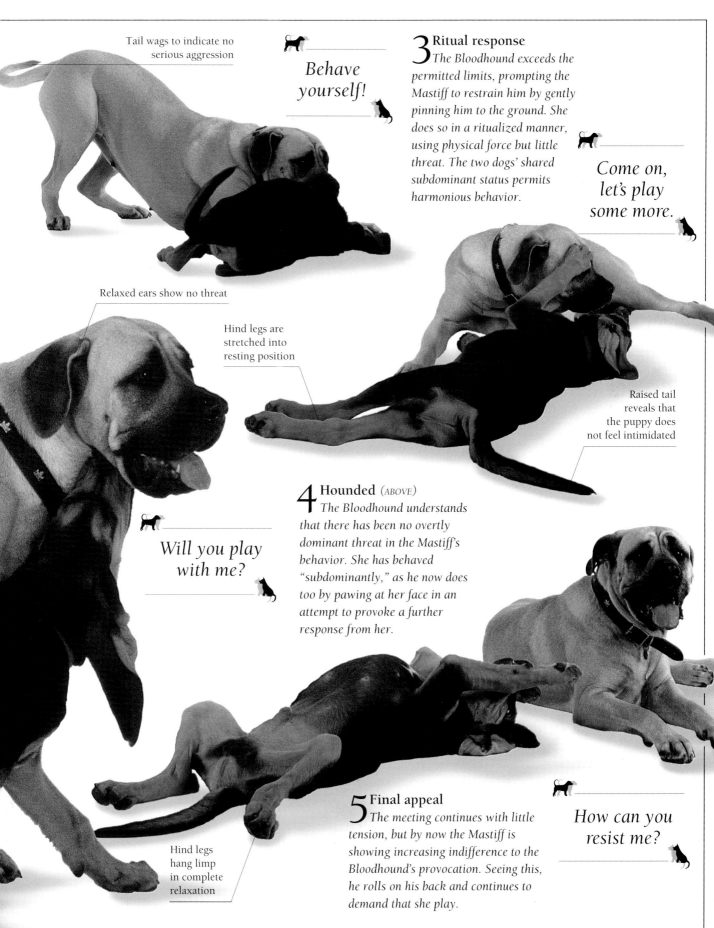

Tail wags to indicate no serious aggression

Behave yourself!

3 Ritual response
The Bloodhound exceeds the permitted limits, prompting the Mastiff to restrain him by gently pinning him to the ground. She does so in a ritualized manner, using physical force but little threat. The two dogs' shared subdominant status permits harmonious behavior.

Come on, let's play some more.

Relaxed ears show no threat

Hind legs are stretched into resting position

Raised tail reveals that the puppy does not feel intimidated

4 Hounded (ABOVE)
The Bloodhound understands that there has been no overtly dominant threat in the Mastiff's behavior. She has behaved "subdominantly," as he now does too by pawing at her face in an attempt to provoke a further response from her.

Will you play with me?

Hind legs hang limp in complete relaxation

5 Final appeal
The meeting continues with little tension, but by now the Mastiff is showing increasing indifference to the Bloodhound's provocation. Seeing this, he rolls on his back and continues to demand that she play.

How can you resist me?

The Underdog

DOGS COMMUNICATE articulately with their bodies. As a result, we find it easy to understand what dogs are saying to each other or, for that matter, to us. Submissive behavior is necessary if pack members are to follow the commands of their leader, and it is the basis for successfully incorporating dogs into our homes. Even the most dominant dogs should exhibit submissive behavior to the human members of their pack. To make more obedient companions, we have bred some dogs to always be submissive.

Relaxed submission
Many dogs, such as this Shetland Sheepdog, submit in a relaxed and contented manner when in the presence of the pack leader. The dog's tail lies limp on the floor as she solicits attention.

Hangdog
This Weimaraner sits down, hunches his shoulders, and droops his head and ears when he is confronted by a more dominant dog. He averts his eyes to avoid contact.

I'll obey, as long as you tell me what to do.

Crouched in submission

Tail tucked firmly between legs

Abject submission
By rolling over, with his tail tucked firmly between his legs and his lips and ears drawn back, this Yorkshire Terrier displays abject submission. Urinating while cowering is the final stage of submission.

Let's not argue.

Tactical withdrawal
By drawing back his head and lowering his whole body to the floor, a Pekingese defuses a potentially explosive situation when confronted by an equal-sized but dominant dachshund.

Forelimb raised

Please leave me alone.

Ears flattened and out of danger

Appeasement gesture
Flattening back his ears, drawing back his lips, and turning his head away, this Whippet drops down on his side. He is poised to lift his foreleg in a dramatic show of submission. His tail remains close to his body, where it is out of danger.

I'm completely defenseless and offer no threat.

Head lowered

Ears folded back

Eyes averted

Pack Rivalry

DOGS TREASURE POSSESSIONS and frequently want whatever another member of the pack has – simply in order to have it themselves. In these circumstances, only very dominant canines achieve their ends through aggression. For subdominant dogs, arguing over who gets the object can become a game of deftness and guile. The holder protects his prize from the other dog's jaws, but if the interloper manages to clamp his teeth on it, the two dogs enter into a tug-of-war (*see pages 76-77*). The desired object then passes back and forth between them, but the ultimate winner is often the pack member that is slightly more dominant.

1 **Jealous onlooker** (*ABOVE*)
While a brindle French Bulldog chews on a dog toy, his pied littermate watches enviously nearby, taking care not to make overtly dominant and provocative eye contact.

If you've got it, I want it.

Hackles (the hair on the neck) remain flat and smooth

Leaning forward, ready to lunge

Short, powerful legs give good balance

Ears are drawn back submissively

2 Mock play activity (ABOVE)
Because his presence has not provoked aggression, the pied French Bulldog now drops into a play position and looks directly at his sibling and at the dog chew that he desires.

Relaxed ears signal no anger

3 Confident grab (BELOW)
Having received no threat through either body language or voice, the pied dog confidently and quickly creeps up and grabs the toy from between the jaws of the other dog.

Toy is gripped with the canine (eye) teeth

Hey! That's mine!

4 Protecting the prize (LEFT)
Showing his mild authority, the pied dog now chews on his prize but keeps a wary eye on the brindle dog. This playful rivalry continues as the two dogs repeatedly swap the toy by athletic – and devious – moves.

Eye contact is held

If you want it back, you'll have to get it.

Marking Territory

BECAUSE THE SENSE of smell is their most important sense, dogs use the odors in their waste products to stake out their territories. Some dogs kick up dirt or grass after urinating or defecating to leave a visible mark as well. Although urine is used most often to mark territory, there are odor-emitting "calling cards" in virtually all body discharges and secretions, including saliva and ear wax.

1 Marking a scent-post
Male dogs, such as this Tervueren (Belgian Shepherd Dog), cock their legs to urinate on upright objects, like trees. Marks are left at the nose level of other dogs. Scent lasts longer on vertical posts than it would on the ground.

Back arches to assist in effort of defecation

Odor from ears conveys social information

Lips produce a unique scent

Anal glands leave a distinctive odor on droppings

Emitting anal-gland scent
Having emptied his bowels, a Greyhound strains to squeeze his individual scent from his anal glands. Both males and females use discharge from their anal glands to leave markers; they also empty their glands when they are frightened.

The dog raises its tail, showing interest, as the scent is discovered

3 Covering tracks (*ABOVE*)
The setter deposits his own urine to conceal the staler smells of previous visitors. Dogs can mark up to 80 times an hour, and always have urine in reserve.

2 Reading scent messages (*ABOVE*)
A male Irish Setter passes the same spot and scents the urine on the tree. Liquid waste tells him whether the dog who deposited it there was male or female. If it was a female, he may be able to tell whether she was ovulating.

Making a mark
A male Golden Retriever urinates to surround himself with familiar scent. Although bitches sniff for other dogs' scents, they only mark frequently themselves when they are in season.

Tail is lifted to avoid soiling

Tree-marking in the wild
In his natural habitat, a North American timber wolf lifts a leg to mark a tree with urine, mapping out territorial boundaries so that he knows when he is back on home ground. Ritual re-marking is often carried out daily. In the unnatural indoor surroundings in which dogs find themselves, the tree is sometimes replaced by the nearest curtain.

Defending Territory

REGARDLESS OF THEIR sex or size, dogs naturally defend what they consider to be either their personal space or their pack's territory. This is why we value them as watchdogs, but the behavior can also create problems. Dogs sometimes become territorially aggressive when we do not want them to, for example when they are left in cars. There is a strong genetic component to this form of aggression, which is why it is greatest in guard breeds such as the Doberman and the German Shepherd Dog.

1 Menacing signs (LEFT AND BELOW)
A Doberman growls as he notices a Husky approaching his territory. This is the first part of ritual threat behavior. If it is not enough to inhibit the trespasser, the dog bares his teeth to display his lethal weapons.

Territorial confidence (ABOVE)
At home on his own territory, this Rottweiler-cross shows total control. With tail held confidently high and maintaining eye-to-eye contact with the intruder, he barks, shows his teeth, and advances.

Nose wrinkles as lips are drawn back to reveal teeth

2 Full threat
With his territory still under threat of invasion, the guarding dog now barks his own threats. This display still constitutes ritual aggression. Dogs usually only enter serious fights when they are necessary.

Back off or else!

Mobile territory

In his temporary territory, a German Shepherd Dog barks aggressively at what he sees to be a threat to his personal space. Dogs occasionally defend areas that they consider to be theirs, including territories as small as an armchair or other resting place. Terriers in particular often defend their owners' cars and other such territories.

Splayed ears reveal ambivalence

Ears are tilted dominantly forward

3 Dogged advance
Disregarding the Doberman's threatening behavior, the intruder advances aggressively. By not backing down in the face of ritual threats, the Husky has provoked the "home" dog to defend his territory resolutely. This confrontation is likely to break out in a fight.

All teeth are displayed in a show of defiance

You don't frighten me.

In Pursuit

W E HAVE REDUCED the dog's desire to chase and kill through selective breeding, but all dogs instinctively chase almost anything that moves because they are descended from wild hunters. This natural predatory instinct is constructively channeled in breeds such as sheepdogs and cattle dogs, allowing them to do what comes naturally, but on our behalf. They are trained to slink forward and round up livestock rather than to attack it. Without proper training, the dog's inherent inclination is to chase and bite its prey.

Tail is elevated

Look, it's running away from me!

Bicyclists' scourge (ABOVE)
The sight of a moving bicycle stimulates this dog to give chase. Because the bicyclist continues on his way, rather than stopping to challenge the dog, the canine's predatory and territorial instincts are satisfied, and chasing bicycles could easily become a habit.

Head lowered, eyes fixed on the sheep

Feet placed for sudden movement

If it moves...

A jogger provokes this dog to give chase. This can occur in any context, not just on the dog's own territory. If the jogger suddenly stops and challenges, the dog learns that chasing is not always a rewarding activity.

Curled tail indicates active excitement

Ears perk forward

I'm going to see him off.

Stalking dinner

A timber wolf in winter camouflage lowers his head and eyes his prey. He wants to get close enough to capture it with only a short chase. Dogs also rarely enter into marathon events. In the wild, the wolf pack coordinates its predatory behavior, but this rarely happens with dogs, even in free-ranging packs of strays.

Chasing constructively

A working dog (opposite) expresses his natural instinct and creeps up on this sheep. The dog has been trained not to bite. Untrained dogs often revel in the chase and then savage their prey.

A DOG'S LIFE

·

DOGS ARE SENSITIVE to the subtlest changes around them. Using the sophisticated senses of the born predator, they observe us much more keenly than we observe them, and they pick up body-language signals that we do not even realize we are sending. For their part, they use their voices to communicate articulately in a variety of ways, howling to call other members of the pack, growling in anger, barking for joy, or whining for attention.

Dogs have all the skills of their wild ancestors. Although not as agile as cats, they are still good jumpers. They are far better swimmers – for many, there is no greater pleasure than a plunge into water. Dogs' senses are also more sophisticated than ours in many ways. They hear better than we do, an ability evolved to help them hear the rustling of a rodent on the move, which now enables them to home in on an opening fridge. Their ability to detect, locate, and identify scents is so refined that it is virtually beyond our comprehension.

Balancing acts
At the sight of food, these two terriers use different strategies to get as near to it as possible. The Scottish Terrier balances firmly on his hindquarters, and the West Highland White Terrier dances on tiptoes.

Old habits die hard
With nimble forepaws, this dog perpetuates the wolf's tactic of digging for rodents that have gone underground. Dogs dig for food, to create cool patches in which to lie, or out of boredom.

Rallying cry (ABOVE)
A German Shorthaired Pointer raises his head and emits a plaintive howl, to call to other members of his pack.

Curiously, just as we use perfume, dogs cover themselves in strong scent and will roll on anything with a pungent odor, including decomposing material.

Taking a sniff
Using his prodigious scenting ability, this Basset Hound sniffs the ground. Dogs can detect some scents diluted to one part per million million.

Homing in
With his head tilted so that sound reaches his ears at fractionally different intervals, this terrier perks up his ears to focus on a noise.

Being scavengers as well as predators, dogs eat a wide variety of foods, paying little attention to whether they are fresh or not. They chew sticks and bones, and some bury what they regard as excess food, to be dug up when times are hard. Because they are pack animals, they are competitive feeders. The dominant dog eats first, and all dogs wolf down their food to prevent other pack members from eating it – even if you and your family are the other pack members.

This same gregarious sociability means that dogs willingly sleep together. The sleeping positions that they assume vary with breed, age, environmental temperature, and the security that an individual feels. As well as grooming by licking, scratching, and chewing themselves, or by rolling in grass or even dust, some dogs will also groom each other.

Brushing up
A young Afghan Hound scratches her neck. Dogs groom themselves by chewing and biting at their hindquarters and scratching at their forequarters. They rub their faces with their forepaws, as cats do.

Manual dexterity
Using both forepaws, this Golden Retriever holds his chew firmly as he gnaws at it.

Vision

ALTHOUGH THEY ARE better than we are at seeing even the slightest movement at a distance, dogs' vision is not as good as ours close up. Their eyes, although not as widely placed as the wolf's, are too far apart to give accurate depth of field. Dogs have the right cells in their eyes and brain to see in color, but practically speaking, color is of little significance to them. The primary function of their eyes is to notice minimal movement and then concentrate on it intently.

The slant of the eyes lets the dog see sideways

Do I look intelligent?

Artificial intelligence
This Boxer spends each day in the reception area of my clinic. Because the placing of her eyes mimics a human face, she appears to be more intelligent than a dog with laterally placed eyes.

Dog sits still as she concentrates

I can act as eyes for my owner.

Natural eyeliner
A Husky's eyes are surrounded by dark skin. This reduces the glare of light reflected from snow, and also makes the eyes a prominent feature for communication.

Night vision
This French Bulldog can dilate his pupils more than we can, to take in more light. His eyes also contain more rods, the cells that register low light in black and white.

Pupils dilate widely to allow more light into the eye

Dog's eye view 250°–290°
Human's eye view 210°

Seeing things differently (ABOVE)

The dog's world differs from its owner's. We need to be able to focus on an object, see its color, and decide whether it is dangerous or safe. Frontally placed eyes with plenty of color-sensitive cone cells give us these abilities, but restrict our angle of vision. The dog's ancestors were primarily carnivorous hunters, so lateral vision was more important to them than color. Dogs' peripheral vision is more acute than ours, and their angle of vision is wider, but this varies according to how far apart their eyes are. Having fewer cone cells in their eyes than we do, their color vision is basically restricted to reds.

I'm concentrating on you.

Brown pigment on inner eyelid makes this eye look different from the other

An original gazehound

An Afghan Hound is typical of the ancient dog types originally bred for their acute vision and speed. Her eyes are more sensitive to light and movement than are ours, and their slanted positioning gives her more peripheral vision.

Raised Voices

THE AVERAGE DOG'S ability to hear is four times sharper than ours. Your dog is better at hearing high-pitched sounds, too – a requirement that evolved in its wolf ancestors, whose diet of large herbivores was supplemented with small animals, such as mice, that make high-pitched sounds. Although wolves bark an alarm signal, the dog's bark is more of a man-made characteristic, actively selected for watchdog value. Howling remains a vocal communication technique, while moaning, whimpering, and whining are perpetuated infant sounds.

Seeking attention (LEFT)
This West Highland White Terrier barks to gain attention. Barking is also used as a warning or threatening sound, in the same way that wolves bark an alarm when there is danger nearby.

We're over here. Where has everyone else gone?

Head turns to identify source of distant sound

Lips are pursed to howl

Collar tags are an efficient means of identification that should be worn by all dogs

Plaintive howl
While her partner listens intently for a reply, a Basenji howls plaintively to contact the rest of the pack. Basenjis were never selectively bred for their bark. As a result they almost never bark, limiting their sounds to a howl or the occasional yip or yelp when seriously frightened or in pain.

Sing-along Spinone

This Italian Spinone belongs to my nurse and spends a lot of time at my clinic, where he howls when he hears doleful songs on the radio. Many dogs howl to music just for the enjoyment of joining in. The howl is not a complaint: if they disliked the sound they would move away.

Top lip drawn down

Leg is turned under in relaxed position

The call of the wild

The howl is the wolf's most important vocal method of communication. Wolves howl to let other pack members know where they are. When cubs "yip" at night, adult members of the pack soon respond reassuringly with howls from wherever they are.

Did you say "Food"?

Ears pricked up to improve hearing

Attentive listening

Dogs sometimes tilt their heads, as this Large Munsterlander (left) and Doberman are doing, when they concentrate on listening attentively to a sound. By shifting their ear positions, they can pinpoint the location of the noise in 0.06 of a second.

A Sense of Smell

BECAUSE THE DOG'S ability to scent is extremely sophisticated, we sometimes assume that it must have some unknown "sixth sense" that helps it follow trails or find its way home. In reality, this sense is a scenting ability so acute that dogs can smell some odors diluted to one-millionth the concentration at which humans can detect them. To do this, dogs sniff air into a special chamber in the nose. This air is not washed out when the dog breathes out, so odor molecules accumulate until there are enough to smell.

Ground scenting

A Yorkshire Terrier sniffs the ground for scent messages in another dog's urine. Like cats but unlike us, dogs have a special apparatus in the nose, the vomeronasal organ, that is responsible for the recognition of sex-related odors.

You smell as if you've eaten something interesting.

Improving scent

By licking his nose, this Chow Chow increases the capture of odor molecules. There are over 200 million scent-receiving cells in a dog's nose. If spread out, the nasal membrane would cover an area greater than his body surface.

Who's the boss around here?

Ears and lipfolds are scented for information

Mutual investigation (LEFT)
Three Basenjis sniff each other as we would shake hands. Information is immediately acquired about dominance, sexual status, and position in the pack hierarchy. Because male dogs use their sense of smell to scent out females in season, they make better tracker dogs than bitches.

Air-scenting (BELOW)
Plumes of odor in the air are sniffed by an Italian Spinone. She searches for odor clues in airborne dust particles and water droplets before lifting her foreleg and "pointing" in the direction of the scent.

Anal glands produce individual scent

Body leans forward

Quiet! I can smell it over here.

Following a trail

A timber wolf follows a ground trail, possibly from prey such as deer. Dogs behave in exactly the same way. The best time for both wolves and dogs to scent is when the ground temperature is slightly higher than the air temperature, sending plumes of scent upward. This occurs in early evening, making it dogs' and wolves' preferred hunting time. The invisible scent trails are marked by the smells of damaged grass crushed underfoot and by changes in the soil, as well as by actual odors from the animal being followed.

Table Manners

UNLIKE OTHER PREDATOR species, such as cats, dogs are omnivores, eating more than just meat. They have far fewer taste buds on their tongues than we have, and are willing to consume almost anything that might offer nourishment. This willingness to try anything is combined with a sensitive vomiting reflex, which permits them to reject foods that are unpalatable or dangerous. Standard or large-size dogs are natural gorgers. Boredom, combined with too much available food, can give them weight problems. Small dogs have not evolved under the same genetic pressure, and are more likely to be selective about what they eat. Females are twice as likely to be finicky as are males.

Hands off
Protecting her food from a human as she would from other members of a canine pack, this Springer Spaniel turns and growls a warning as she is approached, natural behavior that we find socially unacceptable.

Me first, me first!

Professional beggars
Exemplifying their evolution from hunter to scavenger and beggar, these Basenjis stand on their hind legs to get near an offered morsel of food. Dogs can be trained to eat almost anything.

Don't come near me until I'm finished.

Head is held over bowl to prevent intrusion

Dog takes a firm stance to defend her food

Eyes close as dog
concentrates

*Mmmm.
Savor the
flavor.*

Grass is bitten off
with incisors

Careful chewing
*Closing his eyes, this Shar Pei concentrates
on chewing his food. Dogs will usually try
anything, but they have favorites that they
enjoy most.*

Side salad
*Grass makes a tasty snack. Some dogs are
highly selective, searching out and grazing
on particular grasses and weeds.
Some eat vegetation only when
they have an upset stomach.*

Body leans forward

Tongue curls
back to lap water

Lapping it up
*A Boxer dips her tongue into water and forms
it into a cup, throwing the liquid up into her
mouth. Dogs are often very careful with
precious liquids such as milk, not losing a
drop, but are much sloppier with water.*

49

Bones of Contentment

HAVING EVOLVED FROM pack animals that hunted and ate creatures larger than themselves, dogs still enjoy gnawing on large bones. Their teeth and jaw muscles are specially adapted for holding, scraping, and crushing, and they use their forepaws with great dexterity to manipulate bones and hold them in position. As a substitute for bones, most dogs willingly chew on similar objects, such as toys, edible chews, and sticks.

Getting a grip
With great dexterity, this Basenji holds a bone steady between his paws. He tilts his head, to better use his large molar teeth for gnawing on his treat.

This is tasty.

Incisors for tearing

Canines for seizing and piercing

Molars for chewing and grinding

Perfect teeth
This Bull Terrier shows the equipment vital to the carnivore. His jaw is elongated to allow plenty of space for teeth of varying sizes and uses.

Forepaws hold the chew firmly

Starting early
Although still only a few months old, this Boston Terrier chews enthusiastically on an edible stick. Chewing is instinctive behavior in all dogs.

Raised tail shows
enjoyment

On guard
*This dog drops his forequarters to the
ground so that he can more readily chew
his toy. He keeps his hindquarters
raised, in case he has to move
quickly to protect his trophy.*

*Be ready to
move fast.*

Every last bit
Gnawing on a bone, this timber
wolf shows the dexterity and
powerful jaw muscles that have
been inherited by domestic
dogs. Wolves will strip all the
meat from bones, then split
them open and eat the marrow. Chewing
keeps their teeth, which are their most
important weapons, in good condition.

A natural toothbrush
*This Golden Retriever holds his object
with crossed paws and gnaws at it.
Chewing hard objects cleans his teeth,
and is necessary to maintain healthy
teeth and gums.*

*I've done
this for
years.*

One paw holds the chew
firmly on the other

Buried Treasure

T HE DOG'S INSTINCT to cache food, creating a reserve for time of need, is inherited from wolves. It leads well-fed, totally domesticated dogs to bury bones and then dig them up later. In the absence of bones, dogs may bury food such as bone-shaped biscuits, and some will try digging in the carpet if there is no earth available. Dogs are efficient earth movers and will also dig to flush out small animals that have gone underground; to escape confinement; and to create a cool patch of earth in which to lie.

I can smell something.

Dog starts digging with one paw

There's something down here.

Expression shows intense concentration

1 Scent marks the spot

Although it is over a month since she buried her bone here, this dog finds the site through scent. The smell of the bone percolates through the ground.

2 Getting warmer

The smell of the bone intensifies as the dog digs, and she becomes more intent. Some breeds, such as terriers, were bred to dig out small animals in this way.

Marrow is licked from the bone

3 One at a time
The hole is now too deep for digging with both forepaws simultaneously. The dog changes technique and dips in with one paw to drag out earth with a scooping action. Completely ambidextrous, most dogs will use both forepaws in turn. Similarly, forepaws and hindpaws will be used equally when filling the hole.

What's that I feel?

4 Success!
Having found her prize, she reaches in and pulls it out in her mouth. Burying and then digging up food provides natural mental and physical activity for dogs. Denying them these outlets can lead to unwanted destructive behavior.

Raised tail reveals heightened excitement

Leg is drawn out for balance and to tip the head down to reach the bone

6 Enjoying the meal
Having recovered her treasure, the dog settles down for a good gnaw. Dogs willingly chew on the filthiest of finds, but in this instance the dog's fastidious owner has cleaned the bone. The hole in the ground remains. It will only be filled in if she chooses to bury the bone again after having her chew.

5 Any more?
Even after finding her cache, this dog's digging instinct has been so aroused that she continues to paw at the hole. The scent rising from the earth is now at its most powerful, and she might be checking for more buried food.

Rolling

MANY MAMMALS ROLL on their backs either to groom themselves or for what appears to be simple pleasure. Dogs indulge in this behavior when they are contented and feel they are in no danger. Your dog is most likely to roll after it has become wet in the rain or after a swim. Some dogs are especially fond of carrying out this activity in sand or dry earth. Rolling for fun or to groom is a distinct activity from rolling in foul-smelling scent. We can only guess why dogs choose to muck-roll, but it is likely that, like wolves, they do so to mask their own scent.

Fox droppings are sniffed

Legs kick up in apparent delight

Pleasure roll (BELOW)
With joyful abandon, a Chow Chow rolls onto his back, pedaling his legs in the air. At the same time, he arches his back up and down, and flips his head from side to side. It seems he does so for the pure pleasure of it.

Life is a joy!

1 **Catching the scent** (ABOVE)
Coming across another animal's droppings, an Italian Spinone stops to capture the scent in his nose. This will be your first sign of premeditated rolling.

54

Rolling on scent

In exactly the same way as your dog rolls in what we consider to be offensive-smelling muck, a timber wolf in the wild may roll its forequarters in decomposing material that is producing strong odors, such as a rotting carcass. Many natural hunters cover themselves in foreign odors, most probably to hide their own scent from their quarry. Their prey have sensitive noses, and are less alarmed by odors such as animal droppings or decomposing material than they are by the wolf's own body scents, which they will recognize as those of a predator.

Mmm...smells like a good disguise.

2 **Anointing one shoulder** (LEFT)
Rather than joyfully flinging himself on the ground, the spinone carefully places one shoulder on the offensive substance and rubs it. Some dogs carry out a full roll, then stand up and sniff the substance again before performing a second roll.

Head is turned and side of face is rubbed in scent

3 **Balancing the smell** (RIGHT)
Having covered one shoulder in pungent scent, the dog now methodically places his other shoulder on the animal droppings to make sure that the odor is symmetrically placed on both sides of the body. After completing this stereotypical behavior, he might indulge in a pleasurable roll.

Neck and ear are rubbed in scent

Half-standing, the dog can anoint his shoulders accurately

Keeping Clean

DOGS LICK, SCRATCH, chew, and shake themselves to keep tidy. Occasionally, they groom each other as well. Shaking is the most simple and frequent grooming procedure for your dog. After resting, being handled, and, most commonly, getting wet, dogs will often vigorously shake their hair back into its natural position. They also lick their coats and pull out any objects that become entangled in the fur. Some dogs trim their nails by chewing them and use their dewclaws (the remnant of a dog's "thumb," found on the inner side of each foot) to clean their ears. Body openings are meticulously licked clean, especially if there are discharges from them.

I hate feeling wet.

Tumble dry
After a bath, a Bouvier des Flandres puppy vigorously shakes the water from his coat. If he did not do this, the water would eventually penetrate through his almost waterproof undercoat.

Water is flung out from fur

Ears show alertness

Ear wax is licked

I wonder what you taste like?

Mutual grooming
A male Japanese Akita licks the ear and other head regions of a young Cocker Spaniel bitch. Licking is usually part of maternal behavior. This type of grooming has distinct sexual associations.

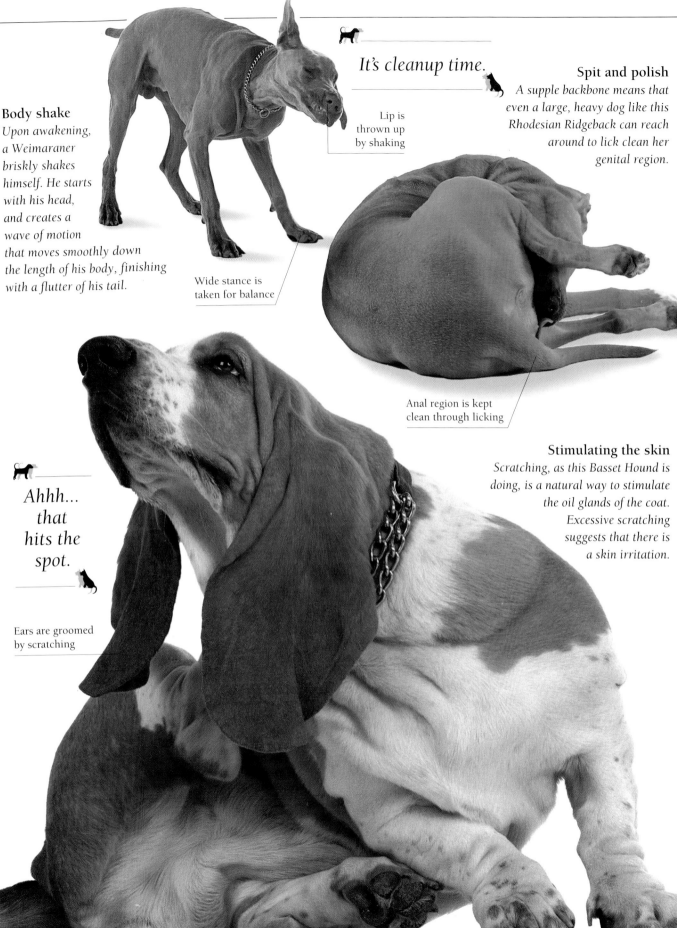

Body shake
Upon awakening, a Weimaraner briskly shakes himself. He starts with his head, and creates a wave of motion that moves smoothly down the length of his body, finishing with a flutter of his tail.

It's cleanup time.

Lip is thrown up by shaking

Spit and polish
A supple backbone means that even a large, heavy dog like this Rhodesian Ridgeback can reach around to lick clean her genital region.

Wide stance is taken for balance

Anal region is kept clean through licking

Stimulating the skin
Scratching, as this Basset Hound is doing, is a natural way to stimulate the oil glands of the coat. Excessive scratching suggests that there is a skin irritation.

Ahhh... that hits the spot.

Ears are groomed by scratching

Sleeping and Snoozing

BECAUSE DOGS NATURALLY coordinate their activities to human timetables, your dog is likely to sleep when you do. With a greater need for sleep than we have, dogs also take "cat-naps," spending half of each day relaxed with their eyes closed. These extra rest periods occur when the pack leader relaxes. Most sleeping time is light sleep, from which the dog awakens easily, but 20 per cent is deep sleep, which is when dogs dream.

Hot dog
By stretching out his hind legs behind him, a Maltese Terrier exposes as much as possible of his body surface to the cool floor. This is a puppy trait that is sometimes retained into adulthood.

Long hair can make it hard to see expression

I'm whacked!

Ears are relaxed

Tongue curls as dog yawns

Creature comfort
A natural comfort-seeker, this Rhodesian Ridgeback has curled up to keep warm in the most comfortable place she can find. Yawning occurs when dogs are completely relaxed, especially just before closing their eyes to sleep, but it can also be a sign of nervousness and apprehension.

This is so comfortable.

Let sleeping dogs lie (*RIGHT*)
*Like this Yorkshire Terrier, which is dozing
next to a human companion, most dogs like
to sleep against an object that protects their
backs. Dominant dogs, however, avoid
contact when sleeping and prefer
to lie alone.*

Hind paws are
turned out

Forelegs become limp

Legs hang relaxed

Complete relaxation
*After vigorous activity, this Golden Retriever
puppy rolls over on his back before falling asleep.
This leaves his vulnerable belly unprotected. Only
dogs that feel totally secure will sleep in this way.*

What?
Me
worry?

Lone wolf
Showing no fear, the leader
of a wolf pack stretches out
in the sun and sleeps alone.
Usually, he first turns around
in circles to flatten the area
that he will lie on. When he
falls into deep, dreaming
sleep, his legs might paddle,
his whiskers flicker, and his
eyelids flutter. Even while
asleep, his jaws can move and
his voice can be activated,
just as can happen when your
dog is in a deep sleep.

On the Move

DOGS ARE BUILT for stamina, so they can work over protracted periods of time. When left to travel on their own, they often trot or canter rather than simply walk. Galloping, however, is reserved for the short bursts of speed needed when chasing, playing, or burning off excess energy. Almost all breeds have supple spines that make them good at tight spaces, but only well-muscled, long-legged breeds like Greyhounds show grace when racing. Others can be quite clumsy.

Flat out
Because he is a true dwarf – with a normal-size body but short legs – this Basset Hound appears clumsy as he gallops. Even so, he can still outrun all but the very fastest humans.

Maximum power and I'm airborne.

Brakes on!

Quick change
An Afghan Hound abruptly changes direction as he runs. This nimbleness of foot evolved to follow the zigzag movements of natural prey such as rabbits.

Forelegs hang relaxed

Feet land close together

Power lifting
With the grace of a ballet dancer, this Wirehaired Fox Terrier uses the powerful muscles of his hind legs to leap from the ground. Some dogs can leap to three times their own height (see pages 62–63).

Balancing act
A timber wolf shows the natural balance inherited by all dogs. He can stand on his hind legs for some time, either to scent the air or to get nearer to what interests him. Where footing is solid, wolves and dogs are adequate climbers, but they usually restrict themselves to clambering over obstacles rather than aspiring to true climbing.

Slalom run

Showing the suppleness of his back, a Tervuren (Belgian Shepherd Dog) weaves through an obstacle course. Agility is enhanced by the fact that there is no canine equivalent of the collarbone. This makes the joints between the front legs and the body extremely flexible.

Howzat!

With only a little training, all dogs can become as skilled at catching as this Whippet. Rapid reactions, the strength of his hind legs, and good eyesight combine to give him nimble dexterity.

Loose shoulders allow paws to land close together

Body is fully stretched out

Flexibility enhances surefooted movement

This is really very easy for me.

Jumping

MOST DOGS ARE surprisingly good jumpers. All but the heaviest breeds and those with short legs are able to jump several times their own height. Dogs will jump spontaneously when they are suddenly confronted by an obstruction such as a ditch or fence. If they have more time, they eye the obstacle and measure their stride before jumping over it. Almost all dogs want to jump, but it can be dangerous for some of them. Giant breeds can suffer internal injuries if they land too heavily, and overweight dogs can tear the ligaments in their hind legs.

2 Airborne
Now in the air, the dog starts to draw up his hind legs. At all times he keeps his eyes focused on the object of his attention. Concentrating too hard on jumping might make him miss his objective.

Legs are tucked tightly into body

1 Cleared for take-off
Using his powerful hind-leg muscles, this Rottweiler-cross propels himself off the ground. At the same time, he draws in his front legs to avoid injuring them, creating an ideal aerodynamic shape.

Paws extended ready for contact

That's a good, gentle landing.

Paws leave ground when body is fully stretched

Eye contact is maintained

Tail curls
forward for
balance

*I'm keeping my
eyes on what
I want.*

3 Over the top
*Having reached his
projected altitude, the dog
continues to draw in his
hind legs but now starts
to extend his forelimbs.*

4 Starting descent
*The dog now uses his tail
more, curling it forward to
assist his balance. He continues
to focus his attention on his
target as he comes down.*

Legs are held almost
straight in descent

Shoulders absorb
impact of landing

5 Coming in to land
*The dog's front legs reach down
with flat paws, for landing. The hind
legs are still fully extended, having
been raised high to prevent injuries.*

6 Down to earth
*With his forefeet firmly planted
on the ground, the dog draws his
hind legs forward as far as possible.
This provides the dog with
maximum propulsion as he
continues to run.*

Forelimbs
land firmly

Paws reach out
for landing

AT HOME WITH US

Schooltime

Concentrating on the reward that will follow, this Golden Retriever sits on command. Both dogs and owners benefit from simple games such as this.

DOGS SETTLE INTO our lives easily because their body rhythms are similar to ours. They sleep when we do, are active when we are, and learn both their own and our feeding times to the minute. There can, however, be problems. Some dogs try to dominate their human companions. Without natural outlets for their sex drives, many male dogs eye legs or sofa cushions as fair game. Neutering can remedy some habits without dramatically changing a dog's personality, but it cannot cure all unwanted behavior.

Close for comfort

Dogs are inveterate comfort-seekers and social animals, enjoying themselves most when the "pack" is together.

As pack leader, it is your attention that your dogs seek. They rely on you for mental and physical stimulation. You feed them, groom them, house them, play with them, and protect them. In turn, all of their behavior involves you.

Learning manners

On meeting a cat, this Border Collie's urge is to chase, but dogs must inhibit some instincts to share our homes.

Flexible friends
Bred as outdoor working dogs, these Huskies move into a home setting as readily as any other dogs. This elasticity of behaviour is the reason why dogs have so successfully integrated themselves into our lives.

Because we are "top dogs" we can teach our pets – they learn to herd flocks, or to turn aggression on and off on command – but we actively teach dogs only part of what they know. Throughout life, dogs observe the world and teach themselves, and then act on what they learn. Some dogs become jealous if their leader shows affection to another dog or even another human. Others become possessive over their food or toys, and threaten not only other dogs but also members of their human family if they come near. As they age, many dogs become more dependent upon their owners. Routine becomes an end in itself, and any change worries them.

Dogs' facial expressions are similar to ours, which helps us to understand when they are happy or sad, bored or alert – although we can misinterpret their actions. Dogs can be destructive when agitated, excited, or worried. We sometimes think this behaviour is wilful, but in fact it is usually a simple expression of anxiety. To make the most of our dogs, we and they must understand where they fit into our home lives.

Ultimate joy
Rolling over and baring her belly, this Brittany Spaniel shows subservience. She is rewarded by the pleasure of having her chest rubbed.

A Dog's Home

WITH THEIR dramatic ability to adapt to a wide variety of circumstances, most dogs have no difficulty in coping with a primarily indoor existence. As sociable creatures, they crave our company and integrate themselves into our routines. The home is their territory, and the human members of the household their pack. Dogs retain virtually all their natural behavior indoors: they exercise themselves, investigate objects, and function as part of a pack. Inveterate pleasure-seekers, dogs seek out the most comfortable lifestyle possible and sometimes vigorously defend it.

I trust you; you protect me.

Freedom of movement (LEFT)
As household pets, most dogs are denied the freedom of going in and out when they please, and live in what amount to luxurious prisons. Using a cat-flap as his personal entrance and exit, this Yorkshire Terrier can decide when he wants to be indoors or out.

Sitting brings the owner's face closer to the dog

Relaxed facial expression

Greetings
Seeing his pack leader sitting down, this Cocker Spaniel goes over, stands on his hind legs, and acknowledges his owner's superiority by trying to reach up to him.

Stands comfortably on hind legs

Ears are laid in
relaxed position

Daily routine (LEFT)
*Bred to retrieve, a Golden
Retriever fulfills his
"fetching" instinct in the
home by collecting the mail
each morning. Less
conveniently, some dogs do
the same with our
personal items.*

Tail raised
for balance

*It just
feels right
carrying
things.*

Indoor exercise (RIGHT)
*A lack of natural outlets for
expending energy causes this
Cocker Spaniel to burn up
his energy indoors. Your dog
may become destructive if it
is not given enough exercise.*

*If you come
any nearer, I'll
get fierce.*

Family quarrel
*When challenged to
move off a bed that he
considers to be his
own personal space,
this small terrier
bares his teeth and
threatens his owner.*

Dominant
stare is held

Scavenging

YOUR DOG IS likely to take food wherever – and whenever – it finds it. Scavenging is rewarding, because it meets the dog's need to hunt and seek its own food as well as satisfying its thirst and hunger. Because they have fewer taste buds than many other animals, dogs will eat whatever is at hand. If they are hungry, they will take decomposing meat and even animal droppings. "Stealing" food is perfectly natural behavior, which is why it can be difficult to train dogs not to scavenge at home. Dogs certainly do not believe they are stealing the food.

Drink problem (LEFT)
After checking that no one is about, a Weimaraner takes the opportunity to lap up tea from a mug left on the floor. Most dogs will risk trying the taste of almost anything.

Let's see if there's anything tasty to eat in here.

Head disappears as dog investigates the bag thoroughly

Searching the shopping
Finding an unattended shopping bag satisfies this Cocker Spaniel's need to hunt and eat. Many dogs consume whatever they can find, which explains why about 30 percent of dogs are overweight.

Docked tail wags with excitement

Cleaning up

Having come across a rotting carcass, two timber wolves scavenge what meat they can from it. Although wolves primarily hunt for their food, they will also scavenge when hungry. Through centuries of selective breeding, we have successfully reduced the dog's desire to hunt while accentuating its willingness to scavenge. Today, in some parts of the world, scavenging is one of the common reasons why dogs are tolerated. Their robust stomachs and strong desire for food make them perfect natural waste-disposal units.

Guess who's coming to dinner!

Long coat can conceal body language

Uninvited guest

Not having been trained that it is anti-social behavior in human terms, a Briard naturally – and innocently – stands up to eat a meal straight off the dinner plate that she has spotted.

First Encounters

CANINES ENJOY COMPANY. By introducing ourselves into their lives almost at birth, we convince dogs that humans make friendly companions. The same technique can be used to integrate any other species into a dog's life. It is best to do this when the dog is less than 12 weeks old. After that age, greater care must be taken to ensure that neither its natural predatory instincts nor its fear of strange animals is stimulated.

Herd reaction
Breeds used in agriculture, such as these Australian Shepherds, will naturally try to herd livestock like these goats. Herding is simply the dog's chasing instinct modified through human intervention.

Eye contact is held

Ears are perked forward, showing active interest

You're just like my littermates.

Early encounter
A young puppy examines a kitten, which confidently holds its ground. By meeting cats now, this puppy becomes less likely to chase them when he is older.

Leg is raised as puppy starts to withdraw from kitten

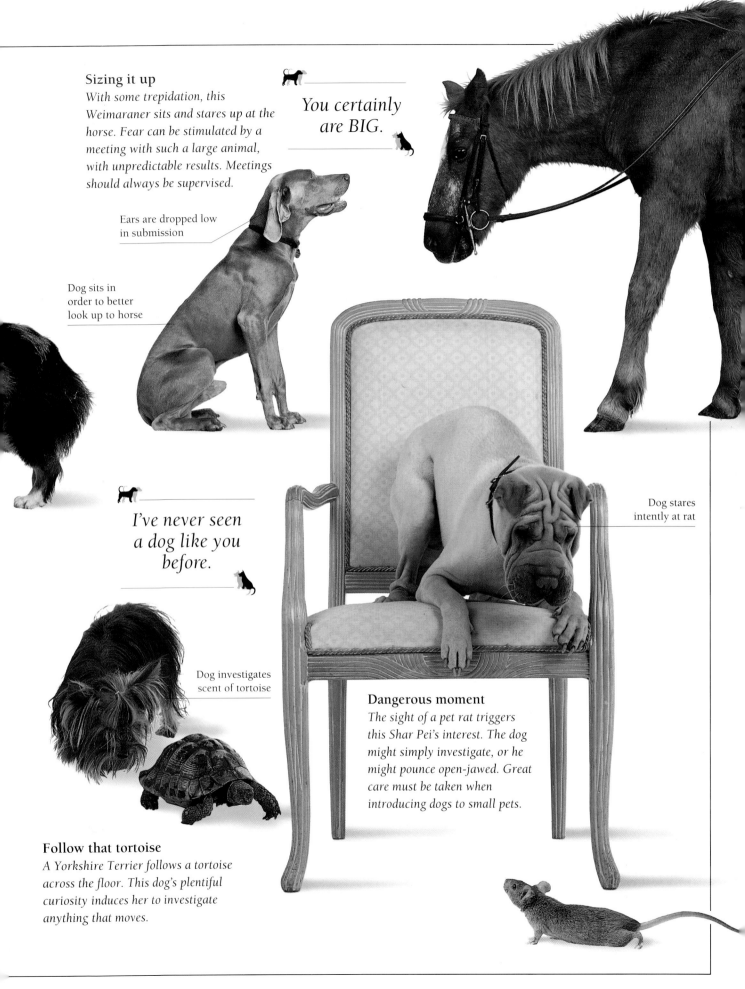

Sizing it up

With some trepidation, this Weimaraner sits and stares up at the horse. Fear can be stimulated by a meeting with such a large animal, with unpredictable results. Meetings should always be supervised.

You certainly are BIG.

Ears are dropped low in submission

Dog sits in order to better look up to horse

I've never seen a dog like you before.

Dog stares intently at rat

Dog investigates scent of tortoise

Dangerous moment

The sight of a pet rat triggers this Shar Pei's interest. The dog might simply investigate, or he might pounce open-jawed. Great care must be taken when introducing dogs to small pets.

Follow that tortoise

A Yorkshire Terrier follows a tortoise across the floor. This dog's plentiful curiosity induces her to investigate anything that moves.

Seeking Attention

BECAUSE THEY ARE so gregariously sociable, and because they consider us to be their pack leaders, dogs crave our attention. Being touched is soothing and reassuring for dogs, just as it is for us. Stroking your dog reduces its blood pressure, its heart rate, and its skin temperature. It calms its sense of arousal. Dependent dogs demand attention most, but even dominant, aggressive canines solicit attention from a strong human leader.

Pick me up, I'm worried.

Leg raised as high as possible

Soft touch
A Weimaraner raises a forepaw to tap his owner and get attention. Dogs can be trained to "shake hands" from this basic gesture.

Hey, look, I'm here.

Emotional blackmail
This Chihuahua stands and scratches at his owner's leg to get his attention. Although this is a sign of submission, dogs such as this in fact often dominate their owners into picking them up.

Head is raised to bark or howl

Double demands
While her owner reads, one of these Golden Retrievers woofs to attract attention. The other gathers herself as close as possible, hoping to be comforted through touch.

Cheek-to-cheek
Seeking his owner's attention, this Gordon Setter puts his face as close as he can to hers. Although elderly, he is mimicking the way he behaved as a puppy with his mother.

Dog enjoys
body contact

*I do
hope she
strokes
me.*

Dog presses herself
against chair

Jealously Guarded

ALL DOGS NATURALLY guard and protect what they consider to be theirs. They often behave possessively about prized objects, sleeping locations, or even the attentions of special people. Children are not seen as dominant, and may therefore be confronted with this dangerous form of aggression. Because of this, adults must always supervise meetings between dogs and children.

Purse-mouthed command bark

1 The voice of annoyance
Seeing the other dog playing with a toy, this Golden Retriever barks to demand the toy for herself.

Head is thrust forward assertively

I want it because you have it.

2 Visual threat (ABOVE)
The retriever continues to threaten and bares her teeth. Responding to this display, the Italian Spinone drops the toy and looks at the aggressor.

3 Winning possession
Showing submission to the more powerful retriever, the spinone rolls over, leaving the toy unattended. The retriever can now take possession of the toy.

Submissive roll

Guarding food

To prevent the loss of any of his food, this German Shepherd Dog puppy threatens the tan puppy, who submissively backs away. The German Shepherd Dog puppy is dominant because of his size and his temperament.

Guarding his prize

Standing over his meal, this dominant timber wolf threatens anyone or anything that comes near. He will continue to do so until his hunger is satisfied. Similar behavior occurs in dogs, and is not dependent on sex or breed. Terriers are known for being possessive, but even a gentle breed such as the Golden Retriever guards food. Often, a dog is possessive of the attention of its owner, behaving aggressively toward any potential rival.

Don't you dare come near. It's mine.

Body pulls away

Eyes look away to show submission

Puppy moves forward confidently

Tests of Strength

TUG-OF-WAR IS A DOG'S favorite sport. It serves a variety of purposes. Some dogs are jealous of others' possessions and want to have them. Others play tug-of-war for the simple fun of the game, with no end purpose other than pure enjoyment. In normal circumstances the self-confident dog ultimately wins, but sometimes superior dogs playing with others lower in the hierarchy let the underdog win, simply to prolong the activity. Tug-of-war reinforces social positions among dogs that live together, so if people enter into the game, they should always make sure that they show high rank by winning.

Winner takes all
This retriever puppy watches the dachshund marching away with the toy. A game has ended with the dachshund taking permanent possession of the prize.

Dog looks back to ensure that the puppy does not follow

Canine teeth are used to grip toy

... and you're not getting it back.

Toy is gripped firmly

Equal and opposite (ABOVE)
This Golden Retriever and Italian Spinone stand side-by-side as they try to get a better grasp on their toy. These dogs are equal in size and confidence. Tugging is simply a game, and is not being used to exert authority.

I love contact sports.

Youth and age
While this older Labrador Retriever tries to pull the toy away, the young Golden Retriever runs in and grabs it. Although adult dogs are usually gentle with puppies, situations like this can lead to displays of possessive aggression.

Head is lowered defensively

Final whistle
A growl from the dominant dog tells the other one that the game is over. In canine terms, possession is now final.

Just for fun
Showing complete relaxation and indicating that this game of tug-of-war is for sheer pleasure, one dog lies flaccidly on his back while the other tugs on their toy.

Bet you can't get it away from me.

Something to prove
Bracing his hind legs, this puppy gives the toy a fierce pull. If he wins this game of tug-of-war with a human, his self-confidence increases.

Toy is playfully pulled away

Leg lifts as dog jumps away

Legs braced ready to pull back

Stirring things up
To provoke a response from her partner, this Basenji teasingly shakes the toy. The other dog responds by grabbing at it. Specially made dog toys are best for these games.

Games with People

ALTHOUGH DOGS ARE often content just to enjoy the luxuries of life with us, they still need mental and physical activity. It is in their nature to be constantly alert, and under natural circumstances they are keen observers of the world around them. Without activity they become bored, and bored dogs can be destructive. Playing games with canines keeps their minds active and – if you play the right types of games – stimulates their bonding to you and reaffirms your role as pack leader.

Playing to win
A terrier pulls possessively on a toy made specially for tugs-of-war. Dogs, especially dominant ones, should never be allowed to win at this game when playing with humans. If they do, it enhances their feeling of dominance.

Harmonious relationship (BELOW)
Hearing his owner sing, a Basset Griffon Vendeen joins in the chorus. Seemingly frivolous activities such as this actually serve to strengthen the bond between you and your dog.

Lips are pursed to howl

A difficult catch (ABOVE)
This Wirehaired Fox Terrier must concentrate to play successfully with such a large ball. Because the ball is too big for him to catch in his mouth, he learns to move it with his muzzle. Teaching this game is the prelude to "playing football" with your dog.

Balloon bounces
off dog's nose

Paw is raised to
touch tentatively

*It jumps
away
every time
I touch it!*

Hide-and-seek
*This mature Gordon Setter enjoys pawing his owner
when she "hides" from him. Playing hide-and-seek
with people or toys stimulates the dog's natural
desire to search and investigate.*

Eye contact is
maintained

Ears show alertness

*It may not be
a bird, but
it's still fun
to chase.*

Forelegs are used
to balance

Legs prepared to
land softly

Mission almost impossible
*By jumping at a virtually uncatchable balloon, these
dogs are given the opportunity to use their ingenuity
while at the same time exercising their bodies. They
depend on you to provide the object of the game and
to act as referee.*

Dog starts
to follow
the balloon

Happy Dogs

WE CAN TELL when dogs are happy by watching their mobile ears, bright eyes, wagging tails, and expressive body language. This is hardly surprising, because they share many expressions and emotions with us. Dogs cannot, however, smile. When they pull back their lips in a greeting they are acting in a subservient manner as they would to a canine pack leader, although occasionally some dogs do learn to mimic a human smile. Dogs need not be excited to be happy: contentment and relaxation also bring pleasure.

Accomplished mimic
Although he looks fierce, this Dandie Dinmont Terrier is simply copying a human smile. This is learned behavior, not inherited.

Wrinkling the nose makes the dog sneeze

Legs are held in begging position

Hind paws are splayed out for balance

The height of delight
Standing tall, this Miniature Poodle shows her pleasure by walking on her hind legs. This brings her closer to the object of her attention, the face of her owner.

Mother love
A young wolf rests his head on his mother's back. Happiness is a human definition, but there is little doubt that this wolf is relaxed and contented. Dogs are also happy in this way when life is pleasurable and enjoyable, and sad when denied physical activity, mental stimulation, or contact with their human "family" or other dogs. There is a direct link between emotions and health: sadness or depression can lead to poor health in humans, and the same probably applies to dogs. It is healthy to be happy.

Open offer (BELOW)
*Wagging his tail and lifting his leg,
a Golden Retriever subserviently
exposes his belly and asks to be
stroked. Dogs that are happy in a
stable relationship with their
owners are likely to
show this kind of
relaxed behavior.*

Relaxed contentment (RIGHT)
*This pleasure-seeking Golden
Retriever has ensconced himself in
the most comfortable place he can
find. Dogs need mental stimulation,
but are also happy when they are
relaxed and at ease.*

Legs are relaxed

Belly is
exposed

Tail hangs limp

Sheer bliss.

Joy ride (BELOW)
*These Bearded Collies find it exciting
to stick their heads out of the car window.
Although this is a potentially dangerous habit,
most dogs enjoy it because the sensation of wind on
their faces mimics the enjoyment of a high-speed chase.*

Heads and Tails

THE "NATURAL" DOG has a long tail, a moderately long muzzle, and erect ears. Dogs use these to signal their feelings, but we sometimes make the signals more difficult to understand by altering dogs through breeding or surgery. Modifications were first made to enhance dogs' work abilities: for example, spaniels' tails were docked to prevent entanglement when retrieving game. Today, there is no justification for such alterations – they are carried out solely for fashion.

A docked tail moves more rapidly than a natural one

Tail curls as it wags

Complete apparatus
This Doberman madly wags his intact tail to show happiness or excitement. Many Dobermans still have their ears and tails cut. There is no medical reason for this: it is carried out solely to make the dog appear more ferocious.

Tail tucked firmly between the legs

Submissive pose
By tucking his tail between his legs, this Whippet simply, but dramatically, signals submissiveness. This obvious gesture is unlikely to be misunderstood.

Human features (LEFT)
This Boxer exemplifies the flattened, "human" face of many breeds. Her ears are intact, although cropping is still carried out on this breed in some countries, but her tail has been docked.

You can see what I'm feeling, can't you?

Ready to go (BELOW)
Keeping direct eye contact with his owner, this Greyhound lays back her ears and pants. These are signals of submissive anticipation to her human pack leader.

Lips are pulled back submissively

Ears show alertness

Panting with excitement

Blind enthusiasm
With his ears perked forward and his natural tail erect and wagging, this Australian Silky Terrier is obviously alert. Long hair over his eyes sometimes interferes with visual communication.

Firm, erect stance shows confidence

A wagging tail indicates excitement

Panting rids the body of excess heat

Getting Worked Up

CANINE EXTROVERTS BEHAVE in a relentlessly gregarious way, but so do highly strung or neurotic individuals. Prolonged boredom can also induce overexcitement. The tendency to be excitable is partly inherited and partly learned. It is one of the prime characteristics for which dogs have been selectively bred. Terriers exemplify the most excitable breeds, and hounds like Bassets and Bloodhounds the least excitable. Excitement is a gratifying feeling. It acts as its own reward, which is one reason why dogs learn to behave this way.

The doorbell! Something exciting is going to happen!

Tail wags with excitement

Overeager greeting
This excitable Springer Spaniel responds to the sound of the doorbell by instantly leaping up at the door as if shot from a cannon. Her actions are rewarded when the visitor enters, and this reinforces her behavior.

Ardent excitement
Excited by the presence of another dog, this Tibetan Terrier clasps the Miniature Schnauzer and indulges in mock sex activity. Although males behave this way to show dominance, both males and females will mount other dogs when overexcited.

The long goodbye
*Seeing his owner about to
depart, this Cocker
Spaniel growls and snaps
at his trousers. The dog feels he can
dictate what his owner does, and
becomes recklessly excitable when he
anticipates an unwanted departure.*

Powerful greeting
*A Leonberger jumps up to greet his
owner, just as he jumped to greet
his mother as a puppy. Many
dogs become overexcited
when they see their
"leaders," which can be
dangerous behavior
from a dog as
massive as this.*

Body stretches
to reach face

Nubile knee
*Overexcited by seeing his
owner, this Golden Retriever
grabs his leg and uses it as a
sex object. Dogs often
behave this way when
excited by the arrival of
strangers in their homes.*

*Not very sexy-
looking, but it's
all I've got.*

85

Bored Dogs

DOGS DO NOT like being alone. They are a sociable species, and it is unnatural for them not to have companionship or activity. A dog needs to be mentally active for about half of its time, and if it is not its brain actually shrinks in size. Most bored dogs just look glum and lie around, but many become destructive. They dig under fences, burrow in the carpet, and scratch at walls. A playmate is the surest solution, but even this does not always work. Because we keep dogs in artificial surroundings, their mental well-being is as much our responsibility as their physical health.

Abject boredom (LEFT AND RIGHT)
With nothing better to do, this Hungarian Viszla climbs onto a chair, yawns, looks glum, and shuts her eyes. Her brain and temper will benefit from mental stimulation.

Not in the mood
An Italian Spinone refuses a Boston Terrier's request to play. Another dog is usually a reliable cure for boredom, but not the only way. We should anticipate our pet's needs and create mentally and physically demanding activities for them.

Flaccid, hanging ears show lack of interest

Classic play-bow

Sorry, but I'm not interested.

Something to do

With nothing to stimulate his mind, a Cocker Spaniel gnaws on a chew while his partner looks on. Rubbing your hands on your dog's toys increases the likelihood that the toys will be chewed, rather than your furniture.

Unoccupied dog watches the toy

Can I have a try at that?

Legs are extended back in relaxed position

Mental torpor

This glum-looking Golden Retriever is content to simply watch the world go by. He rests because he is cut off from the moment-to-moment stimulation he would find outdoors.

Life's a drag.

Tail hangs limp

Craving Company

IF A DOG IS left on its own, without physical or mental stimulation, a dog can develop stereotypical routines. Just like a caged wolf in a zoo, it might pace relentlessly, or it might run up and down the stairs, bark incessantly, or even urinate and defecate in the house. Separation anxiety and this kind of obsessive behavior occur most frequently in dogs rescued from animal shelters.

Carpet is shaken as if it is prey

Destructive worrying
This German Shepherd Dog vents his frustration on a carpet. Dogs can behave totally out of character when left alone, chewing and tearing things, and digging and soiling anywhere in the house. These are signs of anxiety, not actions of retribution for being left alone.

Signs of change
This Great Dane sees the suitcase and immediately starts worrying. Dogs are creatures of routine; they observe us closely and note any changes in our activities. The Great Dane does not necessarily understand that a suitcase means her owner is going away – although dogs can quickly learn this association – but she does know that her routine has changed, and begins to worry.

Solitary confinement

In the absence of more constructive activities, this Golden Retriever shreds the newspaper that has just been delivered. If he is still unhappy over being left at home alone he might start licking his forepaws obsessively, to the extent that he will need medical attention.

Well, there's nothing else to do.

Dog relaxes as it chews

Where is everybody?

Distress call *(ABOVE)*

Certain breeds, such as this Doberman, are more prone to separation anxiety than others and howl plaintively when they feel they have been "deserted." Barking, especially continuous, rhythmic barking, is one of the most common manifestations of the frustration dogs feel at being left alone.

Fight or Flight

WHEN CONFRONTED with the unknown, dogs show their fear in one of three ways. Their first reaction is usually to try to flee or at least hide. If this is not possible, dogs have two options: to fight or to collapse in a submissive heap. Even the most dominant dog can be frightened by strange sights or sounds, larger animals, or anything new and unexpected. Fear can be learned, but it is also an inherited trait in some breeds, such as pointers and German Shepherd Dogs.

Furnishing protection
Frightened by strange surroundings, this Boxer retreats under a chair, the domestic equivalent of a wolf seeking the security of the den. When approached, she might simply freeze. This is learned, rather than instinctive, behavior.

Body is drawn back in typical cowering position

They can't reach me now.

In a corner
With nowhere to hide, this German Shepherd Dog turns to aggression for security, a common trait within the breed. I sometimes encounter this behavior at the veterinary clinic. A shivering and fearful dog, with ears back and tail between its legs, feels cornered and suddenly threatens when approached.

The best defense is attack.

Eye contact is held

My Dad's bigger than you are.

Ears show worry and concern

Yawning with fright

This Whippet shows the natural physical signs of fear. He yawns, his eyes are widely dilated, and he trembles. He also signals submission by laying his ears flat, and hides behind the security of he pack leader. In extreme fear, a dog will discharge its anal glands.

Leg is lifted submissively

Tower of strength (LEFT)

Dogs feel most secure when their owners are present. They try to hide behind their legs when they are worried or feel they are in danger, just as children sometimes do. This dog is about to ask to be picked up.

A Lifetime of Learning

THROUGHOUT THEIR LIVES, dogs are constantly learning. We use this trait, training dogs to work for us in a variety of ways, from acting as eyes or ears for blind or deaf people, to guarding property and protecting us on command. Even when they are not actively trained, dogs monitor our routines and teach themselves about the world they see. With age, mental activity slows down, and the brain actually shrinks. Routine becomes more important. But even in old age, a dog's mental activities can be preserved by constantly providing stimulating activity.

Aggression to order (ABOVE)
On command, this trained guard dog attacks a mock intruder. Trained to "retrieve" villains rather than attack them, these dogs can be aggressive one moment, then gentle once the target is under control.

How about a game?

Old dog, new tricks (ABOVE)
Although he is quite old, this Golden Retriever still finds it enjoyable to play with a new and interesting object. Through constant daily exercise he retains a youthful enjoyment of life.

Double trouble (RIGHT)
This Groenendael (Belgian Shepherd Dog) looks quizzical as she catches sight of her image in the mirror. Dogs learn throughout their lives, but some things remain inexplicable.

Tail hangs limp, showing no alarm

I'm irritable.
Don't bother me.

Teeth are
displayed

As old as you feel (ABOVE)
Seeing the Basenji playing with a ball,
an elderly Gordon Setter ambles over
to join in. Dogs remain curious and
sociable in old age if they have
stimulating lives.

Do not disturb (RIGHT)
A puppy backs away from his grandmother, who
is snarling because she is surprised by his
unexpected approach. Old dogs can get
very set in their ways and should
not be suddenly disturbed.

Dog retracts head
in puzzlement

Head is tilted
quizzically

I don't
understand.
Who is that?

THE GROWING FAMILY

The soft answer
The puppy on the ground inhibits her bite, turning a fight into a game. Playing like this avoids causing serious damage, and at the same time helps to determine rank.

OGS VARY TREMENDOUSLY, but they all share common characteristics, especially in breeding. The brief courtship and the physical linking of male and female dogs in mating are the same in the tiniest lapdog and the largest of the defense breeds. So is the behavior of the pregnant female: she becomes quieter, grows possessive of articles such as toys, prefers to stay under tables or chairs, and sometimes becomes snappy. These changes, which are motivated by hormones, also occur during false pregnancies.

At birth the mother is in control, severing the umbilical cords, drying the puppies, and helping them to find her milk. The puppies are born with very few senses, and are completely dependent upon her. But the sensory abilities develop within weeks, and with them comes independence. Soon the puppies are exploring their world, learning to manipulate both each other and any objects that they find, and demanding food as well as milk from their harassed

Topsy-turvy
These six-week-old puppies play rough-and-tumble, improving their coordination, balance, and reflexes.

Childhood games
While one puppy nonchalantly chews on the leg of another, a third puppy joins in the game. Play is a juvenile activity, accentuated by selective breeding to continue through life.

mother. This is the only time in the lives of most dogs that they are part of a true pack. The mother is the pack leader, but a hierarchy develops among the puppies. In their games, teamwork is learned and behavior is set for life.

Mother love
With their mother standing contentedly, these four-week-old puppies take a meal. They are dependent upon her until they reach the age when, in the wild, they could hunt for themselves.

Fight for a place
Through this kind of play-fighting, young dogs determine their future places in the developing hierarchy.

Three's a crowd?
These three-week-old puppies huddle together for security and warmth. As pack animals, they will continue to enjoy contact with others, including us, even when fully grown.

Because we control their breeding, we can accentuate or diminish the characteristics of dogs. In this way we have created the different breeds. Some dogs are easily trained, others are independent. Certain breeds thrive on companionship, while others are very territorial. Some breeds are more excitable than others. By choosing carefully, you can select a canine companion who will enhance your life and that of your family.

Choosing a Partner

ALTHOUGH IT MAY appear that the male initiates courtship, it is actually the female who decides when – and with whom – she will mate. She does not necessarily choose the most dominant male. Females prefer familiar partners and might simply roll over in submission to over-dominant dogs. While males are always sexually active, females normally have only two short spells each year when they ovulate and then willingly mate. Before and just after ovulation, bitches become more playful, soliciting interest from male dogs.

2 Role reversal
During pre-mating games, the female clasps the male from behind and mounts him. Sometimes she will also carry out pelvic thrusts. Although he is disconcerted, he does not become aggressive because of the prospect of mating.

Wait a minute, shouldn't I be doing that?

Front paws surround dog's midriff

Ears pricked forward in alert position

Front legs sink into play-bow position

1 Play-bowing
Having scented that the female is in season, the male dog confidently approaches her. She replies with a play-bow, which invites him to join in play activity while telling him that she is not yet ready to mate.

How about a game?

3 Brief interlude (RIGHT)
Standing still and with his tail wagging with excitement, the male allows the female to investigate him. She licks her nose to allow scent molecules to be caught more readily so that she can scent him better. After a short pause, play continues.

Tail raised in
excitement

5 Standing ready
*Once sure that the
male is an acceptable mate, the female
stands still. She draws her tail to the
side, displaying her vulva. She
only behaves like
this after ovulation.*

Tail
drawn
aside

4 Playing around
*Play-wrestling is often initiated by
the female. It allows her to make
frequent body contact with her partner.
Both dogs roll and tumble, growling all
the time, while the male takes the
opportunity to thrust with
his pelvis.*

*I'm ready
when you are.*

Heavy panting
to cool off
after activity

97

Mating

AFTER all the elaborate procedures of courtship, the act of mating is completed quickly. As soon as the bitch stands for him, the dog mounts her, grasping her body with his forelegs and pushing his chest onto her back. During sexual congress, the male may sometimes gently hold on to the female with his teeth, and also lick areas of her head, especially around the ears. The male ejaculates quickly, but the two dogs remain physically locked together in a "tie" for about half an hour. This period prevents other dogs from mating with the female.

1 Standing receptively
As the female stands waiting with her tail turned to one side, the male excitedly sniffs and licks her vulva. If she resumes play, he will mark a nearby spot with urine. However, if she remains still he knows that she is ready to mate.

Dogs are physically united with each other

2 **Check and mate** (LEFT)
When the male approaches, the female turns her tail away from him. Initially he stands squarely to her side and rests his head on her back. He licks or nibbles her and, if she shows no resentment, prepares to mount.

3 **Copulation** (BELOW)
While the bitch stands still, often with her eyes partly closed, the male clasps her waist with his forepaws and starts making pelvic thrusts. Ejaculation starts almost immediately.

Female stands passively

Forelegs clasp female's body

4 **The tie that binds** (LEFT)
As mating is completed, a balloon-like apparatus at the base of the dog's penis swells up, preventing the couple from separating. He lifts up one of his hind legs to step over her, but they remain locked together in the "tie" for between five and fifty minutes.

Eyes close and dog relaxes

5 **Tidying up**
As soon as the dog's swelling relaxes, the pair "untie" and retire to lick their genitals. This is a simple sanitary gesture that reduces the possibility of infection. After a variable interval, they may mate once more.

Genitals are cleaned

Pregnancy Behavior

ONCE HER SEASON (or period "in heat") has finished, a female dog behaves as if she is pregnant regardless of whether she has successfully mated or not. This happens because the hormone of pregnancy (progesterone) is always produced by the body for a two-month period after ovulation. During this time a bitch tends to be quieter and more reclusive, but she may also be snappy and irritable. In addition, during her pregnancy or false pregnancy, she may become unusually possessive over any belongings, especially soft toys. You may also see her scratch and dig in carpets or earth and create "dens" around the home, often under tables or chairs.

Toy possession (RIGHT)
Finding denlike security under a chair, a female dog exhibits her hormonally influenced maternal behavior by caring for a stuffed toy, sniffing its ears, and then licking them. She behaves this way after her season, irrespective of whether she is really pregnant.

Toy is groomed

Eyes close in contentment

What a weight to lug around.

Late pregnancy
In the last stage of pregnancy, a bitch lies on her side in what is now the most comfortable position for her. The size of her swollen abdomen indicates that she is due to give birth imminently.

Occupying a real den
Few of our domestic dogs have the opportunity to do so, but this pregnant female has dug herself an underground den to which she can retreat to whelp her litter. Housebound dogs will find artificial "dens" under the furniture.

I have to find somebody to look after.

The kitten is groomed as if it is a puppy

Kittens investigate foster mother

Mothering another species
Impelled by her need to nurture, this bitch has adopted an orphan litter of kittens, which she grooms as she would her own puppies. Her behavior derives from her past experience as a mother and from progesterone, which is the hormone of pregnancy.

Tail lies relaxed

Abdomen is distended by growing puppies

Giving Birth

As BIRTH APPROACHES, the mother becomes restless and stops eating. She may be wary of strangers, or react aggressively if disturbed. In labor, the intensity of her contractions varies, and she might pant heavily or take slow, deep breaths. Puppies are delivered at intervals ranging from a few minutes to two hours in length. Some dogs even temporarily inhibit their contractions when they see their owners. Birth can be physically difficult in some modified breeds, such as Bulldogs, which may need veterinary help during delivery. If your dog experiences any birthing problems, you should contact a vet immediately.

1 Last things first

With rhythmic contractions, the mother expels a puppy in its birth sac. Most puppies emerge headfirst, in a diving position, but it is not unusual for them to enter the world tailfirst, as this one is doing. In the meantime, the puppies that have already been born huddle close to their mother for warmth.

Cord is bitten through

2 Severing the ties

This experienced mother has already licked away the sac from the puppy's face, allowing it to breathe. She now turns her attention to chewing through the umbilical cord, severing the puppy from the afterbirth.

3 Licked into shape

The mother dries her puppies with meticulous licking, and stimulates them to empty their bladders and bowels by licking the anogenital regions. These systems are already functioning but are not under the newborn puppies' control.

Easy. Like peas from a pod.

Anogenital regions are licked

102

4 Mother's milk

During a pause in whelping, the mother turns to check on her puppies' feeding arrangement. Inexperienced mothers do not usually feed their young until after the last delivery, but this mother is happy to let her puppies find her teats as soon as they can. She has already eaten their afterbirths.

Ear position shows
her active interest

Legs stretched
out for balance

Puppies immediately seek
milk and warmth

*Just checking that
everything's OK.*

5 Well-earned rest

Having successfully delivered all six puppies, licked them dry, and cleaned up as much of the mess of birth as she can to protect them from possible predators, the mother now relaxes and gives her newborn family an uninterrupted feed. If undisturbed, she will not leave her puppies for the next 24 hours.

6 Dependent offspring

Dry and with full stomachs, these one-hour-old puppies are almost totally helpless and completely dependent upon their mother for warmth, food, and protection. She will only retrieve straying puppies if they cry out, but feeds them without their asking.

Eyes and ears are
closed at birth

Puppies huddle
together for warmth
and to feed

Raising the Family

THE MOTHERING INSTINCT is elicited immediately after birth by the appearance and erratic movement of the puppies, factors that also evoke caring instincts in us. The instinctive behavior in the mother progresses naturally from total concern for her puppies' protection, nourishment, cleanliness, and sanitation, through a stage of teaching discipline, to treating her young as other adult members of a pack when they become competition with her. This rapid evolution in maternal behavior allows the puppies to become independent of their mother by the time they are three months old.

Game for anything
By joining in their games, this mother helps her puppies to develop their coordination and reflexes. Play situations such as this often end in overt mothering activities, such as grooming.

Toilet training
The mother grooms one of her puppies and, by licking its anogenital region, stimulates it to urinate and defecate. These are body functions it cannot initially carry out without her help. To hide signs of the presence of her defenseless young she consumes their body wastes.

Puppy cowers away from mother's rough play

Puppy accepts grooming

I'd better clean him up.

Constant care (RIGHT)
While two of her puppies feed, this experienced mother licks the ear of another. Feeding and grooming are pleasurable activities for her, but both become an increasing strain as the puppies mature and become more active.

Teaching manners

Because she has been bitten too hard during play, the mother disciplines her puppy by growling and pinning him to the ground. This teaches the puppy that during play he must control the severity of his bite.

Who says you can't do two jobs at once?

Swollen teats show that mother is still lactating

Mother licks inside of puppy's ear

Puppies can now feed standing up

Senses of Independence

OR THE FIRST week of life, puppies find their mother or each other through scent, touch, and the heat receptors on their noses. Their eyes and ears do not function until they are two weeks of age but are fully developed after only another two weeks. Taste and smell, present at birth, also develop rapidly over the first five weeks of life. Developing senses give the puppies greater independence: when newborn puppies are cold, they cry to attract their mother, but by three weeks of age the touch receptors on their feet have matured, and their ability to orient themselves is sophisticated enough to allow them to seek her out.

Precocious nose

A five-week-old puppy pauses in play to sniff urine scent on his littermate. Scenting ability is present at birth, and is mature by four weeks of age.

Body heat

In the absence of their mother, these one-week-old puppies huddle together for warmth.

Zzzzzz

Puppy licks and sniffs ear

Call of the wild

A young wolf cub cries for attention, in the same way that dog puppies call to their mother. At birth, wolf cubs only have the ability to squeak and cry, just like puppies, but within four weeks they will growl, bark, and howl in an adult fashion. Rapid development of the senses and faculties is necessary to help the young wolf scent, see, and signal danger, as well as to help it simply to keep up with the pack.

Someone to lean on (ABOVE)

This five-week-old puppy sniffs his playmate's ear, balancing himself by placing a forepaw on her face. Even at this age, all of his sensory abilities have already matured to adult level.

Still little tail movement at two weeks

Present and almost correct

Although they have been open for five days, this two-week-old puppy's eyes are only now becoming functional. It will be another two weeks before her ability to see is completely developed.

It's all dark and quiet.

Sight and sound

Although she has grown rapidly since birth, this one-week-old puppy remains deaf and sightless. In another week her ears will open, and loud sounds will startle her.

Claws are extended for gripping

Little Beggars

URING THE FIRST three weeks of life, the mother decides when to feed her puppies. As soon as they can walk, however, they start demanding food from her. Taking the initiative, they follow her around and try to feed whenever possible – even when she is simply standing still. This behavior not only satisfies their hunger, but also provides continuing contact comfort, acting as a bonding mechanism between mother and young. As the puppies' digestive systems mature, they eat their first solid food. In wolves and feral dogs, the mother first regurgitates food for them, and then carries food to them intact.

Anything in there today?

No resentment as puppy looks for food

Milk is drying up

I actually enjoy this.

Hind legs splayed out for balance

Recycled food (ABOVE)
Sticking his muzzle into his mother's mouth, this puppy tries to stimulate her to regurgitate a meal for him. Wolves introduce solid food to their cubs this way, and some dogs regurgitate in a similar fashion. This is also why dogs willingly eat food that they have just vomited up.

Family provider (*LEFT*)
The puppies gather around their mother, pestering her for solid food. In the absence of humans, she would now be bringing back meat from hunting for them to eat.

Adapting natural behavior (*RIGHT*)
While his mind is still completely open to learning, this Boston Terrier puppy learns to beg for food from a human, his new "mother." He stands on his hind legs to get close to the food, just as he would do to get near his mother's mouth.

Forelegs wave to
keep balance

*Anything
in there
today?*

Old habits die hard (*BELOW*)
Seeing their chance, these six-week-old puppies latch on for a meal. Because it is also comforting to their mother, she stops what she is doing and permits them to suckle, even though they are now old enough to do without milk.

Tail hangs
relaxed

*She's still
everything
to us.*

109

Learning to Move

OVING FROM helplessness to independence depends upon the speedy development of a puppy's ability to investigate its environment. Within weeks, it must learn how to keep up with adults, to avoid predators, and to catch prey. With a nervous system that matures rapidly, a puppy can stand within two weeks of birth, walk at three weeks, and run by five weeks. Its brain is fully mature and it has all the gaits of the adult by the time it is just twelve weeks old.

Tail is used for balance

1 Three hours old (ABOVE)
At birth, this puppy can right himself if he rolls over, and can raise his head. Using heat sensors in his nose, he can also locate his mother and waddle to her for warmth and food.

Eyes are now open and focused

Paws are placed with deliberation and coordination

Wow! This is amazing.

5 Six weeks old
The puppy has developed dexterity and confidence in his movements. His reflexes are well-developed and, combined with his now mature senses, give him all that he needs to investigate the world around him.

Head can be lifted

2 One week old (BELOW)
Although he has more thrusting power in his hind legs, there has been no dramatic change in the puppy's mobility during the first seven days.

I feel so heavy.

Movement is seal-like

3 Two weeks old
Using all four legs, the puppy can now just raise himself off the ground. Improved coordination and balance allow him to take his first steps.

Legs are not yet strong enough to support body

Left...right...left...

4 Three weeks old (BELOW)
The puppy now has all the abilities to make decisions about where he wants to be, and moves in the direction of his choice.

Body is lifted off the ground

Exploring the World

ONCE THEIR SENSES and coordination are well developed, puppies start exploring their surroundings. In a short time, they must learn how to survive in, and benefit from, the environment around them. In addition, they must understand how to live communally with other members of their pack. At first their tremendous curiosity has no fear attached to it. They boldly leave the nest and explore the surrounding territory, willingly approaching all animals, including humans. This is a critical period in the puppies' lives: their early experiences form the backbone of lifelong behavior. Although fear behavior develops at around eight weeks of age, this period of social exploring and open learning continues for another month.

Now, that looks interesting.

1 Off to explore
Seeing two of his littermates involved in physical activity, a third puppy appears to become interested in their behavior and approaches them.

Chewing is "inhibited" and playful

I just felt something on my back – and it wasn't you.

Legs are lifted to kick playmate

Whoops! There's something in my way.

2 Overcoming obstacles
In fact, the puppy's curiosity has been stimulated by something else. Too young to have learned that he could be encountering a serious fight and putting himself at risk, the puppy determinedly takes the shortest possible route to his destination and nonchalantly climbs over the other two puppies.

Hind leg stretches to climb over obstacle

Playing puppies show no concern

Puppy gently bites playmate's neck

3 Soldiering on
Although they are being used as a jungle gym, the two littermates continue their spirited encounter. The inquisitive puppy is too interested in what he sees ahead to join in their activity and continues moving towards the focus of his attention.

4 Activity continues
As the lone puppy goes off to explore what intrigues him, his two littermates continue their play-fight (left). The minds of these puppies are like blank pages: the more they explore their surroundings and learn about each other at this age, the better prepared they will be to cope with anything new and challenging they come across in the future.

Wagging tail indicates excitement

Private Investigators

THE TIME FROM birth to three months of age is the most important in a dog's life. This is when it learns about itself, its littermates, and the world around it. It discovers what is fun and what is dangerous, and how things taste and feel. Skills are honed, and mental and physical dexterity developed by playing with objects. The more a young dog is allowed to investigate its surroundings, the more developed its brain becomes.

Is it edible?
Showing his excitement, this puppy play-bows while chewing on a toy. The chemical senses of smell and taste are the ones first used by puppies to investigate their surroundings.

Raised tail shows interest

Good muscle control has developed

I wonder if it will run away?

Puppy shows good balance

Checking it out
With her foreleg raised and extended, a puppy examines a new object by touching it. She will bat it about before tasting it.

Comfort chew (RIGHT)
Puppies seek out familiar scents. Finding a shoe that carries the scent of her owner, this Golden Retriever puppy settles down for a chew. If she is allowed to chew on an old shoe, she will go on to chew on any others with the same scent.

Young explorers
Two gray wolf cubs investigate a set of antlers. Young canines will investigate, play with, and manipulate any objects they find around them, such as twigs, leaves, or the remains of dead animals.

Feels good, but it doesn't taste very exciting.

Sharp teeth puncture and tear

Toy is held between paws

Sibling rivalry
Three littermates argue over who gets the prize. It seems appealing because they are fighting over a toy, but they would do the same over a recent kill.

Safe toys (LEFT)
Wool provides a chewable feel that this Border Collie puppy finds pleasurable. The best toys for puppies are those that feel good to chew but cannot be swallowed.

Chewing this shoe reminds me of my people.

Puppy is relaxed by familiar scent

Puppy Play

JUST LIKE US, dogs remain playful throughout their lives. This is a characteristic of their behavior that we have exaggerated through selective breeding, because we enjoy watching them play and playing with them. Dogs are most playful while they are young, and through play they learn how to communicate with each other and, most importantly, how to inhibit their bite. Play stimulates inventiveness and teaches problem-solving, timing, balance, and coordination, allowing puppies to experiment in safe conditions.

Face-to-face
Growling and facing each other, these puppies gently try to bite each other's faces. This play activity continues throughout life, and is one of the most common forms of play in adults.

Tail is raised in excitement

Chasing tails
Three littermates bite and chase each other. If they bite too hard, they will provoke a similar response from their playmates, so they soon learn to bite gently.

Turns to "attack" littermate

Assertiveness training

Having been bitten too hard by a larger littermate, the smaller puppy bites back, warning that it will not be intimidated. Social rank is determined in exchanges like this one.

Vulnerable abdomen is exposed

Youthful bravado

Because he has not yet developed fear behavior, this Golden Retriever puppy lies on his back and paws at the German Shepherd Dog puppy's face. Later he will adopt this position only in submission.

Head is turned in submission

Larger puppy tries to escape

Don't do that again!

Formal bow

Asking to play, this puppy lowers itself into the classic play-bow. Dogs use this stance to tell one another that they are not threatening and would simply like to meet. As an adult, this puppy will behave in the same way with humans or any other animals to which it has formed attachments.

Will you play with me?

Body is lowered to ground

Extended Family

TRUE, UNALLOYED pack behavior exists only during the brief period that a litter remains together. Once a puppy leaves its mother and siblings, it develops modified pack behavior, with humans taking the place of other canine pack members. Only puppies that go on to live or work with other dogs find themselves in a situation where they must cope on their own with the admission of new members to their group. In these circumstances, age, sex, size, and self-confidence determine where the new pack members find themselves in the canine hierarchy.

Order of seniority
When meeting an older dog for the first time, this eight-week-old puppy is put in his place by the senior dog's confident show of authority.

Dominant clasp

Mixed bag
This family group incorporates the mother, a daughter from a previous litter, and the grown puppies, each knowing its place in the pack hierarchy.

We know each other well.

Raised tail shows confidence

2 Coordinated attack (RIGHT)
Seeing what is happening, the rest of the litter joins in and threatens the stranger as a group. The puppies act as a team because they know each other very well.

3 Sexual harassment (LEFT)
A litter member mounts the intruder, showing dominance. Mounting and pelvic thrusting are basically sex-related activities, but they are also used to assert authority.

1 Not one of us (ABOVE)
Seeing a small stranger, a 12-week-old member of the pack intimidates it by dominantly placing a paw on the intruder's shoulder. The smaller outsider backs away.

We don't like strangers.

4 Standing his ground (RIGHT)
Although smaller, the intruder gains confidence and snaps back. By doing so, he proclaims that he will not be intimidated.

Family saga (BELOW)
Previous generations will continue to live with their litter, like this mother and one of her offspring. Older dogs are still members of the pack, although with advancing age they relinquish the leadership to a younger generation.

Larger puppy pulls back

Coordinated response to sound

Breed Characteristics

THROUGH SELECTIVE breeding, we have produced dogs with widely varying characteristics. Some are excitable, reacting quickly to their surroundings, while others are more placid. Some are more easily trained than others. Some have been bred to be aggressive guard dogs, others to be docile pets. This chart gives a guide to the levels of these traits in different breeds and, where appropriate, breed groups.

Breeds	Excitability & Activity			Aggression			Trainability		
	High	Med	Low	High	Med	Low	High	Med	Low
Afghan Hound			●		●				●
Airedale Terrier	●			●				●	
Akita			●	●			●		
Alaskan Malamute			●	●					●
American Cocker Spaniel	●				●		●		
Australian Shepherd Dog			●			●	●		
Australian Silky Terrier	●			●			●		
Basset Hound			●			●			●
Beagle	●				●				●
Bearded Collie		●			●		●		
Bichon Frise	●				●		●		
Bloodhound			●			●			●
Boston Terrier	●				●				●
Boxer	●				●				●
Briard		●			●			●	
Brittany Spaniel			●			●	●		
Cairn Terrier	●			●				●	
Cavalier King Charles Spaniel	●					●		●	
Chesapeake Bay Retriever			●			●	●		
Chihuahua	●			●				●	
Chow Chow			●	●					●
Dachshunds	●			●					●
Dalmation			●	●					●
Doberman			●	●			●		
English Bulldog			●			●			●
English Cocker Spaniel		●			●		●		
German Shepherd Dog			●	●			●		

Breeds	Excitability & Activity			Aggression			Trainability		
	High	Med	Low	High	Med	Low	High	Med	Low
German Shorthaired Pointer			●			●	●		
Golden Retriever			●			●	●		
Great Dane			●	●					●
Hungarian Viszla			●			●	●		
Irish Setter	●				●				●
Jack Russell Terrier	●			●					●
Keeshond			●			●	●		
Labrador Retriever			●			●	●		
Lhasa Apso	●				●				●
Maltese Terrier	●				●				●
Miniature Poodle	●				●		●		
Miniature Schnauzer	●			●				●	
Newfoundland			●			●	●		
Norwegian Elkhound			●			●		●	
Old English Sheepdog			●			●			●
Pekingese	●				●				●
Pomeranian	●				●			●	
Pug	●				●				●
Pyrenean Mountain Dog			●	●				●	
Rottweiler			●	●			●		
Rough Collie			●			●	●		
Saint Bernard			●	●					●
Samoyed			●	●					●
Scottish Terrier	●			●				●	
Shetland Sheepdog	●					●	●		
Shih Tzu	●				●		●		
Siberian Husky			●	●					●
Springer Spaniels	●				●		●		
Staffordshire Bull Terrier	●				●				●
Standard Poodle			●		●		●		
Weimaraner		●			●			●	
Welsh Corgis	●			●			●		
West Highland White Terrier	●			●					●
Wirehaired Fox Terrier	●			●					●
Yorkshire Terrier	●				●			●	

121

Assessing your Dog's Character

EACH DOG IS AN individual with its own mind. Dogs have emotions. They feel happy, sad, jealous, angry, and exhilarated. They experience pain, humiliation, elation, and joy. Each has its own unique personality, influenced by genetics, hormones, early learning, and the environment in which a dog finds itself. Looks can sometimes be deceptive – even the most appealing-looking dog retains in some measure the traits of its wild forebears.

The hangdog

Some dogs retain the size of certain wolf breeds but have dramatically altered looks. With his low-set, lopped ears and sad eyes, this Italian Spinone looks unthreatening and easygoing. Visually he gives the impression of a sociable and relaxed personality, but looks can deceive. Some dogs that look soft, gentle, and easygoing to us might in fact be dominant individuals.

Lopped ears look
unthreatening

Large size similar to
that of wolf ancestors

The infant dog

We have created dogs that serve human emotional needs. Dogs that look and act like this Boston Terrier bring out the parent in us. Their large, prominent eyes, together with their flattened faces and small bodies, elicit a caring response from many people. However, this little dog's assertive personality can be quite at odds with the image that it projects.

Large eyes look
innocent and
trusting

Small body
appears infantile
and helpless

Your dog's personality

Many of us enjoy the company of our pet dogs so much that we tend to overlook or brush aside their misdemeanors. It is possible to assess both the positive and the negative aspects of your dog's personality using the following questionnaire. Score each group of questions separately to help you to judge exactly how trainable, domineering, sociable, or active your dog is.

If you would like to help in a worldwide study of dog behavior, please photocopy the completed questionnaire and send it to: Dr. Bruce Fogle, Box DDK, 86 York Street, London W1H 1PD, England.

Check the most appropriate box for each of the statements below.	Almost always (1)	Usually (2)	Sometimes (3)	Rarely (4)	Almost never (5)	Assess your dog's personality by adding up the scores for each section.
1. MY DOG:						**1. TRAINABILITY**
Is poor at learning obedience						*A score of 12 or more means that your dog is trainable and easy to control. Excitable dogs find training difficult because they are easily distracted.*
Is or was difficult to house-train						
Is excitable						
2. MY DOG:						**2. SUBMISSION**
Disobeys or even threatens me						*Dogs with scores of over 20 in this section make the best family pets. If the score is less than 10, contact your veterinarian or a dog handler for professional advice.*
Is dominant toward other dogs						
Barks at sudden noises at home						
Is aggressive to strangers at home						
Is snappy when disturbed						
3. MY DOG:						**3. SOCIABILITY WITH HUMANS**
Is hostile to people						*Scores of over 16 show the dogs that have best integrated themselves into human society. A low score means that your pet is poorly socialized and is a potential fear-biter.*
Will not accept strangers						
Dislikes being petted						
Is likely to snap at children						
4. MY DOG:						**4. SOCIABILITY WITH OTHER DOGS**
Is fearful of other unknown dogs						*Dogs that have scores of 12 or more enjoy canine company. These are the animals that would most appreciate living with fellow dogs.*
Is tense and nervous						
Will not play with other dogs						
5. MY DOG:						**5. ACTIVITY**
Is destructive						*A score of 16 or more means that your dog is relaxed and self-contained. Dogs with low scores need extra physical and mental activity. These are inherited traits over which you have little control.*
Barks when anxious or excited						
Whines/demands my attention						
Demands physical activity						

- What is the breed of your dog?...
- What color is your dog?...
- How old was your dog when you acquired him/her?.......................................
- How old is your dog now?...
- Is your dog male or female? ....
  - Has your dog been neutered?...
    - If so, at what age was your dog neutered?.......................................
    - In what country do you live?...

TOTAL SCORE

A score of under 40 means that your companion is a potential problem dog. You should contact your veterinarian for professional advice. A total score of over 70 means that you are sharing your home with an angel.

DOG CARE
MANUAL

A GUIDE TO CARING FOR YOUR DOG

THE ASPCA AND DOG CARE

HAVING A DOG is only the beginning of a magic equation. There are two other critically important parts: loving your dog and caring for your dog. And of those two, you prove the former by paying careful attention to the latter. In other words, if you love your dog you will care for it properly; and that is what this invaluable book is all about.

Man's Best Friend

As you will learn, when man domesticated his dog he literally coaxed it out of the genes of the wolf. In doing that he asked a number of things of the dog, and we are still asking the same things of our dogs today, almost 250 centuries after the domestication process probably began. We have asked our dogs to keep their natural territorialism and aggression to what, for a wolf descendant, is an absolute minimum. We tell our dogs we don't want them making snap decisions on matters of territory and friends-versus-enemies. We tell them to let us guide them, instead. We ask our dogs not to wander, not to chase cars or cats, and not to be destructive and noisy. We want them to be good canine citizens and fit into our very oversized pack – this thing we call civilization. If dogs are to do all of that, they must be kept clean, they must be kept clear of parasites, and – if we want them to live long, healthy lives without the stress of unfulfilled desires to mate – we must ask them to submit to the surgery we call neutering.

Caring for the Family Dog

We ask a lot of our pets. We really have to if they are to fit in and live the kind of life we want of them. We have to pitch in, too, and follow the many points of advice this book offers. In many ways this book sums up the philosophy of The American Society for the Prevention of Cruelty to Animals, developed over

125 years of experience helping animals. Whether it has been through our shelters, adoption programs, education, Humane Law enforcement, or the Henry Bergh Memorial Animal Hospital, we have helped dogs and other animals in just about every conceivable way.

A Dog's Best Friend

Today we spend far too much of our time dealing with the tragic consequences of the unchecked breeding of dogs. Each year, millions of dogs are euthanized in shelters because there are too few good homes. As a dog owner, you are responsible for all aspects of your companion's care. This includes taking the proper steps to ensure that your pet does not contribute to the surplus of dogs. You can help even more by looking for your new canine friend at an animal shelter.

In Sickness and in Health

Whether the canine friend you find is big or small, young or old, this book provides the step-by-step guidance you will need to ensure a long and healthy friendship. Sharing a home and lifestyle with a friend whose strongest urge is to please you, to love you, and never to judge or criticize you has more advantages than we could begin to list here. Protect that wonderful treasure your canine companion by giving the care that is both needed and deserved. This is, quite literally, the least you can do.

Roger Caras

President

The American Society for the Prevention of Cruelty to Animals.

INTRODUCTION

EVERY VET WISHES he had enough time to sit down and talk with each dog owner, so that he could explain that dogs are not simply people in furry disguises, but are uniquely designed individuals with eating, grooming, training, and health needs that are different from our own and specific to their species. Using color photographs and illustrations, this book shows and explains how best to care for your canine companion. Chapter One contains information on the canine senses and explains how different breeds evolved from the wolf and spread to all parts of the world. Because your dog will share your home for ten years or more, it is important that you select your pet carefully, handle and train it during its first, formative months, play with it, and plan ahead when you go on vacation. Basic care is discussed in Chapter Two, and information on feeding is contained in Chapter Three. A dog's coat varies from the velvety texture of the Doberman's to the luxuriousness of the Rough Collie's, and grooming requirements differ accordingly. The grooming of different coats is illustrated with step-by-step photographs in Chapter Four.

The Dog Owner's Responsibilities

Keeping a dog as a pet is a joy and a privilege, but it is also a responsibility. Regardless of how attractive and well fed your dog is, if it is not properly trained, it is like a loose cannon, liable to misfire at any moment. Fortunately, training a dog to be a well-behaved pet is not difficult. If you teach your canine family member while it is still a puppy to sit and stay on command, you should be able to control it under almost any circumstance. Leash training, basic obedience training, and correcting bad habits are discussed in Chapter Five.

Keeping Your Dog Healthy

Maintaining your pet's good health is central to complete dog care, which is why the health care chapter is the largest in the book. Disorders are described according to body system, and there is information on recognizing the

symptoms of your pet's illness so that you can provide a vet with accurate information, enabling him to prescribe an appropriate course of treatment. Inherited disorders and dangers to humans from dogs are discussed in Chapter Six. Dogs seem to get better faster when they are cared for in their own homes, and Chapter Seven concentrates on nursing, administering medicine, and looking after an elderly dog.

A Child in Canine Clothing

Succeeding chapters describe and illustrate breeding, dog shows, and, perhaps most important of all, first aid. You should watch over your dog in the same way that you watch over a young child. Both are inquisitive – if they see something interesting they want to examine it. Accidents do happen, but by understanding elementary first aid, you can provide vital, immediate care. You should know how to give cardiac massage and mouth-to-nose resuscitation or how to stop bleeding and bandage minor wounds. In case of a traffic accident, you should be familiar with how to move an injured dog away from danger and to the nearest emergency facility.

The Last Link with the Natural World

Almost every culture in the world keeps pets, and the dog is the world's favorite. As we evolve from an agrarian to an urban culture, dogs are in many ways one of our most important links with the natural world. We get pleasure from caring for our gardens and from caring for our pets. This is a primitive satisfaction, but the fact that it is enduring is a good omen for the future of the natural world around us.

Chapter 1

INTRODUCING THE DOG

OUR RELATIONSHIP with the dog is much more varied, intense, and interdependent than with any other living species. The pact works because we understand each other so well. Both of us are naturally playful, gregariously sociable animals that instinctively defend our territories and hunt for our food. The dog's superior physical design and senses were obvious to our ancestors, and once these attributes were harnessed, the dog became – and still remains throughout the world – our best animal friend. That relationship continues to evolve and develop, with dogs more popular now than they have ever been.

EARLY DOMESTICATION

Dogs were probably first domesticated from wolves throughout the Northern Hemisphere, and then in this altered form accompanied people, or were taken by them, to all other parts of the world. Wolves may originally have been simply camp followers, willing consumers of ancient refuse. It is equally likely that young wolves were raised in human settlements and treated as pets. Because of the wolf's adaptable nature, taming soon led to controlled breeding, or domestication. The first known domestic dogs date from around 12,000 years ago.

ORIGINS OF THE DOMESTIC DOG

Guardian *(right)*
According to ancient Chinese mythology, the "guardian" Foo Dog was a loyal protector of people and their property, and drove away evil spirits. As well as producing guard and protector dogs, the Chinese also bred the first small lapdogs, such as the Pekingese.

Canine god *(left)*
The dog was worshipped in Ancient Egypt as a messenger of the dead. It was represented by the jackal-headed god Anubis.

Ancient hunting dogs *(below)*
Mastiff-type hunting dogs appear in this frieze from Ashurbanipal's Palace at Nineveh in Assyria, carved over 2,600 years ago.

Beware of the dog *(above)*
By Roman times, a vast variety
of breeds had evolved. To guard
and protect remained a primary
role, as shown in this Roman
mosaic of a guard dog.

Aristocratic hounds *(right)*
In Renaissance Europe, dogs
were specially bred to hunt with
the aristocracy, as seen here in
Andrea Mantegna's 15th-century
portrait of the Duke of Mantua's
grooms with their hounds.

Fashionable lapdogs *(left)*
Although lapdogs like the
Pekingese had existed in China
for thousands of years, and small
breeds like the King Charles
Spaniel had been kept by the
European nobility for centuries, it
was not until the 18th century
that pet dogs became common.
This painting by Richard Collins
shows a pet spaniel enjoying tea
with the family. Pedigree breeds
were initially the companions of
wealthy, aristocratic families, but
gradually became widespread
among the lower classes.

THE FIRST DOG BREEDS

Distinct dog breeds have been in existence for thousands of years. In Israel, archaeologists have found a grave over 10,000 years old containing a human skeleton with its arm around a puppy. The puppy's skeleton was similar to that of the Canaan Dog, a species still found in the Middle East today.

Dingoes arrived in Australia with settlers more than 3,000 years ago. Salukis have been bred in the Middle East for several thousand years, while the Pekingese in China has not changed in 2,000 years. In the New World, native people kept dogs, varying from the Alaskan Malamute to the Chihuahua in Mexico. Similar developments occurred in Europe, producing guarding and herding dogs from the indigenous wolf, while the smaller Asiatic wolf was the progenitor of breeds that spread through the Middle East into the heart of Africa.

Alaskan Malamute
This powerful, wolflike dog was bred by the Malamute people of Alaska.

Newfoundland
The Newfoundland was the result of breeding European dogs with native island dogs.

Boston Terrier
One of the few wholly American breeds, the Boston Terrier was first developed in New England as a fighting dog.

Chihuahua
This tiny dog is the oldest breed on the American continent. It may have been introduced to Mexico by traders from China.

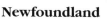

WILD AND FERAL DOGS

Closely related to the Papua New Guinea Singing Dog, the Dingo first arrived in Australia with the Aborigines. Feral dogs, often called pariah dogs, still exist in many parts of the world. They usually form packs and breed successfully. Abandoned domestic dogs will often revert to this behavior.

Dingo

AMERICAN WOLF

The large variety of sizes and colors of the North American wolf provided ample genetic material for different dog breeds to develop.

Wolf-free South America
Northern wolves migrated south as far as Central America but no farther. By the time the Spanish Conquistadores came, however, dogs were found throughout South America, probably having migrated with human traders.

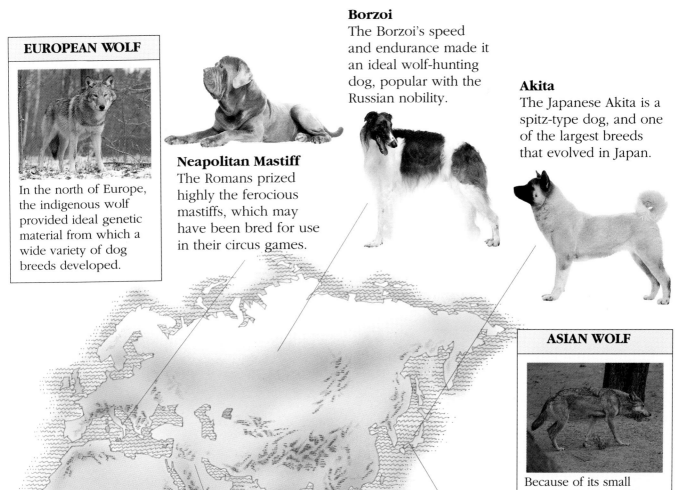

EUROPEAN WOLF

In the north of Europe, the indigenous wolf provided ideal genetic material from which a wide variety of dog breeds developed.

Neapolitan Mastiff
The Romans prized highly the ferocious mastiffs, which may have been bred for use in their circus games.

Borzoi
The Borzoi's speed and endurance made it an ideal wolf-hunting dog, popular with the Russian nobility.

Akita
The Japanese Akita is a spitz-type dog, and one of the largest breeds that evolved in Japan.

ASIAN WOLF

Because of its small size, the Asiatic wolf provided excellent genetic material for the creation of toy breeds such as the Pekingese.

Basenji
The unique barkless Basenji is only one of the many native African canine breeds.

Saluki
With a longer pedigree than any other breed, the Saluki has been prized for millenia in the Middle East for coursing and hunting.

Australian Cattle Dog
The Australian Cattle Dog was produced by crossing a Dingo with a variety of breeds, including the collie.

Japanese Chin
This elegant toy dog was introduced to Japan from China over 2,700 years ago. For centuries it was kept as a pet in the imperial Japanese court.

THE DESIGN OF THE DOG

The classic design of the dog is exemplified by the world's most popular breed, the German Shepherd Dog. This dog has a heavy coat for good insulation against the cold, no bony attachment between the front legs and shoulders, which allows for prolonged running on "shock absorbers," a long muzzle with specialized teeth to grip and crush, and powerful muscles that do not tire easily. This is also the basic design of the wolf, and of its relatives, the husky breeds of dog.

Through selective breeding, humans have improved certain aspects of this model but have also produced breeds with shortened life expectancies and many medical problems.

WHAT IS A DOG?

Erect tail for signaling

Large head with good brain capacity

Long muzzle with well-spaced teeth

Powerful hind-leg muscles for leaping

Short, dense coat for insulation

Deep chest with large lung capacity

Firm, stocky legs with well-spaced toes

The basic dog shape
The typical dog is an all-rounder – well muscled, built for endurance, with balanced proportions of height to length, and with the ability to use all its senses to their maximum capacity.

SELECTIVE BREEDING

Giant breeds (*left*)
The St. Bernard has been selectively bred for size and thickness of coat. The result is a dog with great physical strength, able to work in freezing temperatures.

Body designed for endurance in cold temperatures

Miniature breeds
Because it once served as a mobile hot-water bottle, the Pekingese was designed to be compact, furry, and affectionate.

Strong muscles in the hindquarters propel the dog forward

Long tail for balance

Agile strength
Powerful hind-leg muscles allow this German Shepherd Dog to jump effortlessly, an ability we utilize when we train dogs for specific tasks, such as police work.

Flexible spine for running at great speeds

Speed and endurance
This Lurcher can run much faster than the wolf from which it is descended. This breed is a classic example of how, through selective breeding, humans have redesigned the original model to emphasize one particular characteristic.

Strong shoulders for cushioned landing

Playful temperament *(below)*
Redesign involves temperamental as well as physical changes. This Bichon Frise is typical of the breeds of dog in which humans have perpetuated lifelong active, playful, puppy-like behavior.

Faulty craftsmanship *(left)*
Lovable it may be, but with its bandy legs, squashed face, breathing problems, and skin disorders, the Bulldog shows how we have abused our control over dog design.

THE CANINE SENSES

The dog is a hunter and scavenger that lives within a pack structure in which it must recognize friend and foe. Its senses have therefore developed for these purposes – excellent sight to enable it to see the slightest movement of potential prey; a sense of smell far beyond human comprehension with which it scents game, territory odors, and even emotional states in other animals; acute hearing to distinguish sounds over great distances; but poorly defined taste, allowing it to eat things that other animals consider offensive. It also has a refined sense of touch, which is why the dog makes such a good companion for humans.

THE FIVE SENSES

Sight

Laterally placed eyes, as on this Whippet, provide good peripheral vision, which is important for dogs used for hunting and chasing. The more frontally placed eyes of the Pug offer better binocular vision but are not very good at seeing things close up.

Whippet

Pug

Smell

Smell is the dog's most important sense. Inside the nose is a surface area as great as the area of its entire body. A moist nose can capture more molecules of scent than can a dry one.

Touch *(left)*

The contact comfort of infancy that most mammals enjoy is a lifelong pleasure in dogs. Pleasure of touch is important in animals that play together, huddle together for warmth, and use touch in the form of licking or pawing as a means of signaling rank within the pack.

Taste *(right)*

The sensation of taste is closely linked with that of smell. For example, this Boxer is dribbling saliva because it can see and smell something appetizing to eat. Dogs have far fewer taste buds than do humans and can only register tastes as pleasant, indifferent, or unpleasant.

Hearing *(below)*

Erect ears, as on this Basenji, are more likely to take in sound than the exaggerated lop ears of the Bloodhound. Hearing is almost pitch perfect; for example, dogs are able to tell the difference in car engine sounds produced even by similar models.

Basenji

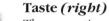

Bloodhound

CANINE SIXTH SENSE

Do dogs have extrasensory perception? Many owners believe that their dogs have a sixth sense. This enables them to know, for example, when it is time to go for a walk or when the family's children are approaching the house on their way home from school. Dogs are also credited with telepathic abilities that enable them to pick up their owners' feelings.

Scientific evidence suggests that dogs have an electromagnetic sense that makes them sensitive to earth tremors and vibrations. This may help them to predict earthquakes and find their way home across hundreds of miles.

UNDERSTANDING A DOG

Because they are pack animals, dogs, like their wolf relatives, have developed a subtle and sophisticated range of communication methods based upon body language and odors. Many of these actions are easily understood by humans, but some, such as urine marking, are open to misinterpretation.

Understanding canine communication is the best way to provide effective care and companionship for your dog.

PACK BEHAVIOR

Pack members
These Siberian Huskies are able to work together as a true pack with a human leader. In the absence of fellow canines, dogs look upon humans as other members of the pack.

Attention fixed on handler for leadership

Separation anxiety
Howling, barking, pacing, and destroying objects are all signs of stress caused by being left alone *(see page 207).*

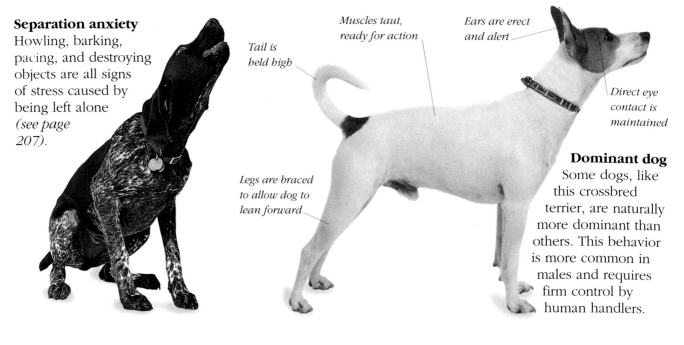

Tail is held high

Muscles taut, ready for action

Ears are erect and alert

Direct eye contact is maintained

Legs are braced to allow dog to lean forward

Dominant dog
Some dogs, like this crossbred terrier, are naturally more dominant than others. This behavior is more common in males and requires firm control by human handlers.

Ears are flattened

Leg is raised

Submissive dog
To avoid aggressive confrontations, dogs have a system of ritual submissive behavior. By lying down and lifting a leg, this Lurcher signals to more dominant dogs, and to humans, that it is not a threat.

Belly is exposed

Tail is tucked between legs

Scent marking *(left)*

Urine scents left in strategic positions are markers to other dogs, giving information on who left them and how long ago the depositor passed through.

Dog looks away to avoid confrontation

Scent signaling *(right)*

Urine scenting, as this Italian Spinone and Alaskan Malamute are doing, is much like humans shaking hands. This provides information about the sex and state of mind of the other dog.

Dog sniffs genitals to ascertain stranger's sexual status

Play-fighting

Dogs play-fight with each other all their lives, but especially when they are puppies. This young German Shepherd Dog is learning how to assert dominant authority. There is some degree of theatricality to this behavior, with all moves exaggerated. Some dogs, however, can get overexcited and bite their playmates.

Puppy submits to older dog

Meeting new dogs *(above)*

With experience, dogs use a complex body language to avoid conflicts when meeting, as this Basenji and young Afghan Hound are doing.

Play-bow

One of the most attractive body-language signals is the play-bow, shown here by an Irish Soft-coated Wheaten Terrier. Dogs commonly use this "Will you play with me?" signal to invite other dogs, or humans, to chase them, or to have a rough-and-tumble game with them.

THE DOG AS A PET

When introduced into homes as young puppies, dogs readily adopt humans as members of their pack. Some people, on the other hand, ascribe human characteristics to their pets. However human it may seem, your dog always thinks like a dog and acts like a dog.

Breeding has enhanced the canine qualities that humans find desirable, such as affection and loyalty. At the same time, it has diminished other normal, but undesirable, characteristics, such as constant territory marking, to make the dog indisputably the world's most popular pet.

BUILDING A GOOD RELATIONSHIP

The dog looks for attention from its owner

Physical contact is reassuring to the dog

The human pack
Dogs are social animals that thrive in a group where there is a well-established hierarchy. Your dog should become part of the family, a member of the human pack but always the lowest-ranking member. All dogs seek attention and physical contact from their owners.

DOG OWNERSHIP WORLDWIDE

Over 200 million dogs are kept as pets worldwide. Australia, North America, and France have the highest dog populations in ratio to households, while Japan has the fastest growing number of dogs. Germany has a relatively small dog population. In China and Iceland, the number of dogs kept as pets is low because of strict controls.

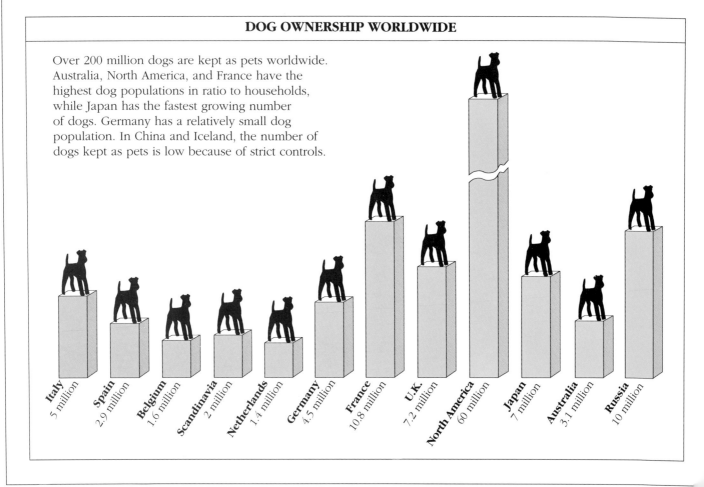

Italy 5 million

Spain 2.9 million

Belgium 1.6 million

Scandinavia 2 million

Netherlands 1.4 million

Germany 4.5 million

France 10.8 million

U.K. 7.2 million

North America 60 million

Japan 7 million

Australia 3.1 million

Russia 10 million

WHY DO YOU WANT A DOG?

Show dog
Showing dogs is a hobby for some and a passion for others. In order to win a show, the dog must be presented at the top of its form, fit, and well groomed *(see pages 302–303)*.

WORKING DOGS

With their supple intelligence and readiness to cooperate, dogs are trained to assist humans in different ways. A guide dog for the blind, such as this one, a hearing dog for the deaf, or a service dog for a physically disabled person, willingly fills the void created when an individual loses an important ability. Some dogs are trained to use their refined sense of smell to detect illicit drugs. Other dogs can follow ground or air scents to aid in avalanche and earthquake rescues.

Lapdog *(left)*
Small lapdogs can provide humans with an opportunity to satisfy their lifelong enjoyment of caring for living things.

House dog *(left)*
A family pet gives you an enormous amount of companionship and affection. Dog owners exercise outdoors more often than non-owners and report fewer minor health problems. They might even be less at risk from heart disease.

Guard dog
Because of their natural desire to protect their pack and their territory, all canines, but especially the larger breeds, offer us security and protection.

BASIC DOG TYPES

Dogs inherited a range of behavior from wolves. But by accentuating or diminishing specific traits or characteristics, humans have created dog breeds with different personalities. They have also created a range of shapes and sizes. Some of these present-day breeds are less fearful than their ancestral relatives, while others are more aggressive. By Roman times there were shepherd dogs, warrior dogs, sight and scent hunters, terriers, and companions. Kennel clubs still emphasize such divisions in their classifications.

BREEDING FOR DIFFERENT TASKS

Herder
These collies are typical of herding breeds with an enhanced desire and ability to herd and control flocks of domestic animals.

Sight hound (right)
This Borzoi is typical of breeds already highly developed thousands of years ago to help in hunting by using their superior vision to sight game and their immense speed to chase it.

Companion (above)
Maltese Terriers like these two were first bred thousands of years ago. The breed is thought to have been named for the island of Malta. Today, companionship is the dog's most important role.

BREED CATEGORIES

The American Kennel Club and the Canadian Kennel Club group recognized breeds into seven categories: sporting, hound, working, terrier, toy, non-sporting, and herding. Other countries have slightly different categories.

Scent hound

These Bloodhounds have an infinitely superior ability to follow both air and ground scent. Scenting breeds invariably have long noses to house their larger-than-average smelling faculties.

Long, sensitive nose to pick up different scents

Warrior

Historically, guard and attack dogs were massive in size, like this Neapolitan Mastiff. Today, however, guard dogs are bred more for physical dexterity than size.

Gundog *(below)*

In the 19th century, breeds like this Irish Setter, together with pointers and retrievers, were developed for use in recreational hunting. Today, setters are primarily companion dogs.

Terrier *(left)*

Although terriers have existed at least since Roman times, Britain has produced more breeds of terrier than any other country. This Border Terrier originated in the Scottish Border region.

Chapter 2

BASIC CARE

OWNING A dog can enrich your life. By living with a canine companion we are reminded that we are not unique and separate from the rest of nature but have an interdependent relationship with it from which we both benefit. As the dominant member of the partnership with our dogs, we have an obligation to care for them as best we can. We are responsible for their proper training, feeding, handling, breeding, and housing, as well as acting as a leader of the family "pack", and providing them with companionship and security. Combined with grooming and health management, this care ensures a happy and secure future for our dogs.

BECOMING A DOG OWNER

ake sure you select a
dog that fits into your
lifestyle both now and as you
expect it to be in years to
come. The amount of
exercise, food, grooming, and
general attention a dog needs
varies with its shape and
temperament. Size is not
everything. Some small dogs
can actually need more
exercise than their much
larger relatives.

DECIDING ON A DOG TYPE

Pedigree
By choosing a pedigree dog such as this
Basenji you know in advance not only its
potential size and energy requirements, but also
a good deal about its temperament. Choose a
temperament compatible with your own.

*Facial expression
is endearing
and unique*

Mixed breed (left)
Mixed breeds are often
endearing and in need of
homes. Because of the
randomness of their breeding
they are less likely to suffer
from inherited diseases
and disabilities than are
purebred dogs.

Cross breed (right)
A crossbred dog, such
as this Jack Russell and
Border Terrier mix,
often combines
beneficial attributes
of both parents.

THE DOG FOR YOUR LIFESTYLE

Family pet *(right)*
A dog like this Large Munsterlander revels in human and canine companionship, and delights in vigorous exercise.

Large, active dog
This Rottweiler needs plenty of space for its daily exercise but is wary of unfamiliar people and dogs. You should only acquire a breed like this if you have ample experience in dog handling, since a large dog can be hard to control without proper training.

Small companion
Compact but robust, this Chihuahua offers companionship like most toy breeds. Yet it is also a surprisingly effective little guard dog.

WHERE TO OBTAIN A DOG

Animal shelter *(left)*
Animal shelters always have surplus dogs requiring good homes. The best shelters interview you before letting you take home one of their charges. Because these dogs have had previous homes, be prepared for unexpected behavioral problems. Such dogs may take a while to settle down.

Purebred puppies
Recognized breeders should be contacted for purebred puppies. You should not buy any puppies from pet shops.

ESSENTIAL EQUIPMENT

It is important to invest in proper equipment before bringing a dog into your home. You should provide it with a bed and a variety of toys. Feeding bowls should be slide-proof, and grooming utensils appropriate for the dog's coat. You should also have ready a collar, leash, identity tag, and, if necessary, a muzzle.

Bean bag bed
Form-fitting bean bags make ideal beds. They are soft, light, retain body heat, and are easy to wash. Most dogs enjoy the security they feel when nestled down on one.

Brass tag   *Steel tag*

Basket
Chew-proof plastic baskets are easier to clean and harder for a dog to damage than wicker models. Line the basket with a well-fitting, washable mattress.

Identity tags
Provide an identity tag on which you can have your dog's name, your telephone number, and that of your vet engraved.

Toy cannot be destroyed

Dog pull
Only use a tug-of-war toy like this with a dog that willingly gives it up when you command it to do so *(see page 163)*.

Chew bone
All dogs enjoy chewing. Gnawing on a nylon bone exercises the jaws and cleans the teeth.

Chew bone

Chew toy
This rubber toy is chewable and also bounces erratically when it is thrown, stimulating a dog to pursue it.

Chew toy

Squeaky toy

Squeaky toy
This squeaky appeals to a dog's hunting instincts. Beware of toys with inner parts that can be swallowed.

Muzzle
A dog should wear a muzzle to prevent it from scavenging, or to restrain it, especially around children, if you think there is even a remote possibility of it biting.

Basic grooming kit *(right)*
A good-quality bristle brush grooms the fine, downy coat close to the skin, while metal brushes and combs remove tangles, mats, and debris from the thicker, longer hair. Be sure to use brushes that are correct for your dog's breed *(see pages 186–189)*.

Bristle brush　　*Wide-toothed comb*　　*Fine-toothed comb*

Leather leash

Leather collar

Collar and leash
A leather collar and leash are ideal for a mature dog. You might prefer using cheaper meshed nylon, especially given the variety of collars needed for a puppy that will grow to a large size. A dog should always wear a collar and identity tag *(see page 169)*.

Bowls
Each dog should have its own food bowl, which should always be kept clean. Use a heavy ceramic bowl or a stainless steel or plastic one, preferably rimmed with rubber so that it does not slide. Fresh water should always be available and replenished daily.

Stainless steel bowl　　*Ceramic bowl*　　*Puppy bowl*

CHOOSING A PUPPY

WHAT TO LOOK FOR IN A PUPPY

Owing to advances in preventive medicine, nutrition, and treatment of diseases such as cancer, it is likely you will share the next decade or more with your dog.

Choose one that is not only right for your lifestyle today, but also one that you think will fit into your daily routine for the next ten years. Choose only a puppy that appears bright, alert, and healthy. Whenever possible, arrange to see the puppy with its mother, since this will tell you something about its temperament. A reputable breeder will let you have a puppy conditional upon a vet examining it and certifying that it is healthy. Puppies should stay with their mothers until they are eight weeks old.

Eleven-week-old puppy
This Boxer puppy is active, inquisitive, and alert. When it first meets new people it does not cower, but comes forward to investigate, which is a good sign of confidence. Puppies that are overconfident, however, can sometimes develop into dominant adults.

Facial expression is quizzical but relaxed, with no sign of fear

Fur is shiny and soft, and feels clean and smooth

Legs are straight, and there is no splaying to suggest poor growth

Muscles are well developed and symmetrical

Relatively hairless skin on the belly is pink and unstained

Feet should show no signs of deformity that could lead to lameness

EXAMINING A PUPPY

1 The eyes should be clear and bright, and free from any discharge. There should be good pigmentation, and no sign of inflammation or irritation.

2 The ears should be pink inside with neither an unpleasant odor nor any sign of crusty or waxy discharge, which may indicate ear mites.

3 The skin should not be oily or flaky, and it should not have any sores or lumps. The hair should be firm and not come out when it is stroked.

6 When picked up, the puppy should feel firm and heavier than you expect. If the puppy is relaxed while being lifted, this is an indication that it might be easygoing as an adult.

4 The gums should be pink and odor-free. Except in breeds such as this Boxer, the teeth should meet perfectly.

5 The anal region should be clean and dry. There should be no sign of diarrhea or other discharge from the genitals.

ASSESSING TEMPERAMENT

Observing the litter
Seeing the mother will give you an idea of the puppy's potential temperament. Watch how the puppy behaves with the rest of the litter. Bossy puppies often become dominant adults, while submissive puppies often develop into insecure adults. The best pets are usually those with temperaments between these extremes.

FIRST INTRODUCTIONS

When it is first brought into your home a new puppy might be disoriented. You should restrict it to one room and let it investigate its new environment, but keep it company so that it does not become afraid. You should provide water, food, a chew toy, and a comfortable bed, preferably in an enclosed pen, which will soon become the puppy's personal "den." Newspaper on the floor will soak up accidents.

For the first few days you should give it the same food that it has previously been fed and change gradually to a new diet once the puppy is over the initial excitement of coming into your home.

A secure den

A puppy pen offers security and means that even when you are out of the room the puppy is being trained to relieve itself on newspaper (see page 156).

THE PUPPY PEN

Puppy can watch all activity of household

Newspaper will soak up accidents

Fresh water should always be available

MEETING OTHER PETS

Introducing a dog to a puppy
An older dog may resent the arrival of a puppy so it is important to supervise their first few meetings. Allow the dog to investigate the puppy when it is asleep.

Puppy demands attention from older dog

SAFETY IN THE HOME

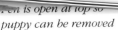
*Pen is open at top so
puppy can be removed*

Making your home safe

A puppy is naturally inquisitive and will want to investigate any new object by smelling and chewing it. Simple precautions, similar to those you would take to ensure that your home is safe for toddlers, should be taken to prevent damage or injuries to your dog. Remove all breakable items and ensure that the puppy does not chew dangerous objects such as electrical cords.

*Make sure
all electrical
appliances are
switched off
at sockets*

*Lemon juice or pepper
can deter puppy from
chewing objects*

*Toys provide
stimulation*

DANGERS IN THE HOME
• Keep outside doors and low windows closed to prevent wandering. • Place electrical cords and all cleaning and decorating materials out of reach. • Temporarily remove valuable objects or items of sentimental value until the puppy is past the chewing stage. • Keep breakable objects well out of reach.

Introducing a cat to a puppy

Dogs and cats can live together peacefully and enjoy each other's company if their first introductions are not threatening. Introduce the resident cat to the puppy with a mesh or wire gate between them.

HOUSE BREAKING

Dogs are naturally clean animals that will not willingly soil their sleeping areas. They enjoy the routine of urinating in specific places. As a dog owner you can determine where these should be, initially on newspaper in the home and later restricted to an area outdoors. Canine droppings are aesthetically unpleasant and a minor health hazard: you should always clean up after your dog. In many places this is the law.

PAPER TRAINING

1 After eating, drinking, playing, or waking up, a dog will need to empty its bladder and bowels. Young puppies must relieve themselves every few hours, so there will probably be a few accidents until a puppy is fully house broken.

2 Sniffing the ground is often the only sign the puppy will give that it needs to empty its bladder or bowels. Some puppies both sniff and race around frantically at the same time. You have only seconds in which to intervene, and place the puppy in the designated place.

Puppy sniffs to find a spot that smells right

3 Quickly pick up the puppy and place it on the paper. Newspaper is best because it is cheap, readily available, and also very absorbent. Keep a small piece of soiled newspaper along with the fresh supply to provide the puppy with its own odor and to encourage it to use the paper again.

4 Praise the puppy after it has urinated. Never discipline a puppy after it has soiled the floor, and never rub its nose in the mess.

Both actions are valueless and will make the puppy scared of you.

Praise puppy for using paper

Accidents
Clean up accidents in the home with an odor-eliminating disinfectant. Do not use ammonia products, since these may remind the puppy of its own urine smell.

TOILET TRAINING OUTSIDE

1 An older puppy can be trained to relieve itself outside. Learn to recognize the warning signs so that you know when it has to be let out to answer the call of nature. In time, going outside to relieve itself will become a regular habit for the puppy.

2 Encourage the puppy to use a remote area for its toilet. A puppy is more likely to urinate where it has soiled before.

3 Having found the right place, the puppy urinates. Dog urine is acidic and burns grass, leaving brown patches. Train the puppy to relieve itself when and where you want it to.

CLEANING UP DOG MESS
Always clean up after your dog. Carry a plastic bag or "pooper-scooper" with you and dispose of the mess in the proper place. When cleaning your own garden, flush the mess down the toilet. Roundworms and tapeworms can be transmitted in dog feces. Your dog must be dewormed regularly.

HANDLING A DOG

Stroking and grooming are comforting to a dog and at the same time teach it that humans are in control. You should handle a new dog as much as possible. If you first see a puppy while it is still with its breeder, ask that it be handled frequently by many different people until it is old enough to be taken home.

Once home, accustom your dog to being picked up and carried. Even large dogs must occasionally be lifted, and it is best to teach them this from a young age. Always be careful when approaching a strange dog. Even a dog that has been trained not to be hand-shy may be wary of a stranger.

CHILDREN AND DOGS

Introducing children to a dog

Even a friendly dog, such as this Golden Retriever, should be introduced to young children in the presence, and under the supervision, of an adult. While a dog may enjoy being stroked by adults, it might not be used to the more awkward touch and handling of children.

A friendly dog enjoys being stroked on its neck and head

Sharing tasks

Children can help care for the family pet. By choosing an enjoyable task, such as feeding, grooming, or walking a dog (always under the supervision of an adult), children will enjoy developing a closer relationship with the pet.

PICKING UP A LARGE DOG

1 Always talk to the dog to reassure it before trying to pick it up. You should muzzle it first if you have any doubts about its temperament. Place one arm around the dog's chest and forelimbs, and the other around its rump. Bending your knees, draw the dog in to your chest. Keep your back straight.

2 Keeping a secure grip on the dog, lift it up. A nervous dog may need to be restrained by a helper, who should gently hold its head and talk to it. A dog should be used to being picked up from an early age and should not struggle to get free. Put the dog down if it begins to panic.

PICKING UP A SMALL DOG

1 Reassuring the dog calmly, place one hand under its forelimbs and chest, and the other around its hind limbs and rump. This gives you firm control over the dog and helps to stop it squirming and paddling.

2 Lift the dog by supporting the chest with one hand, keeping the other under the dog's rump. This method prevents the dog from jumping out of your grasp.

Support the dog's hind legs and rump

APPROACHING A DOG

1 Approach a dog that you do not know well with caution. Do not use jerky movements. Offer a hand at face level for the dog to bend down to sniff. Avoid reaching down from above, since this is an intimidating gesture.

2 If the dog appears to be friendly and does not show any obvious sign of fear or aggression, it can now be stroked. Do not pat it from above, which is a dominant gesture.

COLLARS AND LEASHES

When you get your dog, provide it with a buckle collar and leash. Always leave the collar on the dog, along with the dog's license and identity tag, to ensure that it can be identified if it strays. Choose the type of collar, head halter or harness, and length of leash that is most appropriate for you and your dog. You can protect your dog in case it strays by using a method of permanent identification, such as a tattoo or microchip implant.

Leash training
All dogs should be trained from an early age to walk obediently on a leash *(see pages 198–199)*. Dogs with fine, long necks such as Greyhounds and Whippets require a special, wide collar, whereas small dogs such as Yorkshire Terriers may benefit from a light harness.

TYPES OF COLLARS AND LEASHES

Choosing a leash and collar
Leashes and collars vary in quality, price, and usefulness. They are usually made of leather, cotton, or nylon. Braided or rolled leather is comfortable and long lasting. Meshed nylon is firm, supple, and usually less expensive. An extending leash is very practical. It allows a dog greater freedom than an ordinary leash, while the owner still retains control.

It is important to get a puppy used to wearing a collar from as young as six to eight weeks of age. Start by putting the collar on the puppy for short periods each day. When the puppy is unsupervised, always remove the collar in case it catches on something. A puppy's first walks on a leash should take place in the safety of the home. This will make walking on a leash outside less frightening. The leash should represent the fun of going for a walk.

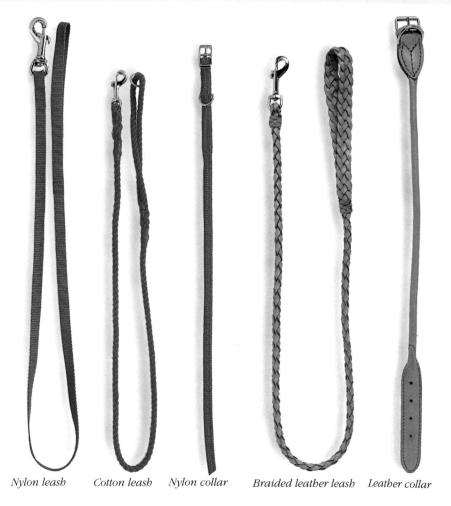

Nylon leash   *Cotton leash*   *Nylon collar*   *Braided leather leash*   *Leather collar*

PUTTING ON A COLLAR

1 Make sure that the collar is the right length for the dog's neck so that it fits comfortably. It should not get caught in the fur of a dog with long hair. Be careful not to fasten the collar too tightly and cause the dog discomfort.

2 You should be able to slip two fingers under a well-fitted collar. The collar will then not come off if the dog tugs backward on its leash, will not cause discomfort, and will be able to be unfastened easily in an emergency.

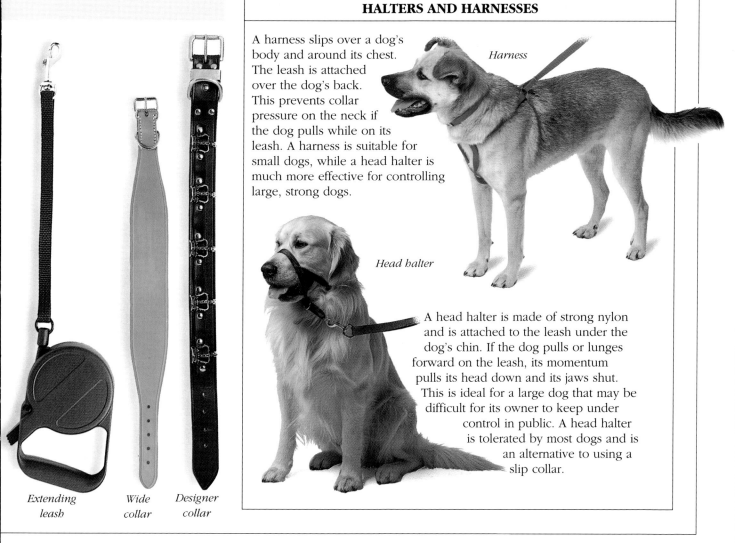

HALTERS AND HARNESSES

A harness slips over a dog's body and around its chest. The leash is attached over the dog's back. This prevents collar pressure on the neck if the dog pulls while on its leash. A harness is suitable for small dogs, while a head halter is much more effective for controlling large, strong dogs.

Harness

Head halter

A head halter is made of strong nylon and is attached to the leash under the dog's chin. If the dog pulls or lunges forward on the leash, its momentum pulls its head down and its jaws shut. This is ideal for a large dog that may be difficult for its owner to keep under control in public. A head halter is tolerated by most dogs and is an alternative to using a slip collar.

Extending leash

Wide collar

Designer collar

PLAY AND EXERCISE

Dogs of every age and size enjoy playing with each other, and with humans and objects. If a dog is denied mental and physical activity, its energy may be released in destructive and unacceptable behavior *(see pages 206–207).* The actual amount of exercise needed varies according to a dog's breed, age, and state of health, but all obedient dogs should be let off their leashes daily and allowed to run in a safe, appropriate place.

By training a dog to retrieve objects you can concentrate this necessary exercise into a shorter period of time. In your absence, toys can stimulate your dog's mind and senses.

TYPES OF EXERCISE

Exercise off the leash
All active breeds, such as this spaniel, revel in daily physical activity. When you have trained your dog to obey your commands, and where regulations permit, you should regularly let it off the leash to enjoy vigorous exercise.

Exercise on the leash *(left)*
In addition to daily rigorous exercise, provide your dog with frequent walks. An extendable leash provides the handler with short leash control when walking among other pedestrians, and adjusts to allow a dog greater freedom in other areas.

Road walking helps keep nails short

Playing games
Playing games with your dog reinforces your authority, because the dog depends upon you to throw the toy. This is also a good way to use your own time efficiently, since it concentrates the dog's activity into a short time.

Chewing toys
When a dog is provided with toys, it can exercise its mind and senses even in its owner's absence. This Standard Poodle finds chewing a toy a satisfying way of filling its time when it is not playing with humans and is restricted indoors.

Playing with each other
Just like humans, dogs enjoy playing with each other, even as adults, as these Italian Spinones are doing.

Playing together with toys
These Brittany Spaniels know each other well and exercise their minds and bodies by playfully tugging together on a rope toy.

DANGEROUS TOYS

Avoid poorly made toys or small balls that can be swallowed. Do not give articles of clothing or shoes as toys, since a dog will not restrict itself only to the items offered, but will chew anything that bears its owner's scent.

Tug-of-war
This mixed breed enjoys playing tug-of-war. However, when playing games such as this, never let your dog win, since this may make it believe it is dominant over you.

Playing with a ball
Games of chase stimulate natural canine behavior. This puppy chases a ball as it would chase prey in the wild.

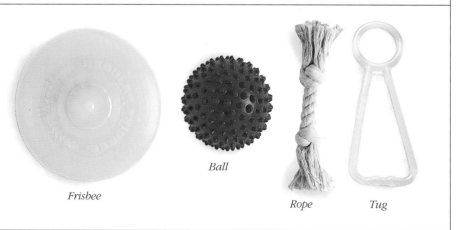

DIFFERENT TYPES OF TOYS

All dogs enjoy playing games with balls and frisbees. These toys help exercise your dog and teach it to chase, capture, and retrieve. Some balls and rubber toys have squeakers, and dogs enjoy "killing" them. Be sure such toys are well made. Knotted ropes and tug toys are ideal for two dogs to play with together. Specially made nylon chews can also help to keep teeth and gums healthy.

Frisbee

Ball

Rope

Tug

DOGPROOFING A YARD

Dogs need daily outdoor activity, preferably in the company of their owners or other dogs. Outdoor activity provides stimulation, but it can be dangerous for dogs on their own. Never let your dog roam freely, except in fenced-in areas where you can quickly regain control of it. Allowing a dog to roam the streets endangers the dog, annoys neighbors, and is illegal in some places. Working dogs can be kept in a well-equipped outdoor kennel, provided that they are regularly exercised.

The dog outdoors
Make sure that your yard is escape-proof and that a dog is not exposed to dangers within it. You can secure it with a high fence.

OUTDOOR KENNELS

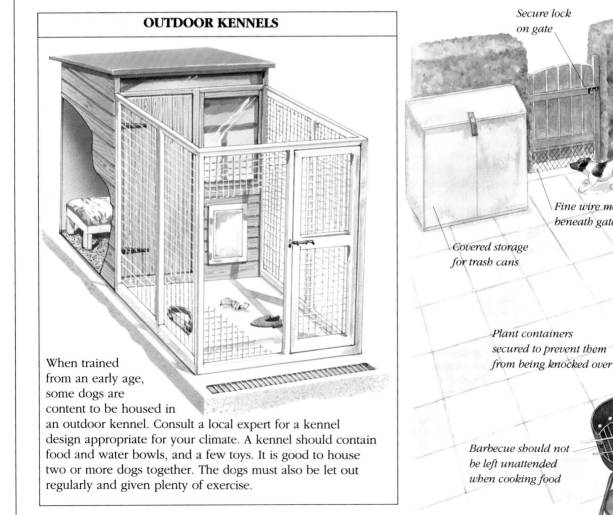

When trained from an early age, some dogs are content to be housed in an outdoor kennel. Consult a local expert for a kennel design appropriate for your climate. A kennel should contain food and water bowls, and a few toys. It is good to house two or more dogs together. The dogs must also be let out regularly and given plenty of exercise.

Secure lock on gate

Fine wire mesh beneath gate

Covered storage for trash cans

Plant containers secured to prevent them from being knocked over

Barbecue should not be left unattended when cooking food

Garden dangers

The greatest danger for your dog in the yard is the possibility of escape. Use sturdy gates, latches, and fencing. Make sure that there are no gaps in the hedges. Fine wire mesh at ground level on gates and beneath hedges is a good additional safeguard to keep small dogs from escaping. Keep all horticultural and other chemicals locked in the garage or a garden shed, and put trash cans in a covered cupboard. Do not let your dog near a barbecue while it is being used for cooking. Avoid placing ornamental plant containers where they can be knocked over, and make sure a garden pond is kept covered. Train your dog to use a specific part of the yard, such as a sand pit or rough grass area, for its toilet. Remove and dispose of all waste. Provide your pet with a doghouse in which it can be kept outside for short periods during warm weather.

TOXIC PLANTS

Many garden plants are poisonous to dogs. In particular, dogs should be prevented from eating all kinds of fungi, and kept away from laburnum trees and mistletoe berries. Keep plant bulbs such as daffodils out of reach. The following plants are potentially dangerous to dogs: columbine (*Aquilegia vulgaris*), hemlock (*Conium maculatum*), oleander (*Nerium oleander*), yew (*Taxus baccata*), lupine (*Lupinus* sp.), boxwood (*Buxus sempervirens*), clematis (*Clematis* sp.), lily-of-the-valley (*Convallaria majalis*), and ivy (*Hedera* sp).

Greenhouse containing garden chemicals

Compost bin

Sand pit for use as a toilet area

Sturdy fencing

Non-toxic plants

Fenced-in area with vegetable garden that is inaccessible to dog

Covered pond

Lockable garden shed

Enclosed doghouse

TRAVELING AND VACATIONS

Traveling with your dog can be enjoyable, but it requires careful planning. If you are driving, make sure your car is well equipped. You should stop every few hours on the journey to allow your dog to exercise, drink, and relieve itself. Never leave your dog in your car in hot or sunny weather. Dogs have poor control of their body temperature and can suffer potentially fatal heatstroke much faster than humans *(see page 290)*.

Obey local regulations on dog control. Remember that your dog will be excited by new sights and smells, but away from home territory it could easily get lost. Make sure that it carries your local telephone number on its name tag. Finally, when you arrive, find out the location of the local vet, in case of an emergency.

USING A DOG CARRIER

Traveling box
A carrier provides safety and security for a small dog when traveling by air or road.

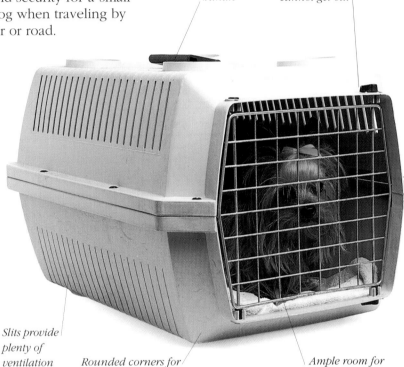

Carrying handle

Locking catch so dog cannot get out

Slits provide plenty of ventilation

Rounded corners for easy cleaning

Ample room for standing and turning

SAFETY IN A CAR

Seatbelt *(left)*
Special seatbelts can reduce the risk of a dog being injured in a car accident, and also prevent the dog from distracting the driver.

Dog barrier *(right)*
A special barrier restricts dogs to their own secure place in the car and prevents them from hurtling forward in the event of a sudden stop.

THE DOG ON VACATION

Backpack (left)
Some dogs can be trained to carry their own food and dishes in special saddlebags when out camping with their owners.

Pack can carry dog's dish, food, and utensils

Lifejacket helps dog to float

Lifejacket
Although they are excellent swimmers, dogs should always wear lifejackets when taken boating on open water a long way from the shore.

QUARANTINE KENNELS

Dogsitter (below)
If you prefer to leave your dog in the comfort of its own home while you travel, a vet can usually put you in touch with an approved "dog-sitting" agency.

Some rabies-free countries maintain quarantine regulations to control the import of animals from countries where this fatal disease exists *(see page 246)*. Other nations require proper identification and proof that a dog has been vaccinated against the disease before it is allowed to enter the country. If you are planning to move to a rabies-free area, make sure that you have the necessary documentation, including all veterinary certification in the country of origin. Where rabies quarantine exists, get a list of approved quarantine kennels from that country's agriculture department, and whenever possible, get someone to inspect the facility for you. Virtually all quarantine kennels permit visiting.

RESPONSIBILITIES OF A DOG OWNER

Enjoying the love, loyalty, and companionship of a dog involves dual obligations. You must maintain not only the dog's basic needs but also the quality of life of your family, friends, and neighbors.

A dog depends upon its human owner to ensure its well-being in its community. This involves your obeying the local legal requirements concerning dogs, as well as protecting your pet from injury or ill health. Your dog relies on you to train it from an early age to be trusting, even-tempered, and sociable with humans and other dogs. Dogs are social animals, and your pet should be treated as one of the family.

SOCIALIZING A DOG

The value of training
Raising a paw is a sign of obedience. All well-mannered pet dogs should be trained to obey commands from their owners, and to be even-tempered and relaxed with strangers. Some large dogs are more powerful than people, and if untrained can be potentially dangerous.

Canine manners
Dogs should be trained to willingly sit together without showing any aggression. Early socialization ensures that your dog is relaxed and comfortable in the presence of other dogs. With so many dogs living in crowded urban environments where they meet other dogs daily, this type of training is essential.

CHOOSING A VET

Routine medical care
All dogs should have an annual medical examination. They should have a stool sample examined twice a year and be wormed if necessary, and routinely vaccinated against infectious diseases. Choose your vet with the help of pet-owning friends. Many vets provide a 24-hour emergency service. Find out the location of your local emergency facilities and keep the telephone number handy. Treatment can be expensive, but health care insurance will help cover costs.

Vaccinations
Vaccination protects your dog from life-threatening diseases.

YOUR DOG AND THE LAW

DANGEROUS DOGS
Responding to public concern, many countries have made it illegal to allow a dog to be dangerously out of control in a public place. You must obey local muzzling laws, but use only a safe, basket-type muzzle that allows a dog to pant freely. A vet or humane society can advise you on any local legislation.

Muzzling
If you have doubts about your dog's temperament or behavior, it is safest to keep your dog muzzled in public, especially around young children.

Identity tags
Every dog must always wear an identity tag and dog license on its collar. You could also have your dog permanently identified with a tiny microchip implant or a number tattooed on its thigh.

Chapter 3

FEEDING

A NUTRITIOUS, well-balanced diet produces a strong-boned, well-muscled, healthy-coated canine. Just like humans, dogs love their food. Unlike humans, however, they have a poor sense of taste and are therefore willing to  eat almost anything. Many pet dogs also lead somewhat boring lives and see mealtime as the highlight of the day. Dog owners should avoid giving their dogs excessive treats or feeding them more often than they should eat, even if they beg. This combination of facts explains why obesity is a problem in almost one out of three pets. Whatever you choose to feed your dog, make sure that it is part of a well-balanced diet, and that it does not exceed your dog's energy requirements.

DIETARY NEEDS

Each dog has its individual requirements, which will change at the various stages of its life. All dogs, however, require minimum quantities of a wide range of nutrients if they are to remain healthy. Dogs are not true carnivores, and cannot exist on meat alone. Therefore, meat, which provides protein, should never form more than half your dog's diet. Meat also provides fat, which contains essential fatty acids necessary for a variety of body functions, including good skin and coat condition. The remainder of a dog's daily calories should come from carbohydrates such as dog meal. A balanced diet has all the necessary vitamins.

THE VALUE OF NUTRIENTS

Protein is needed for growth, tissue repair, and maintenance of metabolic processes

Essential fatty acids give a glossy sheen to a dog's coat

Carbohydrate is an important energy source for dogs fed dry diets. Fiber, which is a form of carbohydrate, promotes regular bowel movements

The well-fed dog
With a well-balanced diet, this Border Collie puppy will grow to have a shiny coat on a well-muscled, straight-boned body.

FEEDING EQUIPMENT

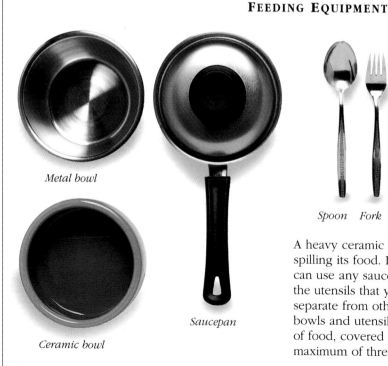

Metal bowl

Ceramic bowl

Saucepan

Spoon *Fork* *Knife*

Plastic lids

Can opener

A heavy ceramic feeding bowl helps prevent a dog from spilling its food. If you cook fresh meat for your dog, you can use any saucepan, but as a hygiene precaution, keep the utensils that you use in preparing your dog's meals separate from other kitchen equipment. Be sure to wash bowls and utensils after each meal. Store partly used cans of food, covered by plastic lids, in the refrigerator for a maximum of three days, then discard.

THE NUTRITIONAL REQUIREMENTS OF AN ADULT DOG

Component	Dietary source	Function in body	Results of deficiency	Results of excess
Protein	Complete dog food, meat, fish, milk, eggs	Builds bones and repairs tissue; maintains growth	Slow growth, weak or deformed bones	Obesity, brittle bones
Fat	Animal and vegetable fats and oils	Provides energy and healthy skin; aids metabolic processes	Dull coat, delayed healing of wounds	Obesity, liver disease
Carbohydrate	Cereals, rice, pasta, dry dog meal, potatoes	Provides energy, and is source of bulk in diet	Possible fertility and whelping problems	Obesity
Minerals				
Calcium	Milk, cheese, bones, bread, and meat	Builds bones, needed for clotting and muscle function	Poor growth, rickets, convulsions	Lameness, joint problems, deformity
Phosphorus	Milk, bones, meat	Builds bones and teeth	Rickets (rare)	Bone resorption
Iron	Meat, bread, vegetables	Builds hemoglobin	Anemia	Weight loss, anorexia
Copper	Meat, bones	Builds hemoglobin	Anemia	—
Magnesium	Bones, fish, green vegetables, cereals	Builds bones; helps in protein synthesis	Convulsions, muscle weakness, anorexia	Diarrhea
Zinc	Meat, cereals	Tissue repair; immune system	Poor growth and skin	Diarrhea
Manganese	Cereals, nuts	Fat metabolism	Poor growth, infertility	—
Iodine	Milk, fish, vegetables	Thyroid function	Goitre, hair loss, lethargy	Thyroid disease
Cobalt	Milk, cheese, meat	Vitamin B_{12} production	—	—
Selenium	Fish meal, meat, cereals	Vitamin E synthesis	Muscle problems	Diarrhea
Sulphur	Meat, eggs	Amino acid synthesis	Poor growth and coat	—
Potassium	Meat, milk	Water balance; nerve function	Kidney, heart problems	Muscle weakness
Sodium	Salt, cereals	Water balance; nerve function	Hair loss, poor growth	Thirst
Vitamins				
Vitamin A	Milk, cod liver oil	Protects skin; bone growth	Skin thickening	Bone pain, anorexia
Vitamin B_1	Peas, beans, whole grains, organ meat	Carbohydrate metabolism	Nerve decay, heart failure	—
Vitamin B_2	Milk, cheese, meat	Energy metabolism	Weight loss, anorexia	—
Niacin	Meat, cereals, legumes	Energy metabolism	Mouth ulcers, diarrhea	—
Vitamin B_6	Meat, vegetables, cereals, eggs	Amino acid metabolism	Anorexia, convulsions, anemia, weight loss	—
Folic acid	Green vegetables	Amino acid metabolism	Anemia, weight loss	—
Vitamin B_{12}	Meat, eggs, milk	Amino acid metabolism	—	—
Biotin	Meat, vegetables	Amino acid metabolism	Scaly skin	—
Choline	Eggs, liver, cereals, peas and beans	Aids fat metabolism and nerve function	Fatty liver, poor clotting of blood	—
Vitamin D	Milk, cheese, eggs, meat, cod liver oil	Aids bone growth; increases calcium absorption	Rickets	Diarrhea, symptoms of calcium deficiency
Vitamin E	Cereals, green vegetables, cheese	Aids cell membrane function and reproduction	Muscle weakness, infertility, anemia	—
Vitamin K	Meat, cereals, green vegetables, liver	Blood clotting	Hemorrhage	—

VITAMINS AND MINERALS

Supplements

Your dog should obtain all the vitamins, minerals, and nutrients it needs from a well-balanced diet. However, occasionally a dog may require supplements – when a puppy is growing, for instance, or when a dog is pregnant, lactating, or recovering from an illness. Vitamin supplements should be given only under a vet's supervision, since too much can be as harmful as too little.

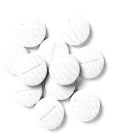

Calcium
Rapidly growing puppies and lactating bitches often need additional calcium.

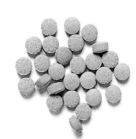

Vitamin pills
Dogs rarely suffer from deficiencies, but tasty vitamin pills can be used as treats.

Bonemeal
Sterilized bonemeal is a good source of calcium. Use under veterinary supervision.

CORRECT FEEDING

In the wild, dogs gorge themselves when any kind of food is available and then live off that nourishment for several days. This food sits in the stomach, where not much digestion takes place, and is passed into the intestines a little at a time. In domestic dogs, this behavior can lead to obesity. Some pet dogs, especially small breeds, are very fussy about what they eat. They turn up their noses at certain foods and blackmail their owners into offering them full menus from which they choose a daily selection.

Your dog should only eat what you want to feed it. The frequency of meals does not really matter, although once or twice a day is the norm. If your dog is overweight, reduce its calorie intake, or increase its consumption of calories through extra activity.

If your dog refuses to eat, seek veterinary advice about its health, then offer it food twice daily, and remove any uneaten remnants after a short period. The war of wills between you and your dog can last up to a week, but the dog will eventually eat whatever you decide to feed it.

Eating bones
Gnawing on bones massages the gums and exercises jaw muscles, but it can also damage the teeth and mouth.

GUIDELINES FOR FEEDING

General rules
1 Provide prepared foods from a reputable manufacturer.
2 Never offer spoiled or stale food to your dog.
3 A bowl of fresh water should always be available.
4 Never feed a dog cat food. It is too high in protein.
5 Always serve your dog's food at room temperature.
6 Dispose of any canned or moist food left uneaten.
7 Discard leftover dry food at the end of each day.
8 Watch your dog's weight. Do not let it get fat.
9 Never feed your dog brittle bones, such as chicken bones.
10 Consult a vet for advice if your dog refuses to eat for 24 hours, since this may indicate illness.

Sharing food
Although some dogs in the same household may be happy to eat together, you should always provide separate food bowls.

CALORIE-CONTROLLED DIETS

REDUCING WEIGHT*		
Target weight	Normal requirements	Dieting requirements
5.5 lb (2.5 kg)	250 calories	150 calories
11 lb (5 kg)	450 calories	270 calories
22 lb (10 kg)	750 calories	450 calories
33 lb (15 kg)	1000 calories	600 calories
44 lb (20 kg)	1250 calories	750 calories
55 lb (25 kg)	1500 calories	900 calories
66 lb (30 kg)	1700 calories	1020 calories
77 lb (35 kg)	1880 calories	1140 calories
88 lb (40 kg)	2100 calories	1260 calories
99 lb (45 kg)	2300 calories	1380 calories
110 lb (50 kg)	2500 calories	1500 calories

*Daily calorie requirements may be less for inactive or neutered dogs in hot climates.

Obesity

If your dog is overweight, increase its exercise, and feed it smaller meals, or a low-calorie diet available from a vet. You should feed about 60 percent of the typical calories required for its ideal weight.

Begging for food
Food becomes an obsession for some dogs, especially if they are bored. If you keep giving in to a dog's begging you will simply reinforce this behavior, and soon have an overweight dog.

DAILY WATER REQUIREMENTS

A dog loses water daily in urine and feces, through panting, and to a limited extent through sweating from the pads. Dogs are as dependent upon water as humans are, and can suffer irreversible body dehydration and damage if it is unavailable for over 48 hours. Although canned dog food is usually three-quarters liquid, this is not enough to satisfy a dog's needs, as it is for cats.

You should fill your dog's bowl with fresh water to the same level each day. If you notice that it is drinking more than usual, contact a vet, since this may indicate an internal disorder.

PREPARED FOODS

TYPES OF DOG FOOD

It is easier to guarantee a well-balanced diet for your dog than for the rest of your family. You completely control what a dog eats, and by choosing from the wide array of prepared foods available from reputable pet-food manufacturers, you can provide all the nutrients necessary to satisfy your canine's feeding requirements. Throughout its lifetime, a dog's energy needs will change. When your dog's energy demands are high – for example, when working, whelping, or lactating – feed foods with more calories. When energy demand drops – for example in old age – feed a specially formulated diet with fewer calories. There are several advantages in feeding complete dry foods. These are convenient, almost odorless, and leave little indigestible residue, making it easy to clean up after your dog.

Standard variety

Premium variety

Dog kibble *(below)*
Dry dog food is an excellent source of fat, carbohydrates, and calories.

Canned foods *(left)*
Meat-based products provide a wide range of protein, fat, and energy and are complete and balanced.

Chunks in gravy

Chunks in gel

Premium variety   *Puppy variety*   *High-energy variety*

Senior dog variety   *Low-calorie variety*   *Standard variety*

Semimoist food
These contain 25–35 percent water and provide the same level of protein and energy as canned foods. Some varieties contain sugar and may cause dental problems.

Complete dry foods
These contain only about 10 percent water. Some dry foods contain more calories per ounce than canned foods and should be fed in smaller quantities. Feed according to the manufacturer's instructions.

DAILY FEEDING GUIDE FOR ADULT DOGS*

Dog type	Calories required	Canned food	Premium dry food	Commercial dry food
Toy 11 lb (5 kg) e.g. Yorkshire Terrier	210	⅓–1 can	½–1¼ cups	⅓–1¼ cups
Small 22 lb (10 kg) e.g. West Highland White Terrier	590	1–2 cans	1¼–1¾ cups	1¼–2⅓ cups
Medium 44 lb (20 kg) e.g. Cocker Spaniel	900	2–3 cans	1¾–3½ cups	2⅓–3⅔ cups
Large 88 lb (40 kg) e.g. German Shepherd Dog	1680	3–6 cans	3½–5 cups	4¼–5⅓ cups
Giant 176 lb (80 kg) e.g. Great Dane	2800	1 can per 15 lb body weight	5 cups + ½ cup per 15 lb over 100 lb	6⅔–9 cups

* These figures are intended as an approximate guide only. Feed according to the manufacturer's instructions.

Assorted flavors   *Cheese flavored*

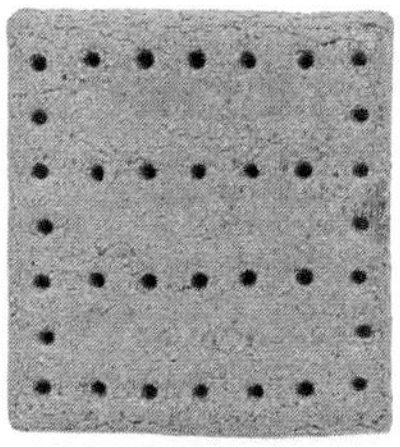

Hamburger   *Pretzel*

Liver rounds   *Meat chunks*

Wholemeal biscuit   *Marrowbone*   *Sterilized bone*   *Beef bones*   *Chicken strips*

Bone

Mixed flavors    *Bacon flavored*   *Ball*   *Toy shoe*   *Beef soft chunks*   *Savory rings*

Biscuits

Biscuits are high in fat and carbohydrate. By weight they contain as many calories as complete foods. Remember to include these calories when calculating a dog's daily needs.

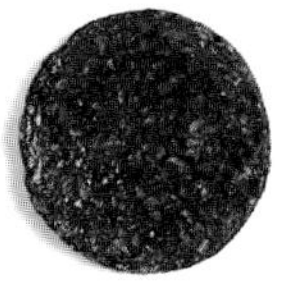

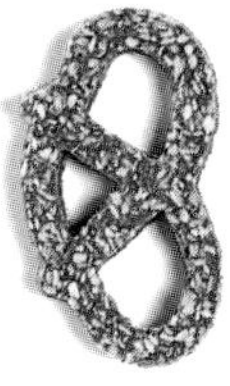

Rawhide chews

These allow a dog to exercise its teeth and gums, which is necessary for good dental hygiene. They contain few calories and may help prevent destructive chewing.

Treats

These tasty snacks are good as training rewards, but they are high in calories, and must be included in any calorie count. Fresh fruits and vegetables can also be given.

FRESH FOODS

FEEDING A BALANCED DIET

Dogs are not complete carnivores and cannot live on meat alone. As a general rule, foods that are balanced for humans are probably balanced for your dog. If you plan to feed your pet fresh food, make sure that you provide it with all the nutritional building blocks it needs to maintain a healthy body. Mix meat or vegetable protein with vegetables, pasta, rice, cereals, or other foods to provide all the protein, carbohydrate, fat, vitamins, and minerals necessary for good health.

Basic diet (above)
Meat and vegetables provide a dog with virtually all the ingredients it needs for a nutritious, balanced diet.

Ground meat (above)
The high level of fat in ground meat is not as harmful to dogs as it is to humans, but is a major source of calories.

Pasta
Pasta and noodles, good sources of carbohydrates, are rather tasteless and often need added flavoring.

Heart
Because of its fat content, heart has twice as many calories as other organs such as kidney. It should be fed in moderation.

Liver
Liver, like other meats, has a high phosphorus but low calcium content. It is also rich in vitamins A and B_1.

Raw vegetables and fruit
Uncooked vegetables and fruit, such as carrots, cabbage, and apple, are good sources of additional vitamins.

SPECIAL FEEDING FOR DELICATE STOMACHS

Chicken
Chicken and turkey are easily digested, and are lower in calories than other meats.

Fish
You should be careful to remove even the smallest bones before feeding fish to your dog.

Rice
Boiled rice is easily digested. Added to chicken, it makes a good diet for a convalescent.

VEGETARIAN FOOD

Tofu

Mixed vegetables

Unlike cats, dogs are not true carnivores. They can survive on vegetarian diets because they can convert vegetable protein and fat into the ingredients necessary for all bodily functions. Consult a vet however, if you wish to feed your dog on a vegetarian diet, since it is difficult to maintain balanced nutrition.

BREAKFAST FOODS

Cereal
Breakfast cereals with milk are good sources of vitamins, and provide a tasty light meal.

Scrambled egg
Light and nutritious, scrambled egg is ideal for puppies and dogs recovering from an illness.

ANALYSIS OF FRESH MEATS

Meat	Moisture	Protein	Fat	Calories per 3½ oz
Tripe	88%	9%	3%	63 calories
Kidney	80%	16%	2.6%	86 calories
Chicken	74%	20%	4.3%	121 calories
Beef	74%	20%	4.6%	123 calories
Pork	72%	20%	7.1%	147 calories
Lamb	70%	20%	8.8%	162 calories
Heart	70%	14%	15.5%	197 calories

Chapter 4

GROOMING

HEALTHY DOGS are naturally good at keeping clean. They groom themselves by rolling and rubbing on the ground, scratching, chewing at matted fur, and licking their coats. Unfortunately, they also like to roll in noxious substances such as other animals' droppings and anoint their fur with what humans consider to be unpleasant odors, and thus sometimes need help with grooming, as well as occasional bathing. Human intervention in dog breeding has led to a variety of coat textures and lengths, each with individual grooming needs. Selective breeding has also been responsible for dog coats that require frequent brushing, stripping, or clipping.

COAT TYPES

GROOMING REQUIREMENTS

Having evolved in the colder regions of the northern hemisphere, the earliest breeds of dog had dense coats for protection from the cold and from predators. Then, as dogs moved into hot climates in the company of humans, their coats became shorter and thinner. The Saluki in Arabia, the Basenji in Africa, and the Australian Cattle Dog illustrate how different coats have evolved according to regional climatic conditions.

The enormous variety of coats found today is due to selective breeding of dogs by humans, who have developed breeds with specialized coats for different purposes.

Dense, short coat is warm and water-resistant

Short coat (above)
These Welsh Corgis have dense, short coats of profuse, downy, water-resistant hair close to the skin, and thick, straight surface hair. This coat should be groomed at least once a week *(see page 187)*.

Curly, waterproof coat is not shed

Curly coat (above)
Kerry Blue Terriers like this one have curly, non-shedding, extremely waterproof coats. Breeds with similar coats are the Portuguese Water Dog, Irish Water Spaniel, and poodles. This coat should be bathed and clipped every two months *(see pages 190–191)*.

Wiry coat
The wiry coat on this Airedale Terrier consists of stiff, dense hair, which needs daily grooming to prevent matting. You should never use conditioners on this type of coat, since they will soften it. Wiry coats do not molt, and need regular hand-stripping or clipping *(see page 187)*.

Dense, wiry coat needs regular stripping

Long coat *(below)*

This Lhasa Apso has a long, straight, coarse outer coat and a thick undercoat, which require daily grooming and regular trimming *(see page 189)*. These long coats – now prized by owners for aesthetic reasons – originally offered dogs protection from the cold.

Long, coarse coat insulates against cold

Smooth coat

Smooth, shorthaired coats such as this Doberman's are the easiest to maintain, but offer little protection from either dog bites or cold weather. Although short and relatively sparse, these coats are shed and require weekly brushing *(see page 186)*.

Smooth coat offers little protection

Silky coat *(below)*

Afghan Hounds have the bodies of racing dogs, but because they evolved in a cold climate, they retained heavy coats for protection against the elements. Silky coats need a lot of care, with daily grooming and regular trimming *(see page 188)*.

CANINE CLOTHING

Although dogs already have their own furry coats, there are some circumstances when items of dog clothing are useful. For example, Yorkshire Terriers have thin coats with no downy undercoat for protection against the cold. Shorthaired Chihuahuas and Dobermans also have very little fur on their bodies. Even fairly well-furred dogs, such as this Cavalier King Charles Spaniel, can benefit from the additional protection a manufactured coat offers when they are ill or of advanced years.

Raincoat

Warm coat

FIRST STEPS IN GROOMING

Routine grooming serves two main purposes. It keeps your dog's skin, coat, teeth, gums, and nails in a healthy state, and it also allows you to constantly reassert your authority over your pet. You should make its daily or weekly grooming a ritual that both you and your dog enjoy and respect.

If your dog refuses to let you groom it, command it to sit and stay. Grooming should always involve a reward for your dog. In most instances, physical contact is enough, but there is no harm in occasionally giving your dog a food reward.

Ears should be free of wax and dirt

Eyes should be clear and free of discharge

Nose should be wet and cold to the touch

Skin folds should be clean, with no sign of soreness

Teeth and gums should have no sign of infection

Facial grooming
Ears, eyes, and teeth should be inspected each week. Breeds with facial skin folds, such as this Shar Pei, need special attention.

CLEANING THE FACE

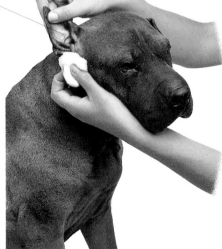

Do not push anything into the ears

1 Gently bathe the skin around the eyes using a fresh piece of moistened cotton for each one. If you notice any discharge or inflammation, you should contact a vet for advice.

2 Hold open the ear with one hand and gently clean inside the flap with a small piece of moistened cotton. Use a fresh piece for each ear. Do not probe too deeply into the ear canal.

3 Loose facial skin must be cleaned regularly with damp cotton. This prevents dirt, dead skin, and bacteria from collecting in the folds and causing irritation and infection.

CLEANING THE TEETH

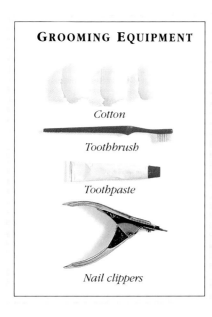

1 You should check a dog's teeth and gums once a week. Make sure that there is no sign of gum infection or tartar build-up on the teeth, since this can lead to gingivitis and tenderness.

2 Gently brush the dog's teeth with a soft toothbrush, using either dilute salt water or a special canine toothpaste, obtainable from a vet.

DENTAL HYGIENE

A vet can provide special canine toothpaste. Never use toothpaste intended for humans.

TRIMMING THE NAILS

WHERE TO TRIM THE NAILS

The pink area inside the nail is called the nail bed, or quick, and contains the blood supply and nerves. Take care to trim the nails without cutting the quick. Ask a vet to trim the dog's nails if you are in any doubt about where to clip them.

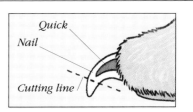

Quick

Nail

Cutting line

Feet are checked regularly for dirt and foreign bodies

1 Spread each of the dog's feet and inspect the area between its toes. Clean away any dirt and debris with moistened cotton.

2 Clip the nails carefully. Smooth any rough edges with an emery board or nail file. Remember to trim the dog's dewclaws if it has them.

GROOMING SHORTHAIRED DOGS

Smooth and short coats are relatively self-cleaning and need less attention than other varieties of fur. Some coats, however, such as that of the Labrador Retriever, are shed heavily. Dogs kept outdoors molt twice yearly, while those housed indoors shed their hair all year round. Even so, if the hair and dandruff are to be kept under control, shorthaired dogs must be groomed almost as frequently as those with longer coats.

Some large breeds like the Doberman and Great Dane have smooth, sometimes thick coats, the hairs of which can act like needles and penetrate the skin at pressure points such as the elbows and hocks when the dog lies down. These susceptible areas should be treated with a conditioner to soften the hair and prevent damage to the skin.

GROOMING A SMOOTH COAT

1 Smooth-coated dogs such as this Boxer do not need a lot of grooming, but they should be brushed regularly. First use a rubber brush or hound glove, to loosen any dead hair and surface dirt.

Rubber brush loosens dead skin and dirt

Brush vigorously with the lie of the coat to remove dead skin and hair

2 Remove dead hair and skin with a bristle brush, taking care to cover the entire coat, from head to tail. A coat conditioner can be put on at this stage to give the coat a glossy sheen.

3 Lastly, briskly polish the coat with a chamois cloth to bring out the shine. Dogs with smooth coats are the easiest to groom, and can look immaculate with regular care and attention.

GROOMING EQUIPMENT

Rubber brush

Bristle brush

Chamois cloth

GROOMING A SHORT COAT

1 A dog with a short, dense coat must be groomed regularly to prevent mats. A slicker brush will remove tangles.

Without grooming, a short, dense coat mats easily

2 Brush thoroughly with a bristle brush, which removes dead hair and remaining dirt and debris. While you are grooming your dog it is important to check for signs of parasites, such as fleas and ticks *(see page 222)*, and for any sores or skin disorders *(see page 220)*.

3 Lastly, run a fine comb through the feathers on the dog's legs and tail. You can also trim untidy hairs from the feathers with scissors, if you wish.

GROOMING EQUIPMENT

Slicker brush

Bristle brush

Comb

HAND-STRIPPING A WIRY COAT

Wiry coats, such as those of terriers, schnauzers, and the Wire-haired Dachshund, must be hand-stripped every three to four months. Dead hair can be pulled out between the thumb and finger in the direction of growth. If done correctly, this should not cause the dog any discomfort. Alternatively, a stripping knife can be used. This instrument has no cutting blade, and the hair is plucked out between the thumb and the knife. If you wish, instead of stripping, the coat can be regularly machine-clipped and excess hair around the face trimmed by a professional groomer.

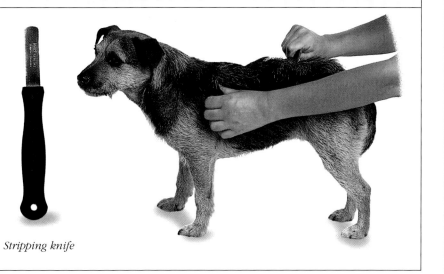

Stripping knife

GROOMING LONGHAIRED DOGS

Luxurious, long coats are elegant and insulating, but they need more attention than short coats. Breeds with silky coats like the Yorkshire Terrier have no downy undercoat, so extra care must be taken while grooming to avoid scratching or irritating the skin.

Rough Collies and Shetland Sheepdogs have long coats combined with dense, thick, protective down. This type of deep coat mats easily without thorough grooming.

GROOMING A SILKY COAT

1 Use a slicker brush to remove any tangles. Mats can be gently teased out. Take care not to pull on the hair and break it.

2 Brush the coat once more, using a bristle brush to bring out the shine. There should be no resistance.

Bristle brush brings out shine in coat

3 Part the long hair on the back and comb each side straight down. Any untidy ends can be carefully trimmed with scissors.

Comb hair on either side of center parting

4 Trim around the feet and ears. The nails should also be clipped *(see page 185).*

Carefully trim feathers around toes and feet

5 Long hair above the eyes can either be trimmed or tied with a ribbon and bow.

After grooming (right)
This Yorkshire Terrier's coat is now silky, neat, and gleaming.

GROOMING EQUIPMENT

Slicker brush

Bristle brush

Scissors

Bow

Comb

GROOMING A LONG COAT

1 Using a slicker brush, gently untangle any matted hair or knots. Be careful not to pull out the hair or cause the dog pain by brushing too vigorously.

Coat should be tangle-free

2 Brush the coat again with a pin brush. You should feel no tangles as you brush through the coat.

3 Comb through the fur with a wide-toothed comb, paying particular attention to the feathers on the legs.

4 Trim long hair around the feet, especially between the toes, where dirt and foreign bodies can become lodged, causing irritation.

After grooming (below)
This Rough Collie is sleek and neat.

5 Using sharp scissors, trim around the hocks so that the long hair does not become tangled and collect dirt and debris.

GROOMING EQUIPMENT

Slicker brush

Pin brush

Scissors

Comb

189

CLIPPING A DOG

Most dogs molt their coats, either constantly or in two seasonal bursts. Some breeds with curly coats, such as poodles, however, do not. The hair simply keeps growing and is maintained through routine clipping.

Although some people like to shape their pet's coat in distinctive ways, such as the lamb clip on the Standard Poodle shown here, all that is really necessary is a regular trim, taking special care around the face and anal region.

Clipping is usually necessary about every six to eight weeks, although a dog's coat can be clipped more frequently in summer, and less often when the weather is cooler.

Most dogs enjoy having a shortened coat. Even if you do not want to completely clip your dog's coat yourself, you should be prepared to trim it to keep it from getting tangled.

CLIPPING EQUIPMENT

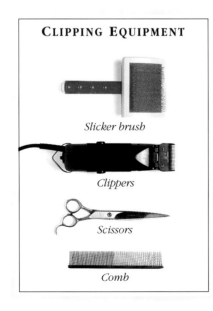

Slicker brush

Clippers

Scissors

Comb

CLIPPING METHOD

Wax can get trapped in long hair inside ears

1 After bathing, drying, and brushing the dog with a slicker brush, pluck the long hair from inside the ears. If this hair is not plucked regularly, it can trap wax, which may cause hearing problems.

2 Holding the skin tight to avoid nicking it, carefully clip the sides of the face from the corner of the ear to the eye, and down the neck toward the body. Continue along the sides of the muzzle, cutting against the lie of the hair.

Be careful not to clip skin on face and neck

Avoid cutting close to eyes

Trim long hair between dog's toes

3 Finish off the muzzle by clipping down the top from the eyes to the nose. Try to keep the strokes even and parallel. Do not cut too close to the eyes.

4 Clip the feet from below the ankle bones downward, and between the toes. Cut against the lie of the hair, taking care to avoid nicking the pads.

5 Comb the tail hair toward the tail tip. Hold the tail at the end of the tailbone and clip the top quarter toward the rump. Three-quarters of the tail should be left unclipped.

6 Carefully clip the dog's groin area, holding each back leg out of the way in turn. The stomach can also be clipped now, but only up as far as the ribcage.

7 Clip down the dog's back from the neck to the tail, holding the ears out of the way. Following the contours of the body, clip down the sides and over the ribcage.

Clip tail into pompom

Trim hair to the same length on each leg

8 Tease the hair on the legs outward with a comb and trim off the uneven ends with scissors. The hair should be the same length on each leg.

9 Holding the end of the tail, trim the long hair into a pompom with scissors. The topknot can be cut into a round, even shape.

Clipped poodle
Trimming reveals any skin problems a dog might have. Consult a vet for advice if there are any areas of discoloration.

BATHING A DOG

Routine grooming keeps a dog's coat in a healthy condition, but bathing is sometimes necessary if a dog has rolled in a smelly substance. Bathing is also beneficial in eliminating certain skin parasites and treating a variety of dry and oily skin conditions. In some circumstances, a vet might suggest medically therapeutic shampoos and conditioners. You must always follow the manufacturer's instructions.

Rinsing is important, since any residual shampoo in the coat can irritate the skin and cause scratching. The dog may need to wear its collar in the bath, so that you can hold on to it and prevent it from jumping out. A rubber mat on the bottom of the bath will keep the dog from slipping.

BATHING METHOD

1 After brushing the dog and plugging its ears with cotton, stand it carefully in the bath on a rubber mat. Hold it tightly by the collar and pour warm water on its coat.

Rub shampoo well into coat to loosen dirt and dead skin

2 Using a canine or tearless shampoo, soap the dog all over except for its head. Hold the dog firmly so that it does not slip or try to get out of the bath. Work up a good lather, massaging the skin against the lie of the coat, but be careful not to splash water or soap in the dog's eyes.

3 Lather the dog's head with a tearless shampoo poured in your hands, and massage the hair gently, being careful to avoid splashing the eyes or getting soap in the mouth.

Keep soap out of dog's eyes

BATHING EQUIPMENT

Cotton

Container

Towels

Shampoos

4 Rinse and dry the dog's head before rinsing the body. This will help prevent it from shaking water everywhere.

5 Rinse the rest of the body in warm water, taking care to remove all the shampoo. If necessary, rub conditioner into the coat, then rinse it off.

6 Squeeze excess water from the coat, then dry the dog with a large towel. Remove the ear plugs and dry the insides of the ears.

7 A hair dryer set on warm, not hot, can be used on dogs with healthy skin, but not on dogs prone to itchiness, since heat exaggerates itch. Brush the hair straight, away from the body.

After bathing
After its bath, a dog often runs around with excitement. Take care it does not instantly roll over and try to cover itself in more natural smells.

Chapter 5

TRAINING

Training is a most important part of caring for a dog. An untrained dog is like a car with faulty brakes. It is unreliable and, until the fault is corrected, potentially dangerous. All but the most dominant dogs enjoy training because it involves mental stimulation. Training also helps prevent the dog from adopting bad habits through boredom. Prevention of bad habits is always easier than eliminating them. If you train your dog as early as possible to instantly obey your commands, walk on a leash, and play games, you are unlikely to ever have to deal with unwanted behavior. If you do have to correct bad habits, it will be much easier if your dog has already learned basic obedience, so that it can be stopped the instant it does something wrong.

PUPPY TRAINING

Informal training should begin as soon as you bring a new puppy home at eight weeks old. Whenever it does anything you eventually want it to do on command, such as sit, say the appropriate word several times while the puppy maintains that position. It will rapidly learn to associate the word with what it is doing. At the same time, praise the puppy to let it know you are pleased with what it is doing. It quickly learns what praise words like "good dog" mean.

If the puppy does something you do not want it to, say "No!" but only when you catch it actually misbehaving. Never discipline the puppy even seconds after it has done something wrong. It will not associate your discipline with a previous action.

Early leash training *(see pages 198–199)* can be started as soon as a puppy is used to wearing a collar and leash.

THE BASIC COMMANDS

The puppy's name
This puppy sits attentively when it hears its name. Each time you play with the puppy, repeatedly say its name. Sharp, two-syllable names like "Sparky" are easiest for a dog to learn.

Puppy stops and listens when it hears its name

Puppy's gaze is fixed on food bowl

Sitting on command
The puppy's attention is drawn to its impending meal. Hold the food bowl above the puppy so that it will sit in order to keep its eye on the bowl. As it does so, say the word "Sit," then reward it with the meal.

TRAINING A PUPPY TO LIE DOWN

1 By teaching the puppy to lie down you are telling it that you are in charge. Begin with the puppy in a sitting position. Give the command "Lie down" while patting the ground in front of it.

2 If the puppy ignores the command, ease it to the ground by gently pressing on its body and pulling its legs forward. Give immediate praise when the puppy is lying down.

TRAINING A PUPPY TO COME

1 While the puppy is sitting, wearing its collar and leash to give you greater control, give the command "Wait." Remain standing in front of the puppy until it is settled. Do not pull on the leash.

Keep the leash loose

Puppy listens to owner's voice

2 Slowly walk backward away from the puppy to the end of the leash. Give the command "Come," and if it looks confused, give the leash a gentle tug. Continue walking and encouraging the puppy to come.

3 Always finish any exercise by praising the puppy. Stroking and food are powerful rewards. An encouraging, pleased tone of voice is important when praising a dog. Remember the puppy understands not what you say but the way in which you say it.

PREVENTING BAD BEHAVIOR

Jumping up
If the puppy jumps up, gently push it down and say firmly, "No!" Command it to sit, and then greet it. A puppy must be discouraged from this type of behavior early on *(see page 204)*.

Chewing objects
Meticulously store away any personal items the puppy might chew. Provide it with several dog toys, giving it praise when they are chewed.

WALKING A DOG

When walking with you, your dog must always be under control. For its own safety as well as a courtesy to others, this means that it should be on a leash. A simple rule of physics applies when walking your dog on a leash: for every action there is an equal and opposite reaction. If your dog strains on the leash and you pull back, all you do is provoke it to strain harder.

As a puppy your dog should have learned to accept a collar and then a trailing leash. You should keep lessons in walking to heel short, no more than fifteen minutes at a time, up to four times a day. Give basic lessons in a quiet area and do not lose patience. If your dog is not performing properly, finish off with a command you know it will follow. Lessons should be enjoyable.

HEELWORK

1 Walk up to the right side of the dog and attach the leash to its collar. Without applying any tension to the leash, hold the handle in your right hand and the middle of the leash in your left hand, with a loop between.

2 The dog should be on your left side with its shoulder just about level with your thigh. There should be no tension on the collar.

Hold leash securely, with both hands

Dog's shoulder is level with handler's thigh

THE CHECK CHAIN

When used correctly, check chains help with training by applying intermittent tension on a dog's neck. They should only be used on dogs that are insensitive to touch, or have thick neck fur. Never use a check chain on a puppy or on breeds like the Chihuahua or the Yorkshire Terrier, which have fragile windpipes. You should not use a check chain on a dog with a respiratory problem.

4 A great deal of concentration is needed when you first begin training a dog. The dog will soon learn to walk correctly. When turning left, you should walk around the dog, and when turning right, the dog should walk around you.

3 Attract the dog's attention by speaking its name. Begin walking, keeping the dog close to your leg. If it pulls ahead or back, jerk the leash gently and say "Heel." Praise the dog when it obeys and walks correctly.

5 When you stop walking, command the dog to sit. You may have to push down its rump at first. It will eventually learn to sit automatically.

PUTTING ON A CHECK CHAIN

1 To put on the check chain correctly, hold it open in a circle as shown, then gently slip it over the dog's head until it hangs loosely around the neck.

2 When the check chain is positioned correctly, it will only tighten when tension is applied. Always keep the dog on your left side.

Incorrect method
If the check chain is put on backward, it will cause discomfort and not loosen after it has checked the dog.

OBEDIENCE TRAINING

TRAINING TO WAIT AND COME

Due to their differing temperaments, some dogs are easier to train than others. With proper training your dog will always be under control, both on and off its leash. Puppies can be taught basic social skills starting at seven weeks. Formal obedience training will begin later.

If you have little or no experience with dogs it is best to undertake obedience training under the supervision of an experienced dog trainer recommended by a vet or your local kennel club or humane society.

1 Using a simple hand signal, tell the dog to sit *(see page 196)*. Whenever you want to teach a dog something new, you should begin by giving the command "Sit," to ensure that you have its full attention.

2 With the dog sitting, give the command "Wait." Holding the leash, walk around the dog, making sure that it stays in the same position all the time.

3 Walk to the end of the leash. Repeat the command "Wait." If the dog moves, go back to it, and start the exercise from the beginning.

4 Call the dog using its name and the command "Come." Always make the dog sit before praising and releasing it.

Dog pays attention to voice and hand signals

Dog sits patiently, waiting for next command

TEACHING THE DOWN-STAY

1 With the dog in a sitting position, give the command "Lie down." Gently pat the ground at the same time *(see page 196)*. Both verbal and visual signals are initially combined in obedience training.

2 Holding the dog's leash so that you can reinforce the instruction if necessary, give the command "Stay." This command is used when you do not want the dog to move from its position until you return to it.

Dog watches handler's hand signal closely

3 Walk a leash length away from the dog, and turn and face it. Use the same palm-of-hand signal to reinforce the "Stay" command if the dog starts to move.

4 After a minute or so, return to the dog, making sure that it is still lying down. An obedient dog should not move even when its handler is out of sight. This training exercise reinforces in the dog's mind that it must submit to human commands.

5 Release the dog from the position. Always praise the dog after every exercise, so that it knows when it is finished. Touch and gentle words are such overwhelming pleasures for most dogs that they willingly obey to receive them.

THE WELL-BEHAVED DOG

The well-behaved dog is a pleasure to its owner and to the community in which it lives. Ensure that your dog is enjoyed by training it to live in harmony with its human and animal neighbors. It should respond to your commands, be friendly to strangers and other dogs, not be scared by distractions, and be content at home without creating havoc.

THE WELL-TRAINED DOG

Sitting on command
Tell the dog to sit. By doing so you will get its attention and demonstrate that you are in charge. A well-behaved dog will sit when anyone, even a stranger, asks it to do so.

Staying in position
Tell the dog to stay, then drop the leash and walk away. If the dog has been properly trained you can turn your back and walk 16 feet (5 m) away without it following.

Ears pricked to listen for instructions

Eyes watch handler closely

Walking on a loose leash
With the dog on your left, walk with it on a loose leash. It should not pull back and refuse to move, or try to run.

THE SOCIABLE DOG

Accepting a stranger (below)
A well-mannered dog shows no resentment when people stop to talk to its owner. Nor does it fidget or show signs of shyness. It should sit or lie down quietly, without pulling on its leash.

Petting by a stranger (above)
A dog should be content to be stroked by a stranger, even on the top of its head – a gesture of dominance. People often approach dogs like this.

Sitting for examination *(above)*

A dog should allow itself to be examined by you, a member of your family, or by a stranger. This means that a vet will always be able to examine it when necessary.

Reaction to another dog *(above)*

Ask a friend with a dog to approach while you are walking your own dog, stop, talk for a short while, and then move on. Well-behaved dogs show interest in each other but no signs of fear or aggression.

Walking through a crowd

Walk the dog along the sidewalk through pedestrian traffic. It can show interest in the various sights and sounds but should not strain on its leash or act shyly or aggressively.

Reacting to distractions *(right)*

When the dog is not expecting it, drop a book or heavy magazine about 10 feet (3 m) behind it. If it has been properly trained, it will show curiosity and interest, but will not panic, bark, run away, or show aggression.

THE CONTENTED DOG

Leaving a dog alone

Leave the dog alone in either your home or garden, then listen for any howling, whining, barking, or pacing the floor. A well-behaved dog might be agitated, perhaps even a little nervous, when you leave, but should show no signs of separation anxiety *(see page 207)*. A toy may comfort the dog.

Toy helps comfort dog

CONTROLLING UNWANTED BEHAVIOR

Dogs sometimes get carried away by their feelings or simply by the desire to act as they please. This can often lead to overexcitement or disobedience. A submissive dog is most likely to jump up, in an effort to lick its owner's face, mimicking the way it behaved as a puppy. It will also jump up to greet visitors whom it looks upon as equally dominant as its owner.

Disobedience is more likely to be found in confident and independent dogs than in submissive or shy ones. Good training prevents bad habits, but if they occur, they can be remedied with patience.

THE EXCITABLE DOG

Jumping up
Dogs often jump up to greet their owners, as this Standard Poodle is doing. In dog terms this is normal.

Remedy
1 To correct this behavior, say "No" sharply, at the same time turning away and avoiding eye contact. Do not make a fuss over the dog.

2 Command the dog to sit. If it has been trained properly, it will obey at once *(see pages 196–203).*

Dog watches owner for instructions

Owner praises and greets dog as it is sitting

3 Now you can greet the dog on your own terms. Praise it for obeying you. It will soon realize that it must not jump up to greet you.

THE DISOBEDIENT DOG

DISCIPLINARY EQUIPMENT

Toy

Water pistol

Plant sprayer   *High-pitched alarm*

Plant sprayers, water pistols, and high-pitched alarms are useful as distractions. Toys can be used to attract a dog's attention or as rewards. Never physically punish a dog.

Dog runs away from owner when called to be put back on leash

Not coming when called *(above)*

A dog may sometimes refuse to come back when called, especially if you only call it to put it back on its leash. It should not associate coming to you with an unpleasant event or a reprimand. However, if you chase it, the dog may think you are playing a game.

Remedy

Use a favorite toy to attract the dog's attention, then play a game with the dog before going home. Do not let it associate you or the toy with being restrained on a leash. When it comes to you, command it to sit, and then praise it.

Favorite toy is used to attract dog's attention

CORRECTING BAD HABITS

Even the most delightful dog is likely to develop habits that you find annoying or unpleasant in the restricted environment of your home. Obedience training from an early age can prevent many of these behavioral problems, and prevention is always easier than cure. If your dog behaves at home in antisocial ways, you must go back to basics and use your common sense to develop a correction method based on the dog's willingness to obey. Remember: a dog does not misbehave to punish its owner. Revenge is a trait in primates but not in dogs.

THE DESTRUCTIVE DOG

Chewing objects
Dogs left on their own, especially puppies, may sometimes chew objects through frustration at being alone and to relieve boredom.

Remedy (left)
Restrict the dog to a small area of its own where it cannot do any damage, such as a special dog crate. This helps a dog to feel more secure, especially if it has a selection of toys to chew and play with, and a radio or television as background noise. A dog should only be confined to a crate for short periods and must also be given plenty of exercise and personal attention from its owner.

THE GREEDY DOG

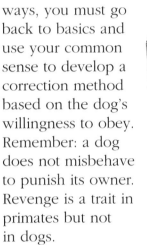

Stealing food (right)
Dogs are scavengers and will eat most food they find. Opportunities to scavenge reinforce this bad behavior, producing a chronic canine thief.

Remedy (left)
Teach the dog to sit before feeding it, and only give it food in its own bowl, not on a plate or from the table. Once it knows it must obey you before eating, it will not steal food in your absence. As a precaution, do not leave tempting food within its reach.

THE OVERSEXED DOG

Hypersexuality
Denied a more natural outlet for its sexual energy, a young, unneutered male dog may mount a human leg or furniture. This occurs most frequently in dogs between one and two years old, although females in season may behave in a similar manner.

Remedy
Distract the dog by spraying it with water from a plant sprayer or water pistol. Any discipline must be carried out immediately so that the dog associates this with its bad behavior. Early neutering may prevent this behavior.

THE LONELY DOG

Separation anxiety *(left)*
Left alone in the house, a nervous dog may chew, bark, howl, or soil the house. Such behavior is especially common in dogs that have not been properly socialized during puppyhood or that have known several homes.

Remedy *(above)*
Before leaving, provide the dog with a special treat, such as a favorite toy that you have rubbed in your hands, or a succulent marrowbone. Do not make a fuss when you leave. The dog may feel more secure in a dog crate *(see opposite)*.

CONTROLLING AGGRESSIVE BEHAVIOR

The most serious problem a dog can develop is to show aggression. A dog can become aggressive to other animals, to strangers, or even to its owner. To prevent this behavior, you must assert your pack leadership. Train your dog to always obey your commands, and reinforce your leadership over it through routine exercises.

AGGRESSION TOWARD OWNER

Possessive aggression
A dominant dog may challenge its owner for possession of favorite objects. Food, old bones, resting places, and toys are all possessions that a dog may aggressively defend.

Remedy
Command the dog to lie down. When it does so, it automatically becomes submissive to the person above it. Give a stern verbal correction.

Alternative remedy
You can assert control over a young dog by lifting its front legs off the ground. A professional trainer should be consulted at once to deal with very aggressive behavior.

AGGRESSION TO VISITORS

Territorial aggression
A resident dog may bark at a visitor to its home, bravely defending its territory and its owner, whom it considers a member of its pack. By standing over the dog and bending down to stroke it, the visitor appears to be acting in a threatening way. A dog may be especially frightened of strangers if it has not been handled during puppyhood.

AGGRESSION TO OTHER DOGS

Dominant aggression
A dominant dog, particularly an unneutered dog, or one not properly socialized with other dogs when young, may bark aggressively at, or even try to fight with, other dogs. Neutering usually solves this problem.

Remedy *(right)*
To remedy this type of aggression, keep a loose leash and command the dog to sit. Since you are the dog's pack leader, it will realize that you are unconcerned about the strange dog, and that it is no threat. Always praise good behavior.

CONTROLLING AGGRESSION

Aggression takes a variety of forms and responds to different methods of control. Obedience training is of paramount importance in preventing this behavior. Seek professional advice from a vet, an experienced trainer, or a dog-training club if your pet shows any signs of not always being under your control.

Remedy
Introduce the dog to new people gradually and offer it rewards for good behavior. The visitor should initially avoid direct eye contact with the dog. By sitting down and offering the dog food or a toy as it remains on its leash, the visitor will appear less intimidating. Do not allow visitors to force themselves on a shy dog; let the dog set the pace.

Chapter 6

YOUR DOG'S HEALTH

DOGS CAN suffer from almost all the physical diseases and ailments that afflict humans. In addition, selective breeding by humans has intensified the incidence of some canine health disorders. Fortunately, modern veterinary care provides a vast array of diagnostic aids, treatments, and even cures. When a dog is not well, it relies upon its owner to notice and take appropriate action. Many dogs may try to hide their discomfort and want to please their owners so much that they attempt to behave normally. Whenever you notice any changes in your dog's routines, demeanor, or behavior, contact your veterinarian for advice.

THE HEALTHY DOG

The healthy dog is vibrant, alert, and almost always enthusiastic about living. Although happy to snooze and relax for most of the day, a fit dog is constantly observing humans, and is always ready for exercise and entertainment of any kind.

Assessing your dog's health soon becomes natural. Once you understand its daily routines and behavior, any deviation from the norm becomes obvious. Dogs are creatures of habit with finely tuned biological clocks. If your dog does not get up when it usually does, is reluctant to play, moves slower, eats less, or behaves in an abnormal way, contact a vet for advice.

As well as observing your dog's behavior, check its health when you groom it. There should be no unpleasant or new odors or discharges from the mouth, nose, eyes, ears, body, or urinary or anogenital regions. The dog should move with natural grace, showing no signs of difficulty when getting up or down. Breathing, appetite, thirst, and frequency of emptying the bowels and bladder should be routine.

If you notice a change in the color, consistency, or quantity of droppings, contact your veterinary clinic for advice. The resident staff can often answer your questions over the phone, and an office visit is unnecessary.

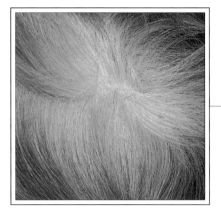

Skin
Normal skin is resilient, clean, and has no dry flakes, odor, or grease. Healthy fur glistens and does not come out when pulled except during molting. According to the breed, the hair should lie evenly on all parts of the body. There should be no sign of parasites, flea dirt, dandruff, sores, baldness, itchiness, or strong odor.

Anal region
The anal region should be clean with no signs of inflammation, lumpy growths, or dried feces. Excess licking or dragging of the rear along carpet or grass means irritation, most frequently caused by blocked anal sacs.

Canine fitness
Healthy dogs are clean, robust, and full of spirit. They enjoy the company of humans and do not resent being touched. Even slight changes from normal behavior can signify illness.

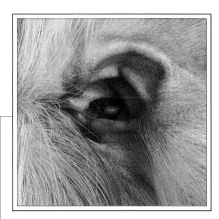

Eyes
A dog's eyes should be bright, clean, and free of discharge. There should be no redness, squinting, or vision impairment.

Ears
The insides of the ears should be dull pink and free of discharge and odor. The flaps should hang symmetrically. Occasional head shaking is normal, especially when a dog wakes up from a snooze.

Mouth
Dogs have whiter teeth than do humans. The gums and tongue should be pink, and are sometimes mottled with black pigment. Gums should form a clean margin with the teeth, with no recesses in which food can get trapped, causing bad breath.

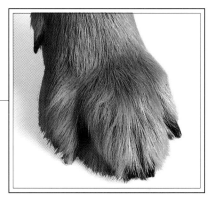

Paws
Paws should be neat, clean, and symmetrical. Check the pads for cuts or burns, and the nails for breaks or damage, and always check between the toes for grass seeds that can easily penetrate the skin, causing swollen, painful abscesses.

SIGNS OF ILL HEALTH

Because your dog enjoys human companionship, it will often try to behave normally even when it is unwell. For example, if your dog refuses to eat unless you feed it by hand, it may be ill but eating just to please you. It may be experiencing pain or discomfort even if it does not cry or yelp. Most dogs are stoic individuals and suffer their pain silently. You can help the vet make an accurate diagnosis by keeping a record of exactly when you notice any signs of ill health.

Be prepared
Keep the telephone number of your local veterinary clinic handy and always give it to anyone looking after your dog. Contact the clinic immediately if your dog appears unwell or is injured.

NERVOUS DISORDERS
(see page 241)
- Fits, convulsions, or seizures
- Staggering gait
- Partial or complete paralysis
- Behavioral changes
- Loss of balance

DIGESTIVE DISORDERS
(see page 231)
- Projectile, bloody, or painful vomiting
- Persistent, bloody, or explosive diarrhea
- Constipation
- Weight loss or excessive weight gain
- Listlessness and abdominal discomfort

SKIN AND COAT DISORDERS
(see page 221)
- Persistent scratching
- Sudden chewing or licking
- Redness or inflammation
- Increased hair loss

REPRODUCTIVE DISORDERS
(see page 237)
- Any unusual genital discharges
- Swelling in the mammary glands
- Swelling in the testicles
- Failure to conceive
- Difficulties at birth

URINARY DISORDERS
(see page 239)
- Straining to pass urine
- Blood in the urine
- Incontinence
- Increased urination
- Increased thirst

INTERNAL PARASITES
(see page 233)
- Visible worms in the feces
- Pot-bellied appearance
- Persistent or bloody diarrhea
- White grains on rear
- Loss of weight

RESPIRATORY DISORDERS
(see page 229)
- Nasal discharge
- Persistent sneezing
- Coughing, gagging
- Excessive snoring
- Labored breathing

EYE DISORDERS
(see page 225)
- Discharges from the eyes
- Failing vision
- Squinting
- Bloodshot inflammation
- Blue-gray cloudiness

EAR DISORDERS
(see page 227)
- Head shaking
- Discharges from the ear canal
- Swelling of the ear flap
- Difficulty in hearing
- Loss of balance

MOUTH AND TOOTH DISORDERS
(see page 235)
- Bad breath
- Dribbling saliva
- Reluctance to eat
- Inflamed gums
- Loose or broken teeth

EXTERNAL PARASITES
(see page 223)
- Scratching
- Excessive licking
- Dandruff
- Hair loss
- Visible parasites

BLOOD AND HEART DISORDERS
(see page 243)
- Nonproductive coughing
- Reluctance to exercise
- Reduced stamina
- Fainting

BONE, MUSCLE, AND JOINT DISORDERS
(see page 219)
- Lameness and limping
- Swelling around affected area
- Paralysis
- Tenderness when limb is touched

DIAGNOSIS CHART

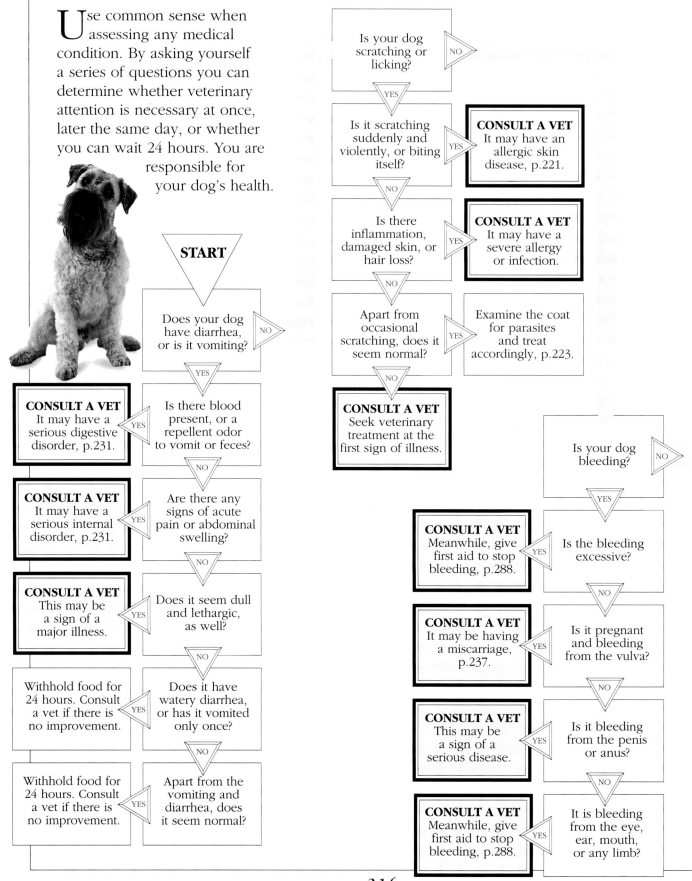

Use common sense when assessing any medical condition. By asking yourself a series of questions you can determine whether veterinary attention is necessary at once, later the same day, or whether you can wait 24 hours. You are responsible for your dog's health.

START

Does your dog have diarrhea, or is it vomiting? — NO

YES

CONSULT A VET
It may have a serious digestive disorder, p.231. — YES — Is there blood present, or a repellent odor to vomit or feces?

NO

CONSULT A VET
It may have a serious internal disorder, p.231. — YES — Are there any signs of acute pain or abdominal swelling?

NO

CONSULT A VET
This may be a sign of a major illness. — YES — Does it seem dull and lethargic, as well?

NO

Withhold food for 24 hours. Consult a vet if there is no improvement. — YES — Does it have watery diarrhea, or has it vomited only once?

NO

Withhold food for 24 hours. Consult a vet if there is no improvement. — YES — Apart from the vomiting and diarrhea, does it seem normal?

Is your dog scratching or licking? — NO

YES

Is it scratching suddenly and violently, or biting itself? — YES — **CONSULT A VET** It may have an allergic skin disease, p.221.

NO

Is there inflammation, damaged skin, or hair loss? — YES — **CONSULT A VET** It may have a severe allergy or infection.

NO

Apart from occasional scratching, does it seem normal? — YES — Examine the coat for parasites and treat accordingly, p.223.

NO

CONSULT A VET
Seek veterinary treatment at the first sign of illness.

Is your dog bleeding? — NO

YES

CONSULT A VET
Meanwhile, give first aid to stop bleeding, p.288. — YES — Is the bleeding excessive?

NO

CONSULT A VET
It may be having a miscarriage, p.237. — YES — Is it pregnant and bleeding from the vulva?

NO

CONSULT A VET
This may be a sign of a serious disease. — YES — Is it bleeding from the penis or anus?

NO

CONSULT A VET
Meanwhile, give first aid to stop bleeding, p.288. — YES — It is bleeding from the eye, ear, mouth, or any limb?

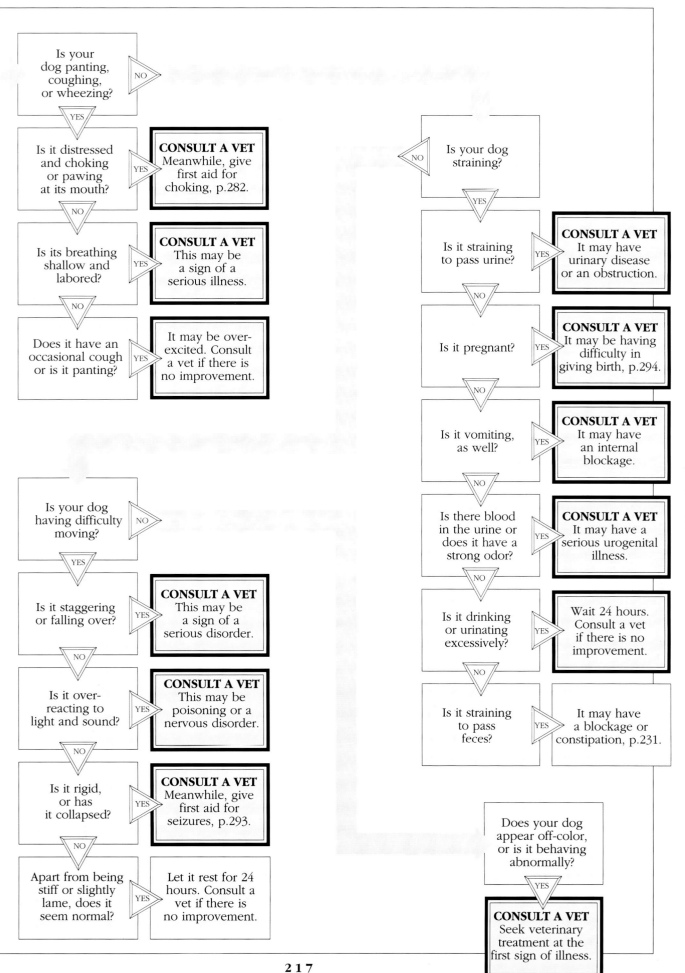

Is your
dog panting,
coughing,
or wheezing? — NO

YES

Is it distressed
and choking
or pawing
at its mouth? — YES → **CONSULT A VET** Meanwhile, give first aid for choking, p.282.

NO

Is its breathing
shallow and
labored? — YES → **CONSULT A VET** This may be a sign of a serious illness.

NO

Does it have an
occasional cough
or is it panting? — YES → It may be over-excited. Consult a vet if there is no improvement.

Is your dog
having difficulty
moving? — NO

YES

Is it staggering
or falling over? — YES → **CONSULT A VET** This may be a sign of a serious disorder.

NO

Is it over-
reacting to
light and sound? — YES → **CONSULT A VET** This may be poisoning or a nervous disorder.

NO

Is it rigid,
or has
it collapsed? — YES → **CONSULT A VET** Meanwhile, give first aid for seizures, p.293.

NO

Apart from being
stiff or slightly
lame, does it
seem normal? — YES → Let it rest for 24 hours. Consult a vet if there is no improvement.

NO — Is your dog
straining?

YES

Is it straining
to pass urine? — YES → **CONSULT A VET** It may have urinary disease or an obstruction.

NO

Is it pregnant? — YES → **CONSULT A VET** It may be having difficulty in giving birth, p.294.

NO

Is it vomiting,
as well? — YES → **CONSULT A VET** It may have an internal blockage.

NO

Is there blood
in the urine or
does it have a
strong odor? — YES → **CONSULT A VET** It may have a serious urogenital illness.

NO

Is it drinking
or urinating
excessively? — YES → Wait 24 hours. Consult a vet if there is no improvement.

NO

Is it straining
to pass
feces? — YES → It may have a blockage or constipation, p.231.

Does your dog
appear off-color,
or is it behaving
abnormally?

YES

CONSULT A VET Seek veterinary treatment at the first sign of illness.

BONE, MUSCLE, AND JOINT DISORDERS

Endurance and agility are important attributes of the natural hunter, and a dog's body is built to enhance these characteristics. The front legs are attached to the rest of the body by muscles, and there is no collarbone, which gives maximum flexibility. The hind legs have massive muscles to power instant acceleration and to maintain speed.

All this superb equipment is susceptible to injury and damage by misuse, especially in breeds whose bone structure has been much altered through selective breeding. Lameness is a common problem in dogs and requires rest. Examine the dog for signs of injury to the limbs, such as swelling or tenderness to touch. Determining the cause of lameness can be difficult and often requires veterinary help.

Fractures
When a fracture is simple and the bones remain straight, healing is assisted with a cast or bandage.

THE DOG'S SKELETON

Basic anatomy
Dogs bear over 60 percent of their weight on their front legs, with the hind legs acting as powerful, pistonlike accelerators.

Skull

Cervical vertebrae

Mandible

Thoracic vertebrae

Lumbar vertebrae

Scapula

Sacrum

Coccygeal vertebrae

Humerus

Pelvis

Radius

Ribs

Femur

Ulna

Sternum

Patella

Tibia

Fibula

Carpus

Tarsus

Metacarpus

Metatarsus

Phalanges

BONE, MUSCLE, AND JOINT DISORDERS

Signs and disorders	Description	Action
Front leg lameness Fractured bones Dislocated joints Torn ligaments and tendons Bruised muscles Osteochondrosis (OCD) Elbow dysplasia Bone infection	With simple fractures there may be a little swelling, but more complex breaks involve substantial damage to the surrounding tissue. Hip, shoulder, and knee joints are most frequently injured or dislocated in traffic accidents. Torn ligaments and tendons are less painful than fractures but cause considerable lameness, with or without swelling. Bruised muscles are tender to the touch, although deep bruising is not always apparent from looking at the skin. In OCD, small pieces of cartilage break off the ball of the humerus in the shoulder joint and float around in the joint fluid, causing pain. The dog's head bobs down on the side of the affected shoulder, but otherwise it seems normal. Elbow pain and lameness are caused by injuries or an ununited anconeal process (elbow dysplasia), in which an elbow bone does not meet the ulna properly, leaving a loose piece of bone that can eventually cause arthritis. Bone infections usually occur after a penetrating injury such as a dog bite.	If a dog is injured in a traffic accident, carry out emergency first aid (see page 278) and get the dog to a vet. Some fractured bones heal well by being splinted or set in a cast, while others require internal fixation with pins, plates, or screws. Dislocated joints are manipulated back into position, or may require surgical repair. Torn ligaments and tendons often need surgical repair, while bruised or strained ligaments, tendons, and muscles respond to professional bandaging, rest, and painkillers. A vet can diagnose OCD according to the history of the dog, its breed, an examination, and X-rays. Sometimes only medication is necessary, but when pain and lameness are severe, the floating pieces of cartilage are surgically removed from the joint. Elbow injuries are treated with drugs, or by surgical correction with screws, while bone infection needs antibiotics that concentrate in bone tissue.

Hind leg lameness
Hip dysplasia
Perthe's disease
Luxating patella
Ruptured cruciate
  ligament
Fractures, dislocations,
  torn ligaments, bruised
  muscles (see above)
	Hip dysplasia, an inherited defect, causes pain and lameness to one or both hind legs. The pain is exaggerated when the leg is flexed, and occurs most frequently in large breeds. A similar pain occurs when the head of the femur loses its blood supply and "dies" (Perthe's disease, or avascular necrosis). This cause of hip pain is most common in small dogs. Small breeds are also more prone to luxating patellas (slipped kneecaps), another inherited defect, while all breeds can suffer from ruptured cruciate ligaments. In both instances weight is not carried on the affected hind leg, but there is no pain associated with either problem other than at the time when the ligament tears.	Contact a vet to determine the cause of lameness. Some cases of mild hip dysplasia respond well to medication, while more severe problems require surgical correction. Surgery is the only treatment for Perthe's disease. The "dead" head of the femur is removed. Luxating patellas can be surgically corrected. Cruciate ligaments are most likely to rupture in overweight, mature dogs, although young, lean dogs of some breeds, such as Boxers, can also tear these ligaments. Weight reduction, rest, and surgical repair are all necessary.

Paralysis Ruptured disks	Mildly ruptured disks cause intense pain, and the dog is reluctant to move. Greater slippage causes a partial or even complete paralysis (see page 241), eliminating movement and also the dog's perception of pain.	If the slippage is severe the dog needs immediate surgery to reduce the damage to the spinal cord. Absolute rest is most important for ruptured disks.
Joint pain Arthritis	Osteoarthritis can occur in any joint, and usually affects older dogs. It can be either hereditary or caused by disease, poor nutrition, or congenital abnormalities. Polyarthritis also causes pain in many joints. It can be caused by infection, autoimmune conditions in which the body destroys its own tissues, or as a reaction to certain drugs. Some giant breeds can develop arthritis in later life as a result of injuries or sprains during their critical period of growth.	Chronic arthritis is controlled with steroid and nonsteroid anti-inflammatories. Giant breeds should have limited exercise while growing. Polyarthritis can be permanently damaging. A vet may take a blood sample to determine the cause and might use antibiotics, anti-inflammatories, and painkillers. It is important to alleviate the dog's pain, since there is no definitive cure for arthritis.
Bone weakness Osteoporosis Hyperparathyroidism	Osteoporosis is usually a direct consequence of a meat-only diet, and can cause stunted growth and bowed legs. A poor ratio of calcium to phosphorus stimulates the parathyroid gland into overactivity (hyperparathyroidism). Affected dogs move slowly and feel discomfort when touched. An excess of vitamins during a puppy's growth stage can produce similar problems, with constant discomfort in the joints.	Feed only a well-balanced diet to avoid osteoporosis. Calcium supplements are often necessary for fast-growing dogs, but never give more than the amount recommended by a vet, since too much can be as harmful as too little.

SKIN AND COAT DISORDERS

Irritating skin conditions are among the most common medical problems that dogs can suffer. Scratching usually begins mildly and is most frequently caused by parasites such as fleas. Continued scratching damages the skin, allowing bacteria to multiply. The consequent inflammation stimulates the skin glands into producing excess discharge and odor. Routine grooming and parasite control prevent these complications from occurring. As a consequence of selective breeding, some breeds, such as the Cocker Spaniel, Golden Retriever, and West Highland White Terrier, have a higher-than-average incidence of skin and coat disorders *(see page 245)*, while others, such as poodles, have a very low incidence.

Rhythmic scratching
If a dog scratches in a classic fashion, suspect fleas even if you see no sign of them.

ANATOMY OF THE SKIN

Protective layers
Thick, outer guard hairs and smaller, softer accessory hairs provide good insulation from the cold. Glandular secretions add shine to the coat, and, more importantly, make it waterproof. The surface of the skin consists of multiple tough layers of dead cells, which are constantly being replaced at their base. Beneath this is an insulating layer of fat.

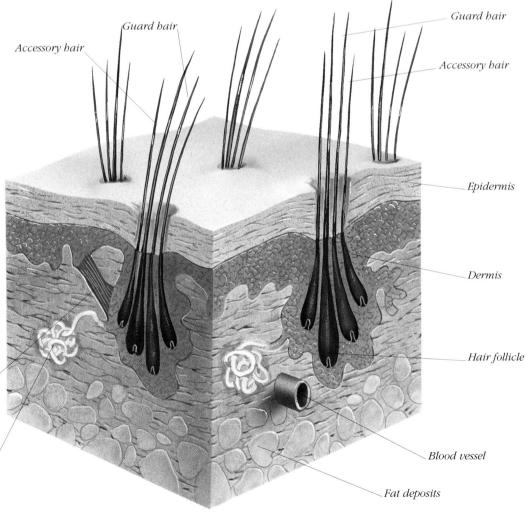

Guard hair

Accessory hair

Guard hair

Accessory hair

Epidermis

Dermis

Hair follicle

Erector muscle

Sebaceous gland

Blood vessel

Fat deposits

SKIN AND COAT DISORDERS

Signs and disorders	Description	Action
Scratching External parasites (p. 223) Allergies Irritation Infection	Scratching and chewing sometimes occur with or without accompanying inflammation. Parasites such as fleas account for most itchiness, although a dog could be scratching an allergic rash caused by inhaling pollen or dust; as a reaction to a contact irritant, such as shampoo or certain plants; or because its coat has just been clipped. Bacterial skin infections can also cause itching.	Eliminating the source of the irritation or allergy is the ultimate goal, although this can be difficult to determine in some instances. In the meantime, a vet can control self-mutilation with anti-inflammatory medication. Elizabethan collars are sometimes necessary to keep a dog from scratching or chewing itself *(see page 259)*. Always consult a vet before treating a dog for any skin problems, since the condition could be caused by a systemic disorder.
Inflammation Allergies Sunburn Foreign body (p. 283) Abscesses Skin infections	Inflammation can be caused by allergy or sunburn, or by foreign bodies lodged in the skin, such as grass seeds between the toes, which cause abscesses. With skin infections (pyoderma), bacteria invade the skin surface, which becomes red and sometimes moist and oozing (acute moist dermatitis). Bacteria sometimes breed between folds of skin and produce lesions (skin-fold pyoderma). Puppies can sometimes suffer from juvenile pyoderma, causing their faces to swell. Deep infections, such as cellulitis, produce hot, painful swellings.	Accurate diagnosis of the underlying cause of inflammation is essential. A vet can treat the inflammation with an appropriate antibiotic or antifungal medication. In hot, sunny countries avoidance of strong sunlight and the use of a high-factor sunblock may prevent sunburn. Bathe abscesses twice daily in tepid salt water.
Skin changes Seborrhea Acanthosis nigricans	Because of an inadequate diet, hormonal imbalance, parasites, or yeast infections, a dog's skin can sometimes become flaky, or its coat can look dull or greasy. Dry seborrhea looks like dandruff, while oily seborrhea is the over-production of oil by the skin. The disease acanthosis nigricans results in thickened, black skin, most commonly in dachshunds. Its cause is usually hypothyroidism.	Skin conditions can be treated with special shampoos and medication, but accurate diagnosis is necessary for complete control of the condition.
Lumps Cysts Warts Tumors Abscesses *(see above)*	Cysts feel like hard lumps just under the skin. Warts are most common in elderly dogs. Warts are often pink, mottled, and crusty around their roots, but they can also be pigmented. Melanomas are pigmented, highly malignant skin tumors that occur most frequently in Boxers. Slow-growing, soft, fluctuating, egg-shaped masses under the skin in older dogs are usually benign tumors.	An accurate diagnosis is essential, since warts, cysts, and tumors require removal by a vet.
Hair loss Ringworm External parasites (p. 223) Collie nose Hormonal imbalance Calluses	Local hair loss can be caused by fungal infections like ringworm, and parasites such as mange mites. Local hair loss on the nose of collie breeds can occur due to sunburn (collie nose). Generalized, especially symmetrical, hair loss often has hormonal origins in the thyroid, adrenal, or pituitary glands, or in the ovaries or testicles. Hair loss on the elbows of heavy dogs is caused by excess pressure on a hard surface causing calluses of the skin.	Ringworm responds to antifungal ointments and oral antibiotics. Mange mites must be treated with an insecticidal shampoo. Collie nose may be prevented by use of a high-factor sunblock. Hormonal imbalances can be diagnosed through blood tests and corrected with appropriate medicines. A skin cream will keep skin supple and prevent calluses, but the dog should also be provided with soft bedding.
Excess licking Lick dermatitis Blocked anal sacs (p. 231) External parasites (p. 223)	Dogs lick their skin to clean wounds and remove debris from their fur, but obsessive licking of any part of the body, especially the forepaws, can be a sign of a serious disorder. Excessive licking can be psychological and result in damage to a dog's skin (lick dermatitis).	Obsessive licking is difficult to control, although it may be controlled by drugs. A vet can treat the skin sores of lick dermatitis with antibiotic medication.

EXTERNAL PARASITES

Regardless of how careful you are in keeping your dog's coat clean and healthy, skin parasites are common and whenever possible will hop onto a canine for a meal. Cat fleas in particular are happy to use dogs (and humans) as hosts, while dog fleas and even human fleas create considerable problems, especially in warm climates. Look for telltale sooty, black specks of flea droppings in your dog's coat and bedding.

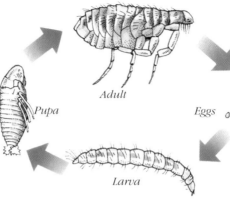

The flea life cycle
Flea eggs can remain viable for up to a year before hatching into larvae, then emerging as adults.

Mange mites and lice are usually transmitted through direct contact with other dogs, although wild animals such as foxes are also sources of these parasites. Ticks can be a problem, especially in regions where they transmit serious infections. Wildlife and domestic animals are sources of these blood-sucking parasites. Most canine parasites prefer dogs to humans, but mange mites can give humans an irritating skin rash.

COMMON EXTERNAL PARASITES

Examining a dog for parasites
Persistent scratching is a common sign of parasite infestation. You should routinely check a dog's skin for signs of dandruff or parasites, and the hair for lice, especially in warm weather.

Flea (above)
This tiny insect moves rapidly through the coat, preferring puppies to older dogs.

***Sarcoptes* mite (above)**
This mite, which prefers the ear tips and elbows, causes severe itching.

Tick (above)
This parasite swells to the size of a small pea when feeding on blood.

***Demodex* mite**
Only visible through a microscope, this mite lives inside hair follicles.

Harvest mite
This mite, known as a "chigger," is visible in autumn as a red dot.

***Cheyletiella* mite**
This highly contagious mite resembles a flake of moving dandruff.

Louse
The louse glues its eggs to the hair and is visible as it feeds on the skin.

EXTERNAL PARASITES

Parasite	Description and signs	Action
Fleas *Ctenocephalides* sp. *Ceratophylus* sp.	Mahogany-colored, long-legged fleas spend most of their lives in carpets and upholstered chairs, only hopping into a dog's fur for a meal. Some dogs are allergic to the saliva left in the bite wound and scratch intensively. Others are irritated as fleas walk around biting them. Dogs also pick up their most common tapeworm *(see page 233)* from flea infestation. Fleas often leave shiny black droppings in the fur.	Place black, hard dirt from the dog's coat on moistened tissue. If blood leeches out and stains the paper red, this confirms the presence of fleas. Treat the affected dog with a suitable insecticide, obtainable from a vet. It is also important to vacuum the dog's environment and treat its bedding with a biological spray that prevents flea eggs from hatching.
***Sarcoptes* mange mites**	These microscopic mites burrow into the skin, favoring the tips of the ears, which become scabby, crusty, and itchy, and the elbows. They cause intense irritation; frantic scratching and subsequent hair loss; and body sores. Humans can sometimes be temporarily affected with itchy pimples like mosquito bites, especially around the waist *(see page 247)*.	Bathe the affected dog weekly for at least four weeks with a veterinary insecticidal shampoo that kills sarcoptic mites. Thoroughly clean or destroy the dog's bedding, since these mites can survive for a short period of time off the dog.
***Demodex* mange mites**	These parasites normally inhabit canine hair follicles, but for unknown reasons they sometimes multiply excessively in either young, shorthaired dogs, or elderly, debilitated ones. There is seldom any itching, but nasty pustules develop as a result of secondary infection.	Examination of a skin scraping under a microscope readily reveals these tiny, cigar-shaped mites. Weekly bathing in a prescription insecticide is necessary until the mites are no longer seen in the scrapings.
***Cheyletiella* mites**	*Cheyletiella* mites are just visible to the eye and produce copious dandruff over the back, a condition known as "walking dandruff." Heavy infestations cause skin scaling but only limited itching. These mites can cause an irritating rash in humans *(see page 247)*.	These mites are easily destroyed with insecticidal shampoos, obtainable from a vet. All dogs that come into contact with an affected dog should be shampooed, and their bedding thoroughly cleaned.
Harvest mites *Trombicula autumnalis*	The small, red, barely visible larvae of these free-living autumn parasites usually infest field mice but also irritate dogs. They especially affect a dog's toes and cause it to lick its feet.	Veterinary insecticidal shampoos destroy these mites, but dogs sometimes need treatment with anti-inflammatory medicines, as well.
Lice *Trichodectes canis* *Linognathus setosus*	Biting lice walk around on the skin and glue their glistening white eggs, called "nits," to the fur. They are intensely irritating and are usually spread by direct contact.	Treatment consists of appropriate veterinary insecticidal shampoos and combing nits out of the fur.
Ticks *Ixodes* sp. *Dermacentor* sp.	Sheep and deer ticks leap into dogs' fur and bury their mouthpieces in the skin. They swell with blood and become engorged, brownish-white, and pea-sized. Some ticks in Australia and North America cause paralysis or carry the virus that causes Lyme disease *(see page 247)*.	Swab the tick and surrounding tissue with rubbing alcohol. Using tweezers, grasp the tick and "unscrew" its mouthpiece from the skin with a rotating action. Treat the area with an insecticide.
Blowfly maggots	Blowflies lay eggs in hair that is matted or contaminated with blood, pus, or feces, especially around the anus. These eggs hatch into maggots that damage the skin. Blowfly maggots are a seasonal problem, most common in longhaired and poorly groomed dogs.	Consult a vet immediately. Maggots can be flushed out with hydrogen peroxide, and the area cleansed with antiseptic. Routinely cut the hair around the anus of a longhaired dog to prevent feces from adhering and attracting flies.
Hookworm larvae *Uncinaria stenocephala* *Ancylostoma caninum*	These microscopic larvae live in damp hay and burrow into a dog's chest and feet, causing bumps and "damp hay itch." The dog scratches vigorously, often damaging its skin. This parasite is mainly found in dogs that are housed in outdoor kennels *(see page 233)*.	Consult a vet, who can treat the affected area with insecticide. The condition can be prevented by using shredded paper or bark for a dog's bedding instead of hay. The bedding should be changed regularly.

EYE DISORDERS

Because dogs communicate so well with humans with their eyes, changes caused by infection, disease, or injury are usually noticeable. The most common problems are discharges and inflammation. A dog may paw at its eyes because of irritation. This can cause accidental damage to the surface of the eye, the cornea, especially in breeds with protruding eyes, such as the Pekingese. More difficult to notice are changes inside the eye. Some of these, such as progressive retinal atrophy, are inherited and can lead to blindness. Other internal changes are indicators of disease elsewhere in the body. Consult a vet at once if you notice any eye abnormality.

Eye inspection
A vet can examine the interior of a dog's eye with an ophthalmoscope.

THE STRUCTURE OF THE EYE

Producing an image
Light passes through the surface of the eye, the cornea, and then through the lens within, which focuses the rays on the light-sensitive cells of the retina. This stimulates impulses that travel to the brain via the optic nerve, producing the image that the dog sees. Extra cells in the retina help dogs to see well in dim light.

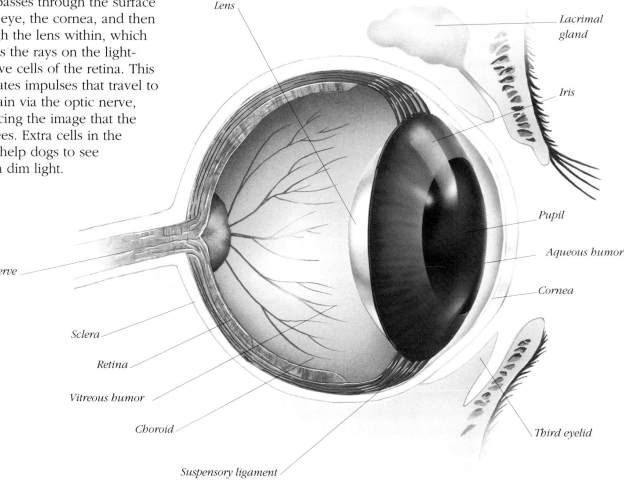

Lens

Lacrimal gland

Iris

Pupil

Aqueous humor

Cornea

Third eyelid

Optic nerve

Sclera

Retina

Vitreous humor

Choroid

Suspensory ligament

EYE DISORDERS

Signs and disorders	Description	Action
Clear discharge Infection Irritation Allergy Poodle eye	Tears usually drain down a canal to the back of the nose. If mucus or inflammation from infection plugs the tear ducts, tears overflow down the face. Excess tears are sometimes produced to wash away irritants or as a reaction to an allergy. Continuous tear overflow can stain the face brown (poodle eye).	Consult a vet immediately, since excess tears are often a sign of other, more important problems. A vet can flush out tear ducts to unblock them and treat infections with antibiotics.
Purulent discharge Dry eye	If the tear glands fail to produce enough tears, the eyeball initially looks dull and lusterless. Then bacteria invade, causing a tenacious yellow discharge. This disorder is most common in older dogs and is a serious problem.	Consult a vet immediately, since a lack of lubrication can lead to infection and blindness. Dry eye can be treated with antibiotics and artificial tears, although it is sometimes necessary to correct it by transferring a saliva duct up to the eye.
Inflammation Conjunctivitis Allergy Distichiasis Entropion/Ectropion Injuries Infected third eyelid gland Glaucoma Foreign body (p. 282)	Conjunctivitis, allergies, or physical irritation from dust, wind, pollen, or shampoo all cause eye inflammation. So do inherited conditions such as distichiasis (ingrown eyelashes) or excessively tight or loose eyelids (entropion and ectropion). Inflammation is also caused by injuries, infection of the third eyelid gland, and glaucoma, an increase in fluid pressure inside the eye caused by injury or disease.	Veterinary treatment is urgently needed. If the eye is uninjured, anti-inflammatories can be used in conjunction with other treatments. Inherited problems may require surgical correction, as does an excessively inflamed third-eyelid gland. Glaucoma needs pressure-reducing treatment for life, although if the pain is too great it is best that the eye be surgically removed.
Clouding (keratitis) Corneal injury or infection Cataract Lens problems Aging Blue eye	When the cornea is damaged through injury or disease it retains fluid and becomes cloudy and blue-gray in color (keratitis). A similar color change occurs in the lens when a cataract forms – which can lead to blindness – or if the lens drops out of its normal position (luxation). Aging produces a gradual clouding of the lens (sclerosis), usually in dogs over ten years old. Blue eye is a clouding of the eye due to a deep inflammation of the cornea, sometimes connected with infectious hepatitis.	Corneal injuries are serious, and an accurate and immediate veterinary diagnosis is necessary. The results of treatment are often excellent but depend upon the extent of the damage. Cataracts and luxated lenses are only surgically removed when the surgery will result in improved vision. Sometimes, using microsurgical techniques, a vet can insert plastic internal lenses into the affected eye.
Bleeding Injuries Prolapse of the eyeball	Eyelids are most frequently damaged in dog fights. Bleeding in the eye occurs after severe trauma from fights or traffic accidents. Breeds with bulging eyes such as the Pekingese are prone to prolapse of the eyeball, a condition in which the eyeball is pushed out of its socket.	Immediate veterinary attention is necessary. Wounds should be cleaned and sutured. A prolapsed eye can be returned to its socket and the eyelids sewn together for a week to keep it in place. Topical and oral medicines reduce swelling and infection.
Failing vision Progressive retinal atrophy (PRA) Stroke (p. 241) Collie eye anomaly (CEA) Retinal dysplasia Aging (see above)	Progressive retinal atrophy, an inherited disorder in which the retina deteriorates, is not outwardly apparent, except for the affected dog becoming confused in strange surroundings and bumping into objects. It can be difficult to spot damage to vision from strokes and also from an inherited retinal disease of collie breeds known as collie eye anomaly. Retinal dysplasia is a congenital defect involving folding or displacement of the retina and can cause blindness.	A vet can examine the inside of the eye with an ophthalmoscope. Because PRA, CEA, and retinal dysplasia are inherited eye disorders, affected dogs and their close relatives should not be used for breeding purposes. Some affected dogs continue to see despite their eye condition. If blindness develops slowly many dogs cope well.
Lumps Eyelid tumors Cysts Tumors in the eye	Eyelid tumors appear as brown or black protruding growths on the edge of the lid. They are most common in dogs over six years old. If the tumor rubs on the eye surface it can cause a watery discharge and may damage the cornea. Cysts can also develop but these look like swellings in the lid. Tumors in the eye initially cause bulging and associated inflammation.	Eyelid tumors are almost always benign and can be successfully removed with surgery. Cysts should also be removed if they provoke irritation. The only treatment for rare tumors inside the eye is total eye removal. With the edges removed, the eyelids are sewn together, producing a good cosmetic result.

EAR DISORDERS

Ear complaints are a regular reason for a visit to a vet. Head shaking, ear scratching, and pungent discharges are the most common conditions, and when these occur, ear mites should be considered as a cause. Dogs with pendulous, well-furred ear flaps, such as spaniels, are more likely to suffer from ear disorders than breeds with erect ears such as the German Shepherd Dog. Deafness can be hereditary in some breeds and is often associated with a white coat. Impaired hearing and eventual deafness is often associated with elderly dogs, especially retrievers. Loss of balance relating to hearing disorders can occur at any age and is usually caused by an infection spreading to the inner ear from the ear canal or the throat.

Examining the ears
A magnifying otoscope permits a vet to gently examine the ear canal for parasites and debris.

THE STRUCTURE OF THE EAR

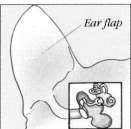

Ear flap

The outer ear
Sound waves are gathered by the large outer ear and channeled to the eardrum.

The inner ear
Sound waves arriving at the eardrum cause vibrations that are transmitted to the ossicles of the middle ear, and then on to the inner ear. These sounds are translated into electrical impulses and conveyed to the brain.

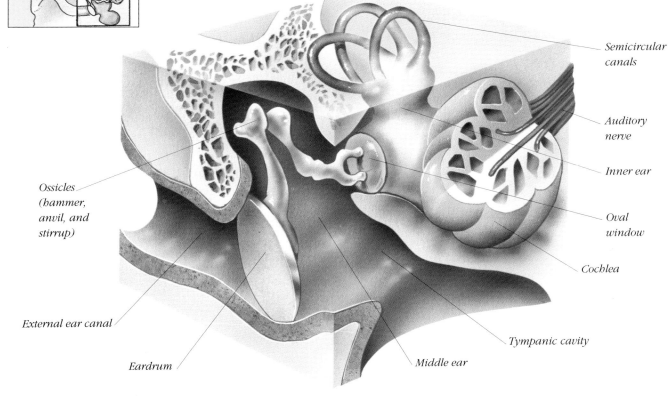

Semicircular canals

Auditory nerve

Inner ear

Oval window

Cochlea

Tympanic cavity

Ossicles (hammer, anvil, and stirrup)

External ear canal

Eardrum

Middle ear

EAR DISORDERS

Signs and disorders	Description	Action
Head shaking and ear scratching Ear mites Foreign body (p. 283) Allergy Infection (*see below*)	Ear mites are common in puppies and spread easily within a litter. They irritate the lining of the ear canal, stimulating wax production, and are just visible to the naked eye. Foreign bodies such as grass seeds in the ears cause sudden, violent head shaking. The ear is quite painful when touched. If a dog has an allergy or an infection, the inside of the ear flap and the ear canal will be inflamed and sensitive.	Consult a vet, who can prescribe eardrops to eliminate ear mites. All dogs and cats that have been in contact with an affected animal should be treated, since these mites can easily be transmitted. Because mites can live outside the ear, insecticidal shampoos are also beneficial. A vet can remove a foreign object with special forceps. The cause of an allergic reaction should be determined and eliminated, if possible; the symptoms can be treated with anti-inflammatory drops.
Discharge Bacterial or yeast infections Ear mites (*see above*)	Infection of the outer ear (otitis externa) often produces discharges. These can be due to bacteria (thick, yellow discharge), yeast (black and runny), or mites (black and gritty). If left untreated, otitis externa can lead to middle-ear infection (otitis media), which can result in severe conditions such as a ruptured eardrum.	A vet can treat discharges with antibiotics and anti-inflammatories. It is best to prevent middle-ear infection by treating infections of the outer ear, since severe cases of otitis media can only be cured by surgically removing the affected parts of the ear canal.
Loss of balance Inner ear infection	Infection can reach the inner ear from the external ear, through the Eustachian tube from the throat or via the bloodstream. This causes the dog to tilt its head in the direction of the affected ear. The eyes often flick in the same direction. Since the semicircular canals in the inner ear control balance, any infection there will make a dog unsteady on its feet.	Confine the dog to prevent it from injuring itself while its balance is impaired. A vet can control possible nausea and treat the dog with high levels of antibiotics by mouth. Surgical drainage of the inner ear is sometimes necessary.
Deafness Excess wax production Seborrhea Tumor Blocked ear canal Aging	Temporary deafness can be caused by excess production of wax or by seborrhea (*see also page 221*), which produces a yellow, malodorous substance that builds up in the ear. This is common in dogs with narrow ear canals, such as poodles. A tumor inside the ear makes the skin appear thickened and dark. The ear canal can also be blocked by the hair inside the ears in some breeds, such as poodles and Yorkshire Terriers. Wax catches in this hair, forming a plug of material and an ideal environment for bacterial multiplication. Some hearing loss is natural in old age.	To eliminate wax or seborrhea, the ear must be cleaned daily with a special liquid, which can be obtained from a vet. Dry the ear thoroughly after cleaning. Tumors must be removed surgically. A vet can remove hair blocking the ear and treat infections with antibiotics.
Swelling on ear flap Hematoma (blood blister) Physical damage	Chronic head shaking – for whatever reason – can cause internal bleeding, especially in older dogs. The ear swells, forming a warm, egglike structure (hematoma). The tips of the ears bleed easily and are prone to damage from dog bites and other injuries.	Consult a vet. A hematoma can be surgically drained and stitched. In the case of physical damage to the ear, stop bleeding and prevent infection by cleaning the wound thoroughly and bandaging the ear to the head (*see page 288*) before seeking veterinary advice.
Hair loss Genetic predisposition *Sarcoptes* mange mites (p. 223) Ringworm (p. 221) Hormonal imbalance (p. 221)	In certain lines of some breeds, such as the Yorkshire Terrier, all the hair on the ears drops off when the dog is mature, leaving only dry, leathery ear flaps. A similar loss occurs on the nose. *Sarcoptes* mange mites often infest the tips of the ears in all breeds, causing itchy, crusty lesions and hair loss. The fungal infection ringworm also favors the ears, causing hair loss but frequently no itch or inflammation. Symmetrical thinning of the hair on both ears is an early sign of hormonal imbalance.	A veterinary examination can determine the cause of local hair loss. Genetic hair loss from the ears cannot be arrested, but selective breeding can reduce this condition. Blood samples can ascertain hormonal imbalances. Treatments are specific to the exact cause of hair loss.

RESPIRATORY DISORDERS

The dog has a very robust respiratory system and suffers from few common breathing disorders. Kennel cough, a bacterial or viral infection of the voice box and windpipe, is the most frequent infectious cause of coughing, while allergy is probably the next most usual cause. Coughing related to heart disease is common in older dogs or in young members of breeds that are prone to hereditary heart problems, such as the Cavalier King Charles Spaniel. Internal parasites, infections, foreign bodies, and systemic illnesses all cause respiratory disorders that can include abnormal breathing, whether shallow, deep, rapid or labored. Contact a vet promptly if your dog shows any signs of respiratory abnormality.

Listening to breathing
Using a stethoscope, a vet can listen to breathing. Radiographs also help with diagnosis.

THE RESPIRATORY SYSTEM

Breathing
As the lungs expand, reducing pressure in them, air is drawn through the nose, down the trachea, into the bronchi and finally into the alveoli, where oxygen is absorbed by red blood cells and transported throughout the body. Carbon dioxide is taken back to the lungs, where it is expelled.

Diaphragm

Alveoli

Lung

Bronchi

Trachea

Esophagus

Nasal chamber

Mouth

Nostril

RESPIRATORY DISORDERS

Signs and disorders	Description	Action
Nasal discharge or sneezing Allergy Infection Tumor Foreign body Cleft palate (p. 235)	All dogs sneeze occasionally, especially when they wake. Allergic sneezing is usually nonproductive, occurring in paroxysms, while infections often produce pus. A purulent or bloody discharge from a single nostril indicates a tumor, or a foreign body such as a grass seed.	Consult a vet for correct diagnosis. Allergic sneezing can be reduced by antihistamines, although eliminating the cause is best. Infections can be viral, bacterial, or fungal and are treated with medication. Tumors can be surgically removed, while foreign bodies are often sneezed forward until they can be extracted by a vet.
Acute coughing or gagging Kennel cough Tonsil, pharynx, or larynx infection Acute bronchitis Inhalation pneumonia Foreign body in the airway	Kennel cough is contracted from another dog and causes inflammation to the voice box and windpipe. Other bacterial and viral diseases inflame the tonsils, pharynx, or larynx, causing the dog to stretch its neck forward, gag, and cough. Bacterial or allergic inflammation to the bronchi in the lungs, causing acute bronchitis or inhalation pneumonia, and foreign bodies in the airways all stimulate acute coughing.	Kennel cough is highly contagious, so isolate the dog and contact a vet immediately if you suspect this ailment. A vet can treat infections with medication and remove foreign bodies with special forceps. Cough suppressants can make a dog more comfortable, although in most circumstances these are not actual cures. These medicines reduce the unpleasant side effects of disease, allowing the respiratory system to return to normal.
Persistent coughing or gagging Poor heart function Collapsed windpipe Chronic bronchitis Lungworms Heartworms (p. 243) Roundworms (p. 233)	A nighttime cough can mean poor heart function *(see page 243)*. Fluid builds up in the lungs, causing a nonproductive gag. As time progresses the cough becomes pronounced, especially after exercise. A collapsed windpipe, a congenital defect of some toy breeds, causes a distressing cough, and even light exercise induces a coughing spasm. Chronic bronchitis occurs in older dogs, causing a persistent cough, especially when they are excited or after they exercise. Lungworms, heartworms, and migrating roundworm larvae all cause light coughing.	Consult a vet as soon as possible, since a persistent cough is a sign of serious disease. Improvement to cardiac function controls heart-related coughing. A collapsed windpipe is potentially life-threatening, and when this occurs in a young dog an artificial windpipe can be surgically inserted. Chronic bronchitis improves with appropriate medication. Lungworm infestation can be treated with appropriate medication, although internal damage sometimes requires surgical repair.
Snoring Elongated soft palate Allergy Aging Narrow nostrils and larynx	Many breeds, especially those with compressed faces, have elongated soft palates that hang at the back of the throat. The soft palate interferes with the larnyx, producing a snore. This also happens when there is allergic inflammation in the throat or simply when the soft palate loses elasticity with age. Narrow nostrils and larynx exacerbate snoring.	In some breeds such as the Pekingese and Pug snoring is a sign of potential heart and breathing problems, so it is best to consult a vet. Surgical reduction of the length of the soft palate lessens or eliminates the condition. Allergic snoring can be treated with appropriate medication, while narrow nostrils and larynx can be enlarged with simple surgery.
Breathing abnormalities Pleural effusions Injury to the ribs Lung disease Heart failure (p. 243) Kidney disease (p. 239) Heatstroke (p. 290) Poisoning (p. 284)	Distressed or unusual breathing can be a sign of a potentially life-threatening problem. Pleural effusions of blood, pus, and other fluids can sometimes cause a persistent cough, as well as breathing difficulties and an unwillingness to exercise. Shallow breathing may indicate an injury to the ribs that makes breathing painful. Rapid breathing may denote lung, heart, or kidney disease.	Immediate veterinary attention is needed, especially if you suspect that the dog has an injury causing painful breathing. Pleural effusions are surgically tapped and drained to reduce pressure on the lungs.
Voice changes Injury to the larynx Allergy Laryngeal tumor Laryngeal paralysis	A dog's bark is altered when its larynx is damaged. Allergic reactions, typically from bee and wasp stings, cause laryngeal swelling. Tumors can develop in old dogs, although they are rare. Laryngeal paralysis occurs particularly in elderly Labrador Retrievers and German Shepherd Dogs, turning their bark into a roar.	Consult a vet. Antihistamines or anti-inflammatories can reduce allergic swelling, while tumors are sometimes surgically removed. Surgery to correct laryngeal paralysis is often unsatisfactory. A safe alternative is the surgical creation of a permanent opening in the windpipe in the neck, bypassing the blocked larynx. This dramatically improves breathing.

DIGESTIVE DISORDERS

The dog is a scavenger and opportunistic feeder. Many dogs will deliberately overeat whenever food is available. It is not surprising, therefore, that vomiting is more common in dogs than in many other kinds of mammals. Regurgitation is also the normal way a wild bitch feeds her puppies until they can hunt for themselves. Constant or projectile vomiting, however, are signs of a serious disorder, as is vomiting blood or bile. Similarly, persistent or explosive diarrhea requires immediate veterinary attention. Constipation can be a serious problem, and even a lack of appetite can sometimes be a sign of illness or internal disorder.

Eating grass
Some dogs enjoy eating grass regularly, while others only do so when they feel abdominal discomfort, since it induces vomiting.

THE DIGESTIVE SYSTEM

Digestion
The dog has a large stomach and a relatively short intestinal tract, an ideal arrangement for an opportunistic hunter and scavenger. Food breakdown starts in the stomach, but almost all the digestion occurs in the intestines. The liver detoxifies unwanted products, while indigestible material and waste travel to the large intestine and are excreted.

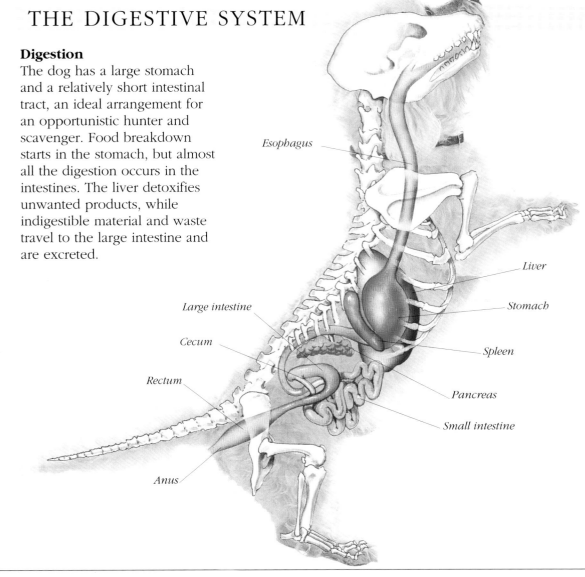

Esophagus

Liver

Stomach

Large intestine

Cecum

Spleen

Rectum

Pancreas

Small intestine

Anus

DIGESTIVE DISORDERS

Signs and disorders	Description	Action
Occasional vomiting Overeating Eating grass Allergy Travel sickness Nervousness Enlarged esophagus	Simple vomiting is common and usually unassociated with discomfort. Though otherwise appearing normal, a dog might vomit as a result of overeating, consuming unusual foods such as grass, eating things to which it is allergic, or as a result of car travel or nervousness. An enlarged esophagus, especially in puppies, can also cause simple vomiting.	Withdraw the dog's food for up to 24 hours and, as long as there is no dehydration, ration its water to small amounts of soda water or occasional ice cubes for eight hours. If vomiting continues, seek veterinary advice.
Persistent vomiting or vomiting blood Gastric torsion Infection Acute pancreatitis Poisoning (p. 284)	Vomiting blood and persistent vomiting are very serious. Gastric torsion (bloat), most common in deep-chested breeds, causes painful vomiting and sudden swelling of the abdomen *(see page 293)*. Infections such as parvovirus, distemper, leptospirosis, and hepatitis all cause listlessness and sometimes bloody or projectile vomiting, in which the contents of the dog's stomach are ejected with great force. Inflammation of the pancreas (acute pancreatitis) may cause pain and vomiting.	Severe vomiting requires immediate veterinary attention. Gastric torsion is a life-threatening emergency requiring immediate surgical correction. Preventive vaccination protects against many of the infectious viral diseases such as parvovirus, while bacterial diseases are treated with appropriate antibiotics. Vomiting associated with acute pancreatitis, especially in small dogs, can be controlled by specific drugs.
Diarrhea Milk intolerance Allergy Chronic pancreatitis Roundworms (p. 233) Colitis Infections Poisoning (p. 284)	Frequent diet changes or food intolerance, especially to milk; allergies; underactive pancreas function (chronic pancreatitis); internal parasites; or inflammation of the colon (colitis) all cause diarrhea. Bacterial and viral infections such as salmonella, parvovirus, or hepatitis can cause explosive, watery diarrhea, sometimes with blood and accompanying lethargy.	Dogs with simple diarrhea should fast for 24 hours and then eat a bland meal such as chicken and rice. Once determined, the cause of diarrhea should be avoided or eliminated. Consult a vet if diarrhea continues for over two days. Explosive, bloody, or painful diarrhea requires immediate veterinary attention.
Overeating or weight gain Pancreatic hypoplasia Hypothyroidism Competition Boredom Overfeeding	Dogs that do not produce enough digestive enzymes (pancreatic hypoplasia) are effectively starving, although they may eat voraciously. An underactive thyroid gland (hypothyroidism) slows down a dog's metabolism, resulting in weight gain on a standard diet, often associated with some lethargy and hair loss. Because of their pack mentality, dogs compete for food and eat more when fed together. Boredom can also cause a dog to eat more, since mealtime is the most exciting event of its day. Overfeeding by a dog's owner is the most common cause of weight gain.	Consult a vet. Pancreatic hypoplasia can be diagnosed through blood tests or stool samples and treated with enzyme supplements. Similarly, thyroid gland activity can be analyzed with blood tests, and deficiencies corrected with medication. If these tests prove normal, then boredom or competition between dogs must be considered as a cause of weight gain. In these circumstances, feed fewer calories under veterinary supervision.
Constipation Blocked anal sacs Abscessed anal sacs Swallowed bones Enlarged prostate gland Pelvic fracture Bowel nerve damage Perineal hernia Atresia ani	If the anal sacs on either side of the anal opening become blocked or infected and abscessed, they cause discomfort. The dog licks or drags its rear on the ground and may be unwilling to empty its bowels. Swallowed bones in the large intestine, an enlarged prostate pressing upon and narrowing the colon, pelvic fractures, and nerve damage are all more serious conditions. A bulge on either side of the anus might be a perineal hernia impacted with feces. Some puppies are born with imperfect anal openings and cannot pass a stool (atresia ani).	Consult a vet. Anal sacs can be manually squeezed empty *(see page 253)* but require syringing with antibiotics when infected or abscessed. Bony impactions require enemas and sometimes anesthesia and manual evacuation of impacted stool, while prostate enlargement can be treated with antibiotics and hormones. Pelvic fractures can be surgically repaired, but nerve damage is often irreversible. Surgical correction is necessary for a perineal hernia and for atresia ani.
Loss of appetite Pain or discomfort in mouth (p. 235) Nausea Anxiety	When a dog asks for food but does not eat it, it might be suffering from discomfort in its mouth. If pain is elsewhere or associated with nausea, the dog may be reluctant to even ask for food. When excited, nervous, or worried some dogs simply lose their appetites.	A lack of appetite is often a very important general sign that a dog is sick, especially in those that routinely enjoy their food. A veterinary examination will determine the seriousness of the condition.

INTERNAL PARASITES

Intestinal parasites seldom cause much inconvenience to dogs, but since the most common, the roundworm, is a potential health hazard to humans, you must ensure that your dog is routinely wormed. Dogs can also act as intermediate hosts for certain tapeworms that can be passed to humans. In addition to roundworms and tapeworms, dogs can become infested with the more serious intestinal hookworms and whipworms, or with parasites that cause diarrhea. Ticks can

Bitch infected by eating contaminated feces

Puppy passes eggs in feces

Adult worms inside bitch

Puppies acquire larvae from mother's milk

transmit a single-celled parasite called *Babesia*, which causes lethargy and anemia. Dogs can contract the disease toxoplasmosis from eating contaminated animals or cat feces.

Puppy infection
Puppies become infected with larvae either before birth, from the larvae passing from the bitch, or after birth from their mother's milk. The puppies pass eggs in their feces, which the bitch consumes, completing the cycle.

COMMON INTERNAL PARASITES

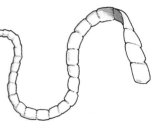

Roundworm (*above*)
Looking like a pale earthworm, this parasite lives in the stomach or intestines and reaches about 4 in (10 cm) in length.

Tapeworm (*above*)
Flat and segmented, the tapeworm attaches itself by its mouth to the intestinal wall.

Whipworm (*above*)
Up to 2½ in (7 cm) long, this worm lives in the cecum. Its eggs can be seen with a microscope.

Signs of infestation
Licking the anal region or dragging the rear are common signs of worm infestation. Check for signs of tapeworm egg sacs in the hair around the anal region. Since impacted anal sacs are just as frequent a cause of excessive anal grooming, check that they are not causing discomfort *(see page 231)*.

Hookworm (*above*)
This microscopic, blood-sucking parasite lives in the intestines. It can cause serious bleeding.

INTERNAL PARASITES

Parasite	Description and signs	Action
Roundworms *Toxocara canis* *Toxascaris leonina*	Roundworms may cause mild vomiting and diarrhea, with curled, round, pink-white worms being passed. Puppies may acquire this worm while still in the mother's womb and have mature worms in their intestines by the time they are only two weeks old. If a puppy inherits a heavy load of *T. canis* worms, it will have a pot-bellied appearance and a dull coat, and either gain weight poorly or suffer weight loss. It might cough, hiccup and, in rare instances, suffer from convulsions. *T. leonina* is acquired by a dog swallowing microscopic eggs.	All puppies should be routinely wormed from two weeks of age. Pregnant bitches should be wormed under veterinary supervision. Only worming medicines that destroy all stages of the life cycle are effective. Even healthy-looking dogs can have roundworms. Adult dogs should be wormed every three months to prevent roundworm infestation.
Tapeworms *Dipylidium caninum* *Echinococcus granulosus* *Taenia* sp.	Tapeworms seldom cause clinical signs. The abdomen can become distended, but the most common finding is small, dried egg sacs like rice grains in the hair around the anus. The worms can also be seen moving in the dog's feces. *Dipylidium caninum* is acquired by the dog eating a flea containing a worm egg. Other tapeworms are acquired by a dog eating carcasses or scraps of animals, such as rabbits or rodents, that contain tapeworm cysts.	Prevent tapeworms by controlling fleas *(see page 223)* and keeping your dog from eating animal carcasses and scraps. *Echinococcus* is of particular importance because it can affect humans *(see page 247)*. This is of most concern in countries or regions with large sheep populations. Worm a dog regularly with a preparation approved by a vet.
Whipworms *Trichuris vulpis*	Whipworms can cause diarrhea with sufficient bleeding to produce anemia. They usually occur in young dogs kept in unhygienic conditions and are most common in warm climates. The worms can be up to 2½ in (7 cm) long. They cause irritation, making a dog drag its rear along the ground.	Consult a vet, since whipworm eggs shed on grass can remain infectious for over a year. Diagnosis is based on a veterinary fecal flotation test. Because this worm is resistant to many drugs, special medicines are needed.
Hookworms *Uncinaria stenocephala* *Ancylostoma caninum*	Hookworms are almost microscopic, living off blood in the small intestine. They can cause severe anemia and diarrhea. When dogs lie on damp, unhygienic bedding, the larval stage of this parasite can cause skin irritation, especially between the toes *(see page 223)*.	Hygiene should be improved and the dog should be wormed with special medication supplied by a vet.
Giardia canis	*Giardia* is a microscopic parasite. Dogs and humans *(see page 247)* can become infected by drinking contaminated water. The parasite causes diarrhea, which is often bloody and accompanied by mucus. Some dogs can contract this parasite by eating droppings from contaminated animals such as beavers.	Take a fresh sample of the affected dog's feces to a vet, who can carry out lab tests and then treat the condition with an appropriate course of medication. *Giardia* is not destroyed by routine drugs.
Babesia	*Babesia* is a microscopic, single-celled parasite transmitted through tick bites. It attacks red blood cells, causing anemia, lethargy, vomiting, and liver problems.	Consult a vet, who can carry out a simple blood test to diagnose the condition. It is best controlled by preventing tick infestation *(see page 223)*.
Coccidia	*Coccidia* is a microscopic protozoan that causes diarrhea, especially in young dogs kept in crowded conditions.	Take a sample of the affected dog's feces to a vet, who can carry out a microscopic examination. *Coccidia* responds to treatment with sulpha drugs.
Toxoplasma gondii	The disease toxoplasmosis can, in rare circumstances, cause diarrhea, muscle weakness, and breathing difficulties. Dogs get it by eating other animals that contain cysts of the single-celled protozoan *Toxoplasma* or by eating contaminated cat feces.	Diagnosis is based upon blood tests. Treatment is difficult, although there is some response to certain drugs. Reduce the risk of infection by clearing cat litter boxes of feces daily. Toxoplasmosis is also a public health hazard.

MOUTH AND TOOTH DISORDERS

Because they no longer use their teeth to catch and kill prey for food, more than 70 percent of domestic dogs show signs of gum disease by the time they are four years old. Bad breath is often the first sign of mouth trouble. This is caused by bacteria multiplying in food trapped between the teeth or by gum infection. Small dogs such as poodles and Yorkshire Terriers, in which the teeth are closely packed, are more prone to gum disease than are larger breeds such as retrievers. Certain breeds, such as the Boxer and bull terriers, can suffer from proliferative gum growth, while other dogs with overshot or undershot jaws are also prone to gum disease. Untreated gum disease leads to tooth decay. Chip fractures from chewing bones and stones also damage teeth and lead to infection. Without early treatment, removal is often the best option.

Examining teeth
Have your dog's teeth and gums examined by a vet at least once a year.

A DOG'S TEETH

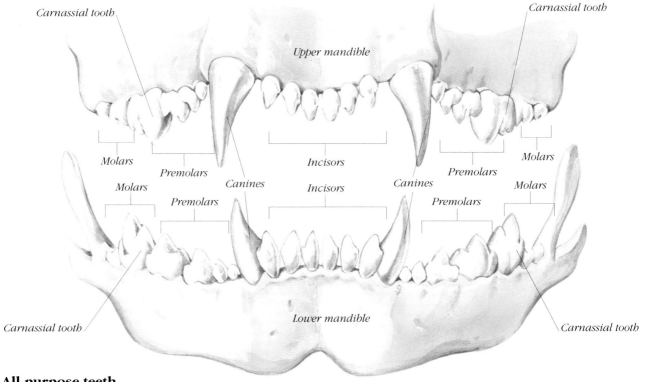

Carnassial tooth

Carnassial tooth

Upper mandible

Molars

Premolars

Incisors

Premolars

Molars

Molars

Canines

Incisors

Canines

Molars

Premolars

Premolars

Carnassial tooth

Lower mandible

Carnassial tooth

All-purpose teeth
Dogs first develop milk teeth that drop out by 20 weeks of age and are replaced with adult teeth. The canines are adapted for tearing, the molars for crushing, and the tiny incisors for scraping. These activities keep the teeth and gums clean and healthy. The carnassial teeth shear food into small pieces.

MOUTH AND TOOTH DISORDERS

Signs and disorders	Description	Action
Halitosis (bad breath) Tartar Gingivitis (gum infection) Tumors Proliferating gum disease	Sensitive, inflamed gums are common in all dogs, but especially in small breeds. Tartar builds up on the teeth, food particles catch between the tartar and the gums, and gum infection ensues. Tumors appear as lumps in the gums. Proliferating gum disease is an inherited condition, common to Boxers and bull terriers, in which the gum grows up to cover the teeth. If left untreated by a vet, this condition can lead to gum infection.	Seek veterinary advice for correct diagnosis. Routine brushing of a dog's teeth will slow or prevent the development of tartar and gingivitis. If tartar has formed, the teeth must be scaled and polished by a vet. Some mouth tumors are malignant and life-threatening, and must be surgically removed. Infection caused by proliferating gums can be treated with antibiotics, but greatly enlarged gums must be surgically removed under anesthesia.
Drooling Salivary cyst Periodontal disease Tongue injuries Foreign body (p. 282)	Salivary cysts look like large, fluid-filled blisters when they occur under the tongue, but they can also develop under the skin in the neck by the corners of the jaw, creating fluctuating masses. Periodontal disease destroys the cement that holds the teeth in place, so that they move when touched. Tongue wounds can be self-inflicted or the result of fights with other dogs. Bites are most common to the tip, while burns occur farther back and are difficult to see.	Salivary cysts require drainage, and the damaged saliva gland must be removed as well, so consult a vet if this is suspected. Once periodontal disease has become so severe that the teeth are loose, they must be removed. Bites and burns also need veterinary attention. Because eating is painful for a dog with such disorders, it is sometimes best to feed small, soft pieces of food that do not need to be chewed.
Reluctance to chew Tooth cavity Tooth root abscess Fractured tooth Distemper teeth	Large cavities are visible as damage to the tooth enamel and often occur at the gum margin. Root abscesses are sometimes more difficult to see. A crack might appear in a tooth or a skin swelling develop. This sometimes affects tear drainage if an upper molar is affected, causing tears to run down the face. Molars commonly fracture, whereas the canines get chipped, often during play. Any contact with the distemper virus while a dog is still a puppy can cause the adult teeth to erupt looking severely eroded, stained, and mottled, and these often decay.	Although it is often most practical for a vet to remove the tooth that is causing pain, routine tooth decay can be treated with fillings, while abscesses and fractures usually require root canal work. Tooth damage from the distemper virus is permanent, and severely decayed teeth should be removed by a vet.
Misaligned bite (malocclusion) Undershot jaw Overshot jaw	The upper and lower teeth should mesh perfectly when a dog closes its mouth, but sometimes the lower jaw is longer than the upper one, causing an undershot bite. This is normal in breeds with pushed-in faces, such as the Pekingese and Bulldog, but is a defect in others. If the lower jaw is shorter than the upper the bite is overshot. This is a defect in any breed, but is most likely to occur in long-nosed breeds such as the Doberman and collies.	No action is necessary unless the misaligned bite causes discomfort. This is most likely to occur in overshot jaws. With a narrow overshot jaw, the lower canines press into the hard palate each time the dog closes its mouth. A vet can fit a removable appliance over the upper front teeth and hard palate. After a few months the lower canines should have moved into a more correct and less painful position.
Abnormalities Hairlip Cleft palate Retained milk teeth No adult teeth	During fetal development, both sides of the body develop symmetrically and then join in the middle. If the final join is not perfect, a hairlip or cleft palate develops. Puppies born with cleft palates have difficulty suckling. The palate is also prone to damage at the midline, in which there is an obvious tear down the center of the hard palate, causing affected dogs to sneeze when they drink. Retained milk teeth are common in small breeds, especially the Yorkshire Terrier. In this case, once the adult teeth have erupted there are commonly eight canines instead of four. Rarely, adult teeth do not appear at all, and a mature dog retains only tiny milk teeth.	Hairlips look unusual but rarely need surgical correction, but cleft palates require veterinary treatment. Sometimes waterproof plasters can be temporarily applied over the damage until the puppy is larger and better able to cope with the trauma of major surgery. In most instances, surgery is the only effective solution. All milk teeth should loosen and drop out just before adult teeth erupt. If the adult teeth have broken through but the milk teeth are still firmly rooted, the baby teeth should be removed under anesthesia by a vet to provide the proper spaces into which the adult teeth can grow. This reduces the likelihood of future gum disease.

REPRODUCTIVE DISORDERS

Early neutering eliminates the possibility of the most serious reproductive disorders. Neutering a male removes the threat of testicular cancer. If a bitch is spayed before her first season, she has virtually no risk of developing mammary cancer. However, if the bitch continues to cycle until she is over two years old, her risk of developing a cancerous tumor has already reached a maximum. Similarly, the

longer a bitch cycles, the more at risk she becomes of developing a life-threatening womb infection. All breeding dogs, especially males, should

be routinely examined for sexually transmitted diseases. When infertility occurs, a vet can look for metabolic conditions that affect fertility.

Mother love
Maternal behavior is hormonally induced in a bitch after each season.

THE REPRODUCTIVE SYSTEM

Mating
The male's testes produce sperm that is passed to the bitch during mating. The sperm meets the released eggs in the Fallopian tube, where union occurs. The fertilized eggs then position themselves along the length of each horn of the uterus, where they develop over the following two months.

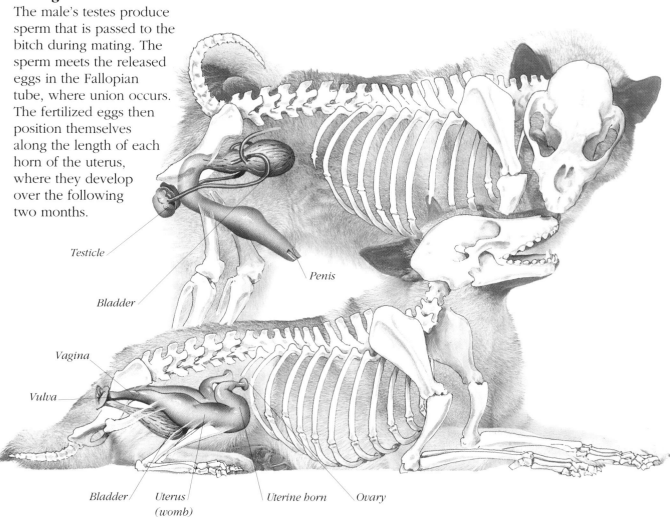

Testicle

Penis

Bladder

Vagina

Vulva

Bladder *Uterus (womb)* *Uterine horn* *Ovary*

REPRODUCTIVE DISORDERS

Signs and disorders	Description	Action
Female infertility Infection Metritis Ovarian cyst Hypothyroidism (p. 231) Hypoestrogenism Physical abnormalities	Sexually transmitted infections such as brucellosis are a major cause of infertility in some countries. Carriers may have a high temperature or swollen joints. Metritis (womb infection) prevents the fertilized eggs from implanting, while ovarian cysts prevent ovulation. Hypothyroidism causes abnormal heat cycles, while hypoestrogenism, under-development of the ovaries, results in low estrogen levels and no heat cycle. Physical problems such as a narrow vagina cause the bitch pain, and the bitch may refuse to mate.	A veterinary examination before mating can determine whether there are any infections in the reproductive system. These can usually be treated effectively with antibiotics. Laboratory tests on a blood sample help to determine whether a bitch has an ovarian cyst, which may be treated with hormones, or removed surgically. A vet may also suggest a hysterectomy. There is no treatment for hypoestrogenism. Physical abnormalities can be corrected surgically.
Male infertility Prostatitis Balanitis Orchitis Physical abnormalities Tumors	Infections that result in an enlarged prostate (prostatitis), and sheath infections (balanitis) can reduce a male dog's fertility, as can inflammation of the testicle (orchitis), due to injury or a disease such as brucellosis. Physical abnormalities can also affect a dog's fertility. With phimosis the sheath has a narrow opening that prevents the dog from extruding its penis, while in paraphimosis, the penis cannot be withdrawn into the sheath and is constricted. A monorchid dog has only one descended testicle, while a cryptorchid has neither testicle descended. Testicular tumors can produce female hormones, resulting in hair loss and enlarged mammary glands.	Stud dogs should be examined by a vet every three months. An enlarged prostate can be treated with hormones, while surgery may be necessary to correct physical defects. In the case of the latter, you can ease the dog's swelling and discomfort until it can be treated by a vet by placing ice packs on the penis and lubricating it with petroleum jelly. Undescended testicles should be removed, since they can lead to cancer. You should never breed from a monorchid dog, since the condition is inherited. Tumors may respond to hormonal treatment, although malignant ones must be surgically removed.
Discharge during pregnancy Miscarriage Pyometra Mucometra	Bloody discharges may mean miscarriage, caused by infection, injury, fetal abnormalities, poor nutrition, and perhaps stress. A discharge of pus may mean pyometra, infection of the womb. Sometimes excess mucus is discharged (mucometra), which is another sign of impending problems.	Contact a vet if there are any vaginal discharges during pregnancy. If the vet determines that the cervix is dilated, medication can be given to help clear up the infection and evacuate the aborted fetuses. If the cervix is closed, the bitch's life is in danger and the only safe option is an immediate hysterectomy.
Extended pregnancy False pregnancy Resorption	Sometimes a bitch may appear pregnant but not produce puppies. This can mean a false pregnancy, in which the dog shows all the symptoms of a real pregnancy (see page 146). Miscarriage without infection may lead to the fetuses being resorbed.	False pregnancies can be treated with drugs that stop the bitch coming into heat, or by spaying (see page 265). There is no treatment for resorption.
Painful or swollen teats Mastitis Mammary tumors Mammary cysts Extended false pregnancy (see above)	Infection can sometimes move up the teat canal, causing a hot, hard swelling of the mammary gland (mastitis). This is painful when touched, while mammary tumors are not. These are most likely to appear in old dogs and can be firm and mobile or soft and invasive. Mammary cysts feel hard, are fluid-filled, and occur most often in old females that have lactated.	Consult a vet, who can treat mastitis with antibiotics. Puppies should be prevented from suckling from the affected gland, and since antibiotic passes into the milk, it is often best that they are bottle-fed. Lumpectomies or a complete mastectomy are usually performed on mammary tumors. Cysts can be drained or left alone.
Panting or whining Eclampsia	If a female pants intensely after the birth, whines, appears unsettled, and has muscle twitches, she could be suffering from eclampsia, or a lack of calcium. This is most common in toy breeds and in bitches with large litters.	Consult a vet at once if eclampsia is suspected, since the bitch will die if not treated soon enough. Eclampsia may be prevented by proper nutrition during pregnancy, given under veterinary advice.
Cannibalism	Some breeds, especially bull terriers, lick their puppies obsessively and sometimes eat them.	Breeds that are prone to cannibalism must be watched 24 hours a day until the puppies' umbilical cords have dropped off.

URINARY DISORDERS

Changes in a dog's normal urinary function warrant immediate investigation by a vet. Straining to urinate can be caused by an infection, mineral sediment in the urine, or bladder stones lodged like plugs in the dog's urethra. In addition to being very painful, this can be life-threatening. Increased frequency of passing urine or increases in amounts passed can mean a urinary infection or a serious metabolic illness, such as diabetes. Incontinence is common in elderly dogs but can also occur for a variety of reasons in young ones. Contact a vet if you notice changes in the color or consistency of a dog's urine.

Excess drinking

This can be a sign of kidney or liver disease, or adrenal or pituitary gland malfunction.

THE URINARY SYSTEM

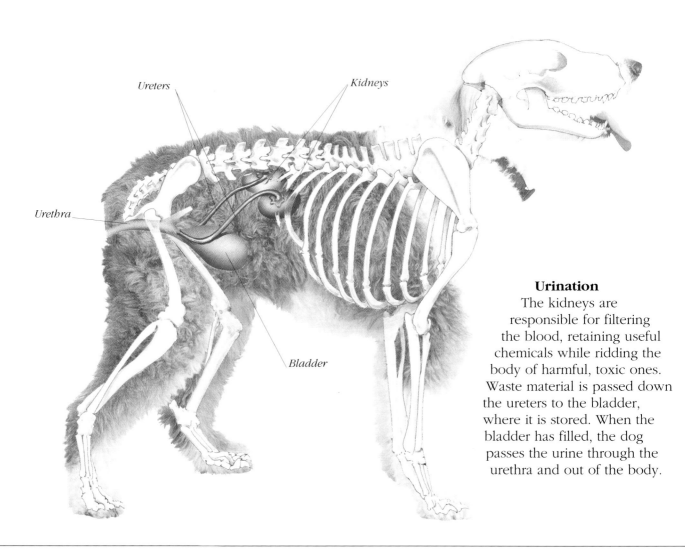

Ureters

Kidneys

Urethra

Bladder

Urination

The kidneys are responsible for filtering the blood, retaining useful chemicals while ridding the body of harmful, toxic ones. Waste material is passed down the ureters to the bladder, where it is stored. When the bladder has filled, the dog passes the urine through the urethra and out of the body.

URINARY DISORDERS

Signs and disorders	Description	Action
Straining to urinate Infections Prostatitis (p. 237) Bladder or urethra stones	Infections of the bladder and urethra cause inflammation and an increased need to urinate even when the bladder is empty. Male dogs can experience the same need when the prostate gland is enlarged or infected, or the penis inflamed. Urine is often clouded with pus and discolored by blood. Vaginal infections can cause females to strain in a similar fashion. Straining is more serious and more painful when caused by stones, which are formed by a build-up of minerals in the bladder. The male dog has a narrow urethra, and stones can sometimes become lodged in it causing nonproductive straining and pain.	Veterinary assistance is vital, since a dog can die in one or two days if it is unable to urinate. When possible, take a fresh urine sample from the dog to a vet. When an infection is the cause of straining, urinary acidifiers may be prescribed in addition to a course of antibiotics, since bacteria often thrive in an alkaline environment. If there is a severe blockage, a urinary catheter can be used to relieve pressure and pain. Bladder stones are commonly diagnosed with X-rays. Treatment usually involves significant diet changes.
Incontinence Hormonal imbalance Bladder displacement Injury to the spine Urinary tract infection Aging	Incontinent dogs are unaware that they are dribbling urine. It might occur when they are lying down, when they get excited, or simply when getting up and down. Incontinence should not be confused with urinating as a sign of submission. It occurs most frequently in females, especially in spayed Dobermans, Springer Spaniels, and Old English Sheepdogs, and is associated with a hormonal imbalance, or with an anatomical displacement of the bladder. Injuries to the spine affecting the nerve supply to the bladder, or damage to the sphincter muscles due to chronic urinary tract infection, also cause incontinence. With old age there can be a natural deterioration of bladder control.	Only some forms of incontinence can be controlled. A dog should be examined by a vet for any sign of physical injury or infection. Female hormones are often prescribed for incontinent spayed females, while male hormones are sometimes used for incontinent male dogs. Contrast X-rays of the bladder may also be taken. If these show that the bladder is sitting abnormally high on the pelvic bone, the condition can be corrected surgically by moving the bladder to a more normal position. A vet can treat infections with antibiotics, while anabolic hormones can improve sphincter muscle tone and control in aging dogs.
Increased urination Kidney or bladder infections Nephrosis Liver disease Diabetes Cushing's disease	Kidney and bladder infections cause dogs to urinate more frequently. Poor kidney filtration, common in old dogs (chronic nephrosis) and in young dogs of certain breeds (juvenile nephrosis), results in increased amounts of dilute urine being passed. Thirst is also increased. Certain liver diseases, as well as diabetes mellitus and diabetes insipidus, a condition in which the body cannot concentrate urine properly, all result in increased thirst and larger quantities of urine. There are similar signs when the adrenal gland produces too much cortisone (Cushing's disease) or when a dog is being treated with cortisone.	Take a sample of the urine to a vet, where it will be checked for sugar, liver waste products, protein, and concentration. Infections can be treated with antibiotics. If filtration has been impaired, resulting in nephrosis, treatment means dramatically reducing the kidneys' workload. This means eliminating most protein from the diet and supplanting it with carbohydrates, sugars, and fats. Diabetes mellitus can be treated with diet changes or insulin, while diabetes insipidus can be treated with hormone drops on the eye that improve the ability to concentrate urine. Blood samples help diagnose Cushing's disease, which can be treated with medication or by removing the overactive adrenal gland.
Decreased urination Dehydration Kidney failure	When a dog is ill and dehydrated for any reason, it conserves as much fluid as it can. Any urine passed is dark in color, often deep gold, and has an almost sticky consistency. There is no straining associated with urination. Quantities of urine voided also drop dramatically during the last stages of kidney failure, and this urine is much more watery. The dog's body has often lost all its fat deposits and most muscle. It is listless and lethargic.	Dehydration can be treated by giving lots of fluids. In the case of kidney failure, immediate veterinary attention is essential to get the kidneys working again. Large quantities of fluid can be administered intravenously. Because waste products build up, peritoneal dialysis is often used, in which quarts of fluids are washed through the abdominal cavity. When possible, kidney dialysis is used to cleanse the blood. These treatments should be employed only if the quality of life of the dog can be returned to an acceptable level.

NERVOUS DISORDERS

A dog's muscles, ligaments, and tendons all depend on the brain and network of nerves to achieve maximum performance. Damage to the nervous system can lead to a lack of sensation, changes in a dog's behavior, loss of balance, partial or complete paralysis, or seizures.

Viruses such as rabies and distemper cause inflammation of the brain and associated changes in temperament and coordination. Other bacterial and viral infections inflame the protective wrapping that envelops the brain, which can result in meningitis, seizures, and loss of balance. Physical injuries to the brain tissue can cause epilepsy, while damage to the spinal cord interferes with the transmission of nerve messages back to the brain. Depending on the part of the spinal cord that is injured, this can result in loss of sensation in the skin, paralysis of a limb, or incontinence. Nerve damage needs immediate attention from a vet.

Light reflexes
By checking light reflexes in the eyes, a vet can determine whether there is damage to the brain.

THE NERVOUS SYSTEM

Nerve network symmetry
Traveling inside the well-protected spinal column, the spinal cord descends from the brain, sending nerves out between each vertebra of the spine to all muscles and organs in the body. Once outside the spinal column, nerves are more susceptible to damage. Unlike muscles, a severed nerve never repairs itself properly.

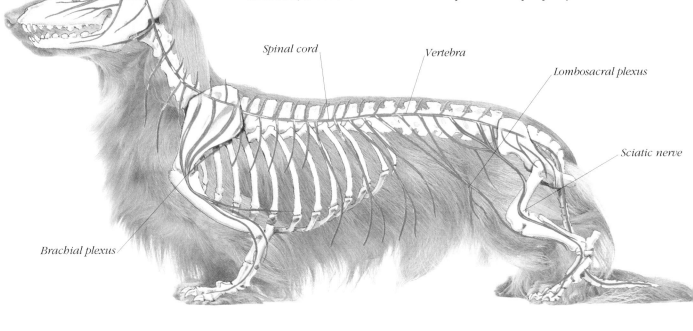

Brain

Spinal cord

Vertebra

Lombosacral plexus

Sciatic nerve

Brachial plexus

NERVOUS DISORDERS

Signs and disorders	Description	Action
Seizures Epilepsy Narcolepsy Hydrocephalus Encephalitis Distemper Trauma Poisoning (p. 285) Eclampsia Tumors	There are several different forms of epilepsy. Grand mal seizures cause loss of consciousness and twitching. Petit mal episodes can last only a few seconds, during which the dog seems to lose concentration. With narcolepsy the affected dog can temporarily fall asleep on its feet. Hydrocephalus causes seizures that can involve loss of consciousness, twitching, urinating, and defecating. Encephalitis is an inflammation of the brain due to infections such as distemper. Physical damage to the brain, either because of trauma, tumors, or poisoning, can cause seizures, as does the condition eclampsia, which is a drop in calcium levels *(see page 237).*	Protect the dog from injuring itself while it is convulsing *(see page 293).* Contact a vet immediately. Seizures are controlled with anti-convulsants. Bacterial encephalitis can be treated with antibiotics, while infections can be avoided with preventive vaccination. Pressure on the brain can be relieved with medication or surgery. Seizures caused by falling calcium levels can be reversed by intravenous calcium. Low blood sugar levels and accompanying seizures occur most frequently in small, lean, young puppies stressed by sudden journeys. They respond to intravenous glucose.
Loss of balance Stroke Inner ear infection Meningitis	After a stroke, a dog is unsure of itself and often avoids food or vomits if it eats. A stroke can affect any part of the body, causing paralysis or a head tilt. Inner ear infections cause a loss of balance and a head tilt on the affected side *(see page 227).* If this is left untreated, the infection moves deeper, causing meningitis and a general loss of balance.	Contact a vet, who can examine the dog's reflexes and its response to light. It is difficult to tell whether a stroke has been caused by a blood clot or a hemorrhage, so it will usually be treated conservatively with appropriate drugs. Ear infection and meningitis can be treated with antibiotics.
Paralysis Compressed spinal cord Wobbler syndrome Nerve injuries Ruptured disk Cancer of the spine Tetanus Scottie cramp Ascending neuropathy Tick poisoning (p. 223)	An instability of the vertebrae in large breeds, such as the Great Dane and Doberman, often results in compression of the spinal cord. This can lead to incoordination of the hind legs, also known as Wobbler syndrome. Mild spinal nerve injuries produce an increased sensitivity to pain. If nerves in the neck are involved there is a lot of pain when the head is moved. If any nerves farther down the spine are affected, perhaps because of a ruptured disk, the affected dog is reluctant to jump or to climb stairs. More severe damage causes a weakness or paralysis of the limbs, and there can be loss of bladder and bowel control, as well. Cancer of the spine can produce similar paralysis through pressure on the spinal cord. Tetanus is uncommon in dogs, but those affected become rigid and almost convulsive. Scottie cramp afflicts some Scottish Terriers and West Highland White Terriers at around six months of age, affecting the nerves to the muscles and causing a rigidity to the legs and back. Ascending neuropathy is often seen in mature German Shepherd Dogs. The hind legs gradually lose their precision until there is a complete loss of their use.	Prevent the dog from moving, then get immediate veterinary advice. Wobbler syndrome responds best to early surgical correction. Nerve injuries are often initially treated with absolute rest, muscle relaxants, and anti-inflammatories. Intravenous drugs are sometimes given to reduce swelling around the spinal cord. If nerve injury is caused by a ruptured disk, discuss preventive surgery with a vet. Some dogs, such as dachshunds, are especially vulnerable, and those that have suffered one ruptured disk are likely to suffer another. Removing the diseased disk eliminates further problems. Drug therapy relieves Scottie cramp. Ascending neuropathy is irreversible, and its cause unknown. Affected dogs sometimes need bandages on their hind feet to protect them from scraping injuries due to their paralysis.
Behavior changes Rabies Fly catching Avalanche of rage syndrome	Some behavioral changes are neurological and not within a dog's control. Rabies causes the most serious changes. A rabid dog usually becomes aggressive. Another form of the disease, dumb rabies, causes unusual friendliness. Fly catching, or snapping at non-existent flies, is a form of psychomotor epilepsy most common in Cavalier King Charles Spaniels. Avalanche of rage is suffered mainly by solid-colored Cocker Spaniels and Springer Spaniels. The dog's placid temperament suddenly changes to fierce and snarling, and then quickly reverts back to normal friendliness.	A medical examination can eliminate possible causes of behavior change. If rabies is suspected, the dog should be confined, away from humans and other animals, and a vet contacted immediately. Fly catching often responds to low doses of anticonvulsant medication. Avalanche of rage syndrome, however, is an inherited disorder. Although it sometimes responds to anticonvulsants, the best method of control is to avoid breeding from animals that perpetuate the disorder.

BLOOD AND HEART DISORDERS

There are very few inherent blood disorders in dogs. Although in some parts of the world blood parasites are common in dogs, changes in the numbers of red or white blood cells are usually signs of poisoning, liver disease, tumors, infections, bone marrow disease, poor nutrition, or allergies. Heart disease, on the other hand, is more common in dogs than in any other domestic species. However, congenital heart defects and heart attacks are rare. Only mature dogs of certain large breeds, especially the Doberman, are susceptible to sudden heart failure.

Progressive valvular heart disease mainly occurs in small dogs, especially those over the age of twelve. For example, in some countries, over half the Cavalier King Charles Spaniels have signs of heart disease by the time they are five years old. Heart disease can be detected during a routine examination.

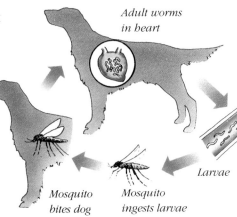

The heartworm life cycle
The microscopic larvae are transmitted via a mosquito bite and develop in the dog's heart.

Adult worms in heart

Mosquito bites dog

Mosquito ingests larvae

Larvae

THE CIRCULATORY SYSTEM

Circulation
The muscular bottom-left chamber of the heart pumps fresh blood through arteries (shown in red) around the body. Veins (shown in blue) bring used blood back to the top-right chamber, from where it flows to the bottom-right, and then to the lungs, where carbon dioxide is removed and oxygen added.

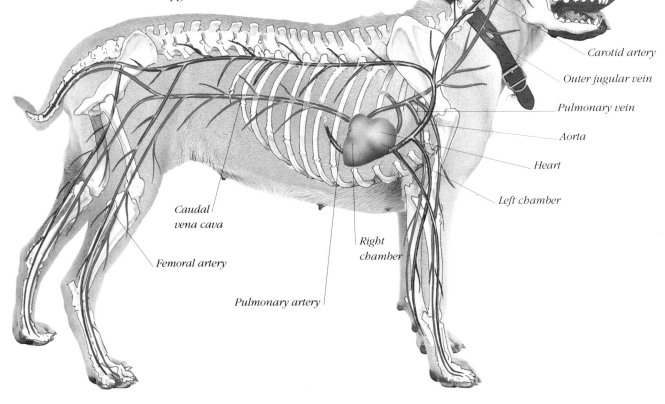

Carotid artery

Outer jugular vein

Pulmonary vein

Aorta

Heart

Left chamber

Caudal vena cava

Right chamber

Femoral artery

Pulmonary artery

BLOOD AND HEART DISORDERS

Signs and disorders	Description	Action
Sudden blood loss Trauma Warfarin poisoning Liver failure Hemophilia Bone marrow damage Autoimmune hemolytic anemia Tumors	Sudden internal or external blood loss causes lethargy, weakness, and sometimes collapse. The dog's breathing becomes labored, and its heart rate increases. The gums are pale. External bleeding, for example due to trauma from a traffic accident, is obvious, but internal bleeding is not readily apparent. Warfarin poisoning *(see page 285)*, liver failure, and hemophilia (including Von Willebrand's disease), all produce coagulation (clotting) disorders. Other bleeding disorders are caused by infections damaging the bone marrow and also occur when the body's natural defense system turns on itself (autoimmune hemolytic anemia). Certain vascular tumors can rupture in the liver or spleen of older dogs, especially retrievers and German Shepherd Dogs, causing a sudden loss of blood.	Control any obvious external bleeding *(see page 288)* and get immediate veterinary assistance. Severe blood loss causes the body to go rapidly into a state of shock. This can be treated with massive amounts of cortisone and fluid replacement. When trauma is not the cause of blood loss, a vet can carry out blood tests to determine whether there is a coagulation or bleeding disorder. Vitamin K is a specific antidote for Warfarin poisoning. Internal bleeding, whether from trauma or from a tumor, usually requires immediate surgical correction. Blood transfusions are best for all forms of blood loss except autoimmune hemolytic anemia.
Chronic blood loss or anemia Heartworms Tumors Infections Inflammation Stomach ulcers	Chronic anemias are slowly progressive. Affected dogs become lethargic, sleep more, and are reluctant to play. Their breathing is shallower than normal, and their heart rate faster. The gums are a dirty, pale pink. Heartworm infestation can cause a gradual weight loss, a persistent cough, and a pot-bellied appearance. Tumors, infections, inflammation, or stomach ulcers can all cause mild bleeding from the nose (epistaxis), or loss of blood in urine (hematuria) or in feces, which leads to excessive demands on the bone marrow and spleen to produce new red blood cells.	Consult a vet. In a heartworm area, a vet can test a blood sample from the dog for heartworm larvae. If it is negative, preventive medication can be given during the mosquito season. If positive, the vet can hospitalize the dog for medical or surgical treatment. When there is chronic blood loss from any body opening, a vet can take a blood sample to check the number and condition of the red blood cells in order to determine the type and severity of anemia. Treatment is directed at eliminating the cause of the anemia.
Lethargy and coughing in older dogs Endocardiosis Cardiomyopathy	Endocardiosis (valvular heart disease) is a common progressive disease in many older dogs. When the left-side valve does not close properly, blood backs up into the lungs, causing a cough, breathing difficulties, a weak pulse, and a murmur that a vet can hear through a stethoscope. If the right-side valve is affected, blood backs up in the liver. As the liver swells, clear fluid builds up in the abdominal cavity, causing a pot-bellied appearance. Sudden heart failure (cardiomyopathy) often involves the heart muscle and occurs most often in large breeds, especially the Doberman. The heartbeat becomes erratic and the pulse weak. An affected dog deteriorates within a few days, pants, and sometimes collapses or faints. The gums are pallid. When pressure is applied they blanch, and it takes a few seconds for blood to return.	Consult a vet if these signs appear. As valvular heart disease progresses, the lowest chambers of the heart enlarge to compensate for the inefficiency of the valves. Affected dogs should be fed salt-free diets, since salt retains unwanted fluid in the body. Drugs might be prescribed to eliminate excess fluid, to dilate peripheral blood vessels, or to improve the efficiency of the heart. Acute heart failure is much more difficult to treat. Electrocardiographs and echocardiography can be used to determine the extent of the damage. Lessen the demand on the dog's heart by reducing exercise and excess weight in accordance with veterinary advice. Cardiac pacemakers are sometimes implanted in large dogs suffering from failure of the heart muscle.
Listlessness in young dogs Congenital heart valve defects Congenital septal defects Patent ductus arteriosis	Inherited heart defects are uncommon in dogs. Affected animals want to play but have little energy to do so. They are often weak and their growth is stunted. In severe circumstances the gums are blue (cyanosis), and puppies suddenly collapse from heart failure. Deformed valves, a septal defect (hole in the heart), and patent ductal arteriosis (failure of a fetal blood vessel to close) all cause blood to leak into other organs, producing a murmur.	Consult a vet immediately if a puppy appears to be weaker or less active than normal. Audible heart murmurs in puppies almost always mean inherited defects, although severe anemia can also produce a murmur. X-rays and electrocardiographs can diagnose the exact nature of the condition. Some forms of congenital heart defect can be surgically corrected.

INHERITED DISORDERS

In the wild, where only the fittest survive, inherited disorders are self-limiting. However, because the dog has been domesticated for longer than any other species, and because so many breeds have depended upon humans for their survival for hundreds of generations, the dog suffers from more inherited disorders than any other animal apart from man. Any body system is prone to hereditary defects. Popular breeds, such as the German Shepherd Dog, seem to suffer from more defects than other breeds, but that is only because there are more of them to study. Similarly, eye and skeleton disorders seem to be particularly common, but this is simply because it was in these systems that the inherited aspect of canine disease was first investigated. As the dog is studied more intensely, the causes of such diseases will eventually be controlled.

Breed problems
The genetics of disease have been investigated most in the German Shepherd Dog.

GENETICS AND INHERITED DISEASE

Recessive genes
Healthy dogs can pass on serious diseases to their offspring if they carry a recessive gene. In this diagram, two dogs are mated, but one carries a recessive gene for blindness (r). Two of their puppies

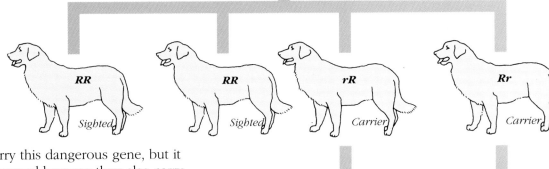

also carry this dangerous gene, but it is suppressed because they also carry the dominant normal gene (R). If these dogs are mated to each other and produce puppies, chances are that one puppy will have two normal genes (RR); two will have a dominant and a recessive gene (Rr and rR), and will be carriers; while the last one will have two recessive genes (rr), and will go blind.

INHERITED DISORDERS

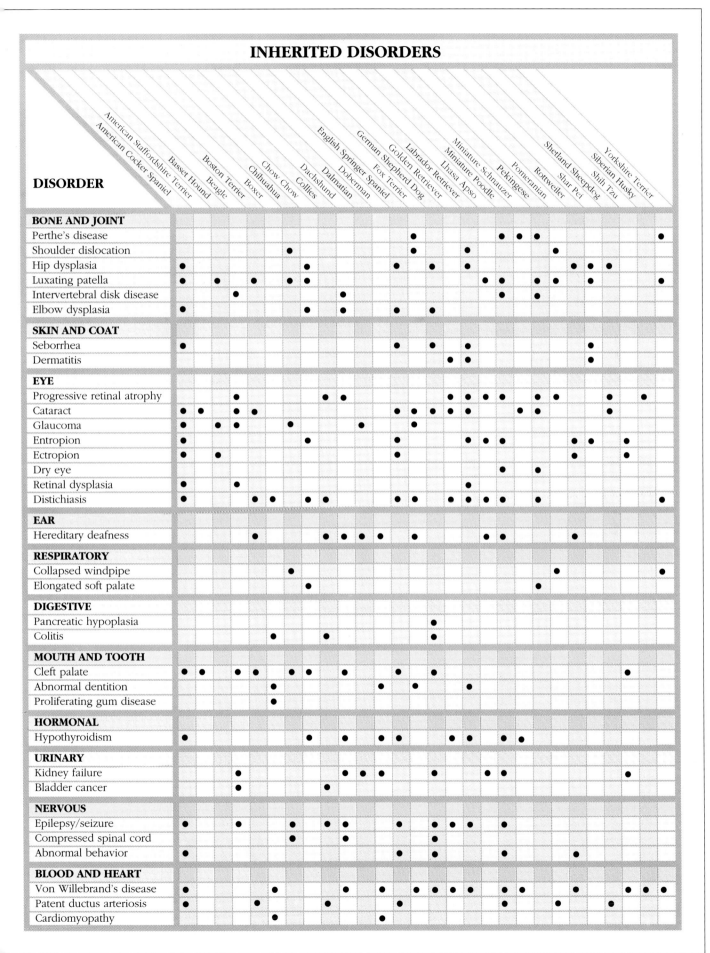

DISORDER	American Cocker Spaniel	American Staffordshire Terrier	Basset Hound	Beagle	Boston Terrier	Boxer	Chihuahua	Chow Chow	Collies	Dachshund	Dalmatian	Doberman	English Springer Spaniel	Fox Terrier	German Shepherd Dog	Golden Retriever	Labrador Retriever	Lhasa Apso	Miniature Poodle	Miniature Schnauzer	Pekingese	Pomeranian	Rottweiler	Shar Pei	Shetland Sheepdog	Shih Tzu	Siberian Husky	Yorkshire Terrier
BONE AND JOINT																												
Perthe's disease																•			•	•	•							•
Shoulder dislocation						•										•		•					•					
Hip dysplasia	•							•							•	•	•								•	•	•	
Luxating patella	•			•	•		•	•											•	•	•					•		•
Intervertebral disk disease				•						•											•	•						
Elbow dysplasia	•							•							•		•											
SKIN AND COAT																												
Seborrhea	•														•										•			
Dermatitis																	•	•							•			
EYE																												
Progressive retinal atrophy				•						•	•					•	•	•	•			•	•			•	•	
Cataract	•	•		•	•										•	•	•	•			•	•			•			
Glaucoma	•		•	•	•			•					•			•												
Entropion	•										•					•				•	•			•	•		•	
Ectropion	•		•													•								•				
Dry eye																				•		•						
Retinal dysplasia	•			•														•										
Distichiasis	•					•	•		•	•						•			•	•	•							•
EAR																												
Hereditary deafness				•					•		•	•	•			•				•	•				•			
RESPIRATORY																												
Collapsed windpipe						•																•						•
Elongated soft palate						•																	•					
DIGESTIVE																												
Pancreatic hypoplasia																•												
Colitis							•			•						•												
MOUTH AND TOOTH																												
Cleft palate	•	•		•	•		•	•			•					•										•		
Abnormal dentition						•								•		•			•									
Proliferating gum disease						•																						
HORMONAL																												
Hypothyroidism	•										•			•		•	•		•	•		•						
URINARY																												
Kidney failure				•											•	•	•				•		•	•			•	
Bladder cancer				•							•																	
NERVOUS																												
Epilepsy/seizure	•			•									•	•		•	•	•		•								
Compressed spinal cord						•								•							•							
Abnormal behavior	•															•	•						•		•			
BLOOD AND HEART																												
Von Willebrand's disease	•					•								•		•	•	•		•			•			•	•	•
Patent ductus arteriosis	•				•						•					•				•			•		•			
Cardiomyopathy						•										•												

DANGERS FROM DOGS

Infectious diseases rarely spread from one species to another. For example, humans cannot catch distemper from dogs, and dogs cannot catch measles from humans. There are a few diseases, however, that can be shared between mammals. Certain parasites can also be passed from dogs to humans, and dogs can be carriers of microorganisms that cause illness in humans and other animals. The most important threats to humans from dogs are injuries from bites, or serious allergy. The risk of being bitten is lessened if you understand canine behavior. Allergies can be helped by keeping your dog's coat and skin in pristine condition.

Rabies
Foxes and raccoons are common carriers of rabies, which is transmitted in saliva via bite wounds.

RABIES WORLDWIDE

Map of vectors
The map shows the main rabies vectors and the few areas of the world that are rabies-free.

Rabies transmission
The rabies virus exists almost everywhere in the world except certain islands and peninsulas. It can affect all mammals, but certain animals are more likely to be carriers than others. In parts of Asia and Africa, the dog is the usual carrier. You should never handle a stray dog in areas where rabies is endemic. If you are bitten and are not protected by vaccination against this potentially fatal disease, you should immediately see a doctor for injections of rabies antiserum.

KEY			
	Raccoon		Mongoose
	Skunk		Dog
	Bat		Cat
	Fox		Rabies-free

DANGERS FROM DOGS

Disorders	Description	Action
Zoonoses Rabies Toxicariasis Ringworm Mange mites Echinococcosis Flea- and tick-borne diseases Tuberculosis	Zoonoses are diseases that can be transmitted between vertebrate species, including man. Of the zoonoses transmitted by dogs, rabies is the most dangerous. The virus is spread in saliva and is usually transmitted through bites. An infected dog undergoes a personality change, often accompanied by profuse salivation. If infectious *Toxocara* roundworm larvae are swallowed by humans they can induce the allergic reaction known as visceral larval migrans, and can cause blindness. Ringworm infection causes circular skin lesions in humans, while *Sarcoptes* and *Cheyletiella* mange mites both produce itchy spots in human contacts (scabies and walking dandruff). Echinococcosis, or hydatid cyst disease, is contracted by humans eating uncooked meat from animals infected with the *Echinococcus* tapeworm. Fleas and ticks can transmit several infections to humans, including Lyme disease, which causes enlarged lymph glands and joint inflammation. Tuberculosis can also pass between dogs and humans, and causes coughing, shortness of breath, and bloody saliva.	All dogs should be vaccinated against rabies where that disease occurs. In countries where this disease is present, humans at risk from dog bites should also be vaccinated against rabies. Routine worming every three months reduces the likelihood of ground being contaminated with *Toxocara* larvae. Owners should clean up their dogs' droppings in all populated areas. Ringworm should be treated medically immediately. Mange mites, fleas, ticks, and tapeworms can all be controlled with the use of parasiticides available from your vet. Consult a vet if you suspect any diseases such as tuberculosis. The dog may be successfully treated with antibiotics, or the vet may recommend euthanasia.
Communicable diseases Campylobacteriosis Salmonellosis Giardiasis Brucellosis Leptospirosis Chlamydial diseases	With these diseases, a dog can be a carrier but may not show clinical signs of infection. *Campylobacter* and *Salmonella* bacteria cause abdominal cramps and diarrhea in dogs and humans. Both often contract the infections from the same source, such as contaminated milk. Neither campylobacteriosis or salmonellosis is common in dogs but victims vomit and often pass blood in diarrhea. *Giardia* can be picked up by dogs drinking contaminated water in streams and ponds, and causes the disease giardiasis, the principal sign of which is diarrhea. Brucellosis causes high fever, shivering, and weakness in humans. Leptospirosis is primarily a disease of rats but can be contracted by dogs from *Leptospira* bacteria and passed in urine. It causes diseases of the kidney and liver. In humans it is known as Weil's disease. *Chlamydia* seldom causes illness in dogs but is reponsible for several diseases in humans and other animals.	*Campylobacter* and *Salmonella* are passed in dog feces and spread through food. If human infection is suspected, a sample of dog feces should be taken to a vet for bacterial culture. If positive, the vet will treat the dog with appropriate antibiotics. Dogs and humans should avoid drinking water possibly contaminated by *Giardia*. Dogs should be routinely blood tested for brucellosis, which is most likely to occur in breeding kennels. This is a difficult disease to eliminate even with appropriate antibiotics. Leptospirosis can be prevented with vaccination. Chlamydial infections respond to antibiotic medication.
Infections from bites *Pasturella* infections Tetanus	*Pasturella* is a normal bacterial inhabitant of most dogs' mouths. When dogs or humans are bitten this bacteria produces purulent infections and abscesses. Although tetanus is rare in dogs, the microorganism that causes it can be passed on to humans through deep wounds.	Immediately clean any bite wound. People at risk from dog bites should have preventative vaccinations against tetanus. If these have not been given, seek medical advice about tetanus antiserum.
Allergies	Just as humans are sometimes allergic to their pets, dogs can be allergic to people, cats, and other animals. They get itchy skin and watery eyes, and sneeze frequently. Humans suffer the same allergic symptoms as dogs, although bronchospasm also affects severely allergic people. This can be caused by an allergy to dog hair but is most frequently a reaction to the proteins in dried dog saliva. In addition, dogs can carry pollen and mold spores in their fur that cause some humans to react allergically.	Keep your dog's coat as healthy as possible. There is less likelihood of allergic reactions to clean, fresh hair and healthy skin. Routinely check for parasites, and do all grooming outdoors so that the home environment is contaminated with as little hair and dandruff as possible.

Chapter 7

HEALTH CARE AND NURSING

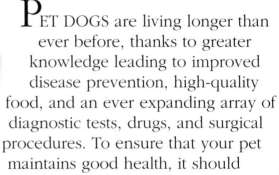

PET DOGS are living longer than ever before, thanks to greater knowledge leading to improved disease prevention, high-quality food, and an ever expanding array of diagnostic tests, drugs, and surgical procedures. To ensure that your pet maintains good health, it should have a yearly medical examination, although older dogs need more frequent and detailed exams, which can include urine and blood tests. In most cases, nothing adverse will be discovered, but if there are any problems, follow the veterinarian's instructions, which may include giving your dog medicine at home, and providing thoughtful, efficient nursing for its full recovery.

VISITING THE VET

EXAMINING A DOG

Since your dog cannot tell you when it is ill, it is up to you to notice any changes in behavior or demeanor that might indicate that it is unwell. The information you give the vet will help him decide where to concentrate his examination of the dog.

In most instances, the vet will first carry out a complete physical examination, while asking you questions about your dog. Whenever possible, you should keep a record of exactly when you first became concerned about your dog. Remember: your dog is totally dependent upon you for its medical care.

Prevention is not only better than cure – it is also less expensive. Consider obtaining health insurance, and take your dog to the vet for a medical checkup once a year.

Eyes
Although there are many inherited and acquired eye diseases, changes in the eyes are often indicators of more complex diseases elsewhere in the body. The eye examination gives the vet clues about where else to concentrate his attention.

Nose
Dogs usually have wet, cold noses. The vet will look for discharges and physical changes, but will not be overly concerned if the dog has a hot, dry nose, although this may indicate fever.

Vet examines dog's nose for discharges or swellings

Ears
The ears are examined for any discharges or unusual odors. A heavily furred, lopped ear, like this Cocker Spaniel's, can act like a valve on the ear canal, raising the humidity within and creating an ideal environment for infection, but any ear is susceptible to infection. The vet will check for tufts of hair and foreign bodies, and also check the color inside the ears.

Teeth and gums are checked for inflammation, decay, and internal disorders

Mouth

The mouth is checked for gum inflammation and tooth decay. At the same time, the vet might press a finger against the gums as a blood pressure test. Pale gums suggest anemia, whereas a tinge of yellow means the dog may have a liver problem.

Skin and coat

A dull coat can result from poor nutrition or indicate a skin problem like parasites or infection. It may also signal disease somewhere in the body.

Nails *(below)*

The vet will examine the nails and nail bed for damage whenever the dog shows signs of excess licking or lameness. Uneven wear can mean that the dog has been favoring one leg. Flaky nails indicate a metabolic disorder.

Coat and skin are examined for parasites and skin disorders

Anal region *(below)*

Examining the dog's rear gives clues about bowel upsets and tapeworm infestation. The anal glands are also checked.

Genitals *(above)*

A bitch's vulva is checked for discharge or inflammation that could mean a disorder of the urinary or reproductive systems. A dog's testicles and penis are similarly examined for swellings, inflammation, or abnormal discharge.

THE VETERINARY EXAMINATION

Having completed the initial stages of a routine physical examination of your dog, the vet will investigate the state of the dog's health in more detail. He will check the dog's temperature and pulse, and listen to its heart and lungs. Lymph nodes in the neck and elsewhere are felt, and the abdomen is pressed to reveal any internal abnormalities. In addition, the joints are flexed for signs of discomfort or resistance.

Once this examination has been completed, the vet may want to carry out further tests. Most frequently, this simply involves taking a sample of the dog's blood, from which a tremendous amount of information can be obtained. It might also mean taking X-rays, scanning the body with ultrasound, or analyzing other body fluids.

CHECKING BODY FUNCTIONS

Taking the temperature
An elevated temperature is often a sign of infection, pain, or stress, or just excitement. A temperature below normal usually indicates a debilitating disease or disorder.

Thermometer is placed in the dog's rectum

Taking the pulse
The vet checks a dog's heart rate, rhythm, and blood pressure by feeling the pulsations in the hind-leg femoral artery. Blood pressure is calculated by feeling just how much pressure is needed to obliterate the pulsations. Blood pressure changes occur due to shock or heart disease.

Feeling the glands
Lymph nodes are part of the body's natural defense system. When local lymph nodes or glands are swollen, this often means that there is infection in the part of the body that they serve. It can also indicate that the defense system itself has become infected.

RELAXING A DOG

A tense dog is difficult to examine. Train your dog at home to sit on command, and to allow itself to have its mouth opened, its ears, eyes, and feet checked, and to be gently prodded and squeezed. The vet will then be able to get the maximum amount of information from a physical examination of the dog.

Listening to chest sounds *(left)*
The vet listens to the dog's breathing and heart sounds, first with, and then without, a stethoscope. Well-developed heart murmurs can be felt through the chest wall, while difficulties in breathing are observed by simply watching the movements of the chest in breathing.

Palpating the abdomen *(right)*
After looking at the shape of the dog's abdomen, the vet will feel it for any abnormal fluids or lumps, then feel deeper to check the size and shape of the liver, kidneys, spleen, bladder, and intestines.

Flexing the joints *(above)*
Individual joints are flexed to check for discomfort. Dogs often tense up during a veterinary examination. This can make it difficult to diagnose mild joint problems.

RESTRAINING AND MUZZLING

1 Most dogs can be held by their owners or a nurse while being examined by a vet. However, if a dog is frightened or in pain, it is safest for the handler and the vet if the patient is muzzled.

2 To make an improvised muzzle, make a wide loop in a bandage or soft rope and slip it over the dog's nose with the knot on top. Take care the dog does not bite.

3 Make another loop in the muzzle and tie it securely, but not too tightly, under the dog's lower jaw. Wrap the ends around the dog's neck and tie them together securely.

ADMINISTERING MEDICINE

There is a wide range of medicines available to treat a variety of canine medical conditions. Drugs are available to cure infections like pneumonia, to correct metabolic disorders such as hormonal excesses or deficiencies, or to control certain types of cancer. Some medical conditions like diabetes are controlled through daily injections.

Unfortunately, very few canine medicines are available as tasty, chewable tablets. Some pills even have an unpleasant taste. Dogs can be deviously clever at hiding pills in their mouths, only to spit them out when their owners are not looking. Never call your dog to you just to give it medicine, or it might become fearful each time it hears its name. It is much better for you to go to the dog.

GIVING A PILL

1 Command the dog to sit. With one hand, open its mouth, and with the other hand, drop the pill as far back as possible, over the hump of the tongue.

2 Hold the dog's mouth closed and its head up slightly. Stroke its throat with your other hand. When it swallows and licks its lips, this means that the pill has gone down. Always praise the dog when it has swallowed the pill.

GIVING AN INJECTION

1 Injections should only be given at home after discussing the procedure with a vet. Prepare the syringe and command the dog to sit. Lift the fold of skin at the scruff of its neck.

Slowly empty syringe into scruff

2 Insert the needle sideways through the skin of the dog' scruff. This avoids underlying muscle. Be careful that the needle does not come out the other side of the scruff. Slowly empty the syringe into the skin.

GIVING A PILL TO A DIFFICULT DOG

1 Hold the dog firmly between your legs, with your knees behind its shoulders, so that it cannot escape. Open its mouth by holding its snout with one hand and its lower jaw with the other. Be careful it does not bite.

2 Having dropped the pill as far back on the tongue as possible, close the dog's jaws and massage its throat while still holding the chin up. Praise the dog after it has swallowed the pill.

Hold dog firmly between your knees so you have both hands free

MEDICINE IN FOOD

Hiding a pill

Simply dropping medicine into the dog's food bowl does not guarantee that it will be swallowed. It is better to hide a pill in a small piece of a dog's favorite food. Most dogs willingly take their medicine hidden in chunks of meat. Others will accept pills sandwiched in bread. You might even try mixing medicine in peanut butter, or your dog's favorite treat. Always check with your vet first, however, since some foods should not be given with certain types of medicine.

Pill is hidden in piece of cheese

LIQUID MEDICINE

If a dog refuses to swallow pills, they can be crushed, mixed in sugar water, and syringed sideways into the mouth. Cough syrup can also be given to a dog in a syringe.

TREATING EYES AND EARS

Infections, injuries, and allergic reactions involving a dog's eyes and ears are surprisingly common and are usually treated with drops and ointments. It is always safest to consult a vet for advice before attempting to treat any condition yourself.

Never use old medicines to treat new disorders. Although the new problem may look the same as the old, the wrong treatment may make it worse. For example, anti-inflammatory drops are perfectly safe when there is conjunctivitis, but if the condition is associated with invisible damage to the cornea, these drops will make that damage worse. Even if the condition completely disappears in a short time, do not shorten a prescribed treatment without consulting a vet first for advice. Ear infections have a nasty habit of recurring at a later date.

ADMINISTERING EARDROPS

1 A dog's ears frequently need veterinary attention. Dogs that suffer from chronic ear problems should have their ears routinely cleaned with wax-dissolving drops. Preventive treatment reduces the likelihood of infection and the need for veterinary attention. First, lift the flap of the ear and clean away any visible wax with a cotton ball dampened with warm water or a wax-removal solution provided by a vet.

2 While holding the head still, and with the ear flap laid back, insert the nozzle of the bottle in the ear in a forward direction toward the tip of the nose. Squeeze the appropriate number of drops into the ear.

3 Without letting the dog shake its head, withdraw the bottle, drop the ear flap back into position, and, with the palm of your hand, gently but firmly massage the ear. This lubricates the entire ear canal with medication.

CLEANING THE EARS

When using cotton swabs, you should only clean the outer part of the ear that you can see. Do not use swabs in the ear canal itself, since they can act like plungers, forcing wax farther down. A foreign body, such as a grass seed, can become lodged in the ear. This should only be removed if it is visible *(see page 283)*. Consult a vet if you suspect that anything is lodged inside the ear canal.

APPLYING EYEDROPS

1 Several common eye disorders can stimulate excess tear production, or a discharge from the eyes *(see page 224)*. If left unchecked, these discharges can stain the dog's facial hair. Before applying any medicine, with moistened cotton gently soften, then wipe away any debris from the corners of the eyes.

Gently clean away any eye discharge

2 Using either a commercial eyewash solution or one provided by a vet, irrigate the eye. Do not use eyedrops intended for humans. Be careful not to get any cotton fibers on the eye itself.

Allow the eye to bathe in the drops for a few seconds

3 Gently restrain the dog and hold the eye open. Bringing your hand to the eye from above and behind so as not to frighten the dog, gently squeeze the required number of drops onto the eye. Allow the eye to bathe in the medication.

APPLYING EYE OINTMENT

1 You may have to administer eye ointment for certain conditions. This should be applied in a line along the inside of the lower eyelid. Do not let the applicator touch the dog's eye.

2 Hold the dog's eye closed for a few seconds so that the ointment warms to the dog's body temperature and disperses over the eye. The eye will initially look greasy but will soon clear.

EMPTYING ANAL SACS

If a dog licks or drags its rear along the ground, this may mean that its anal sacs need emptying. Wearing a rubber glove and holding a tissue, place your thumb and forefinger on either side of the anus and squeeze gently. Ask a vet for guidance.

NURSING A SICK DOG

Only seriously ill dogs require hospitalization. In most circumstances, dogs get better faster when they are cared for by people they know in their own home.

You should provide your convalescent dog with a warm, dry, comfortable bed, and make sure it has free access to its toilet area. This might mean carrying the dog there several times each day.

Follow the vet's advice by giving medicine at appointed times, and offer fresh water and nutritious food. The vet will tell you which foods you can offer and how much water to provide each day. Herbal medicines may be beneficial, but should not replace life-saving drugs.

THE CONVALESCENT DOG

Intensive care
A dog must sometimes be hospitalized for a few days while its condition is stabilized. Visits from its human family should be discussed with the vet.

RECOVERY PEN

When a sick dog has to be kept quiet, with its movements curtailed, it can be kept at home in a recovery pen. For small dogs, a large cardboard box is usually sufficient. Larger dogs can be kept in a child's playpen or a special dog crate. Provide warm bedding, food and water bowls, and newspapers in case of any accidents.

Keeping warm (left)
Body temperature can drop when a dog is sick. With a vet's advice, provide your dog with comfortable bedding and a lukewarm, insulated hot-water bottle for warmth.

Administering fluid (right)
A convalescing dog must consume enough fluid each day to equal the amount it loses in its urine and feces and by panting. The vet will tell you how much liquid is required daily. If a dog is unwilling to drink, try spooning or syringing nourishing liquids into the side of its mouth.

Tempting a sick dog to eat *(left)*

With veterinary guidance, be creative with the foods you offer your dog. Its appetite will be stimulated by smell. Warming food to between room and body temperature releases the odor and gets a dog's taste buds activated. Avoid foods that might cause diarrhea, but cater to a dog's preferences.

HOME NURSING

A dog will not always understand why you are doing seemingly aggressive and unpleasant things to it, but you must follow the vet's instructions. Nursing a dog back to good health should be done as gently as possible, but this invariably involves "being cruel to be kind." If you do not feel that you can carry out the vet's instructions and nurse your pet at home, it is in your dog's interests that it be hospitalized for the duration of its recovery.

Bed sores *(right)*

Pressure can produce bed sores in heavy dogs. Dress affected areas, such as the elbows, daily with softening skin cream.

Elizabethan collar

If your dog has been fitted with an Elizabethan collar to prevent self-mutilation and removal of its bandages or stitches, it must wear the collar in your absence. A collar can be made from cardboard or a plastic bucket.

ALTERNATIVE MEDICINE

Evening Primrose oil

Garlic pills

Herbal nerve pills

Seaweed powder

Many herbal and natural forms of medicine are known to be therapeutic. Some are sources for refined prescription drugs, so always check with a vet before using these medicines with other medication.

CARING FOR AN ELDERLY DOG

Superficial aging changes, such as graying hair or tooth loss, occur much earlier in some dogs than in others. As a dog gets older, messages travel more slowly through the nervous system, and hearing and vision deteriorate. Joint discomfort may develop, the skin loses its elasticity, and muscles shrink. The signs of old age vary according to each individual and may not be noticeable at first.

You can make an elderly dog's life more pleasant through special feeding, gentle grooming, and vigilant attention to its comfort and general well-being. Remember to be gentle with it and be patient with its behavior.

SIGNS OF OLD AGE

The old dog
An elderly dog likes to take life easy, but still enjoys playing. You should not force an elderly dog to do things, but should respond sympathetically to its behavior.

Coat becomes thinner and drier

Muscles shrink and body becomes weaker

Hearing deteriorates, resulting in deafness in some dogs

Lenses in the eyes become a cloudy blue-gray

Hair turns gray on muzzle and around ears

Joint fluid dries up, causing inflammation and discomfort

LIFESPANS OF COMMON BREEDS IN YEARS

Breed of dog	10	11	12	13	14	15	16	17
Cavalier King Charles Spaniel, Great Dane, Newfoundland								
Afghan Hound, Boxer, Chow Chow, St. Bernard								
Bloodhound, Bernese Mountain Dog, Labrador Retriever, Pointers, Rottweiler, Old English Sheepdog								
Airedale Terrier, Basset Hound, Dalmatian, German Shepherd Dog, Scottish Terrier, Staffordshire Bull Terrier								
Beagle, Chihuahua, Doberman, Papillon, Pomeranian								
Collies, Jack Russell Terrier, Pekingese, West Highland White Terrier, Yorkshire Terrier								
Boston Terrier, Golden Retriever, Setters								
Cairn Terrier, Cocker Spaniel, Maltese Terrier, Poodle (Standard), Schnauzers, Shih Tzu								
Dachshunds, Poodle (Miniature and Toy)								

SPECIAL CARE FOR AN OLDER DOG

Brushing teeth *(right)*
Gum infection allows bacteria to get into the bloodstream. Reduce this risk by routinely brushing your elderly dog's teeth *(see page 185)*.

Feeding *(above)*
Changes in the amount of exercise taken, the ability of the intestines to digest and absorb nutrients, and of the kidneys and liver to filter and detoxify waste products from the bloodstream all call for diet changes. Consult a vet for advice.

Eye care *(left)*
You should regularly clear away excess mucus with damp cotton and clean the skin around your elderly dog's eyes.

Ear care *(below)*
Wax can rapidly build up and cause infection. Regularly check inside the ears.

Grooming *(left)*
Elderly dogs groom themselves less than young dogs do because their bodies are not as supple. Gently groom your dog with a soft brush. Remember that its skin is thinner and more sensitive than when it was younger, so be gentle.

Gently massage stiff joints after sleep

Massaging joints
Joint discomfort is very common, especially among large breeds. If your dog is not getting routine exercise, you can gently massage its muscles and joints by flexing its limbs when it is relaxing.

EUTHANASIA

Improved medical attention means that many dogs live to reach their maximum age, but then their quality of life gradually drops below a comfortable level. Deciding when this has happened is difficult, but your vet will be able to offer advice. Euthanasia is painless. It is simply an injection of an overdose of anesthetic. However, choosing euthanasia is perhaps the most difficult decision involving your dog your family will ever make.

Chapter 8

BREEDING

WITH A worldwide surplus of unwanted dogs, it is irresponsible to breed from a dog without first arranging for good homes for the litter. It is cruel to allow a bitch to go through the rigors of whelping only to have the puppies destroyed. You should also not allow your dog to breed if it has an hereditary disorder. If you do decide to breed from your dog, it can be delightful to watch how magnificently most females cope with whelping and with caring for their puppies. The experience can be made much easier for them if you provide the best possible diet and environment, as well as proper health care and nursing assistance.

DECIDING TO BREED

Thousands of unwanted dogs are humanely destroyed each year, so it is important that you consider having your dog neutered or spayed to avoid unwanted pregnancies. Only breed from a dog if you can provide good homes for the puppies and if neither the male nor the female are carriers of serious hereditary defects. Dogs usually reach sexual maturity by the age of about ten months but do not reach emotional maturity for another year. Allow a bitch to have at least three estrus cycles before mating.

Choosing a mate

If you decide to breed from your pedigree bitch, it is best to arrange for her to be mated with an experienced stud dog at its owner's premises.

THE BITCH'S REPRODUCTIVE CYCLE

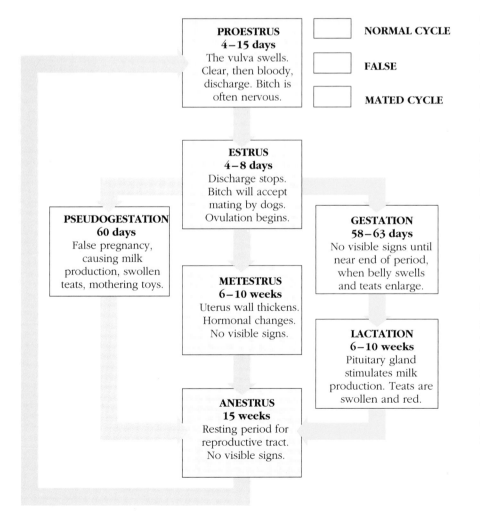

PROESTRUS
4 – 15 days
The vulva swells. Clear, then bloody, discharge. Bitch is often nervous.

NORMAL CYCLE

FALSE

MATED CYCLE

ESTRUS
4 – 8 days
Discharge stops. Bitch will accept mating by dogs. Ovulation begins.

PSEUDOGESTATION
60 days
False pregnancy, causing milk production, swollen teats, mothering toys.

GESTATION
58 – 63 days
No visible signs until near end of period, when belly swells and teats enlarge.

METESTRUS
6 – 10 weeks
Uterus wall thickens. Hormonal changes. No visible signs.

LACTATION
6 – 10 weeks
Pituitary gland stimulates milk production. Teats are swollen and red.

ANESTRUS
15 weeks
Resting period for reproductive tract. No visible signs.

The normal cycle

Most breeds have two estrus cycles each year. Initially, the vulva appears swollen, and within a day there is a clear discharge, which becomes tinged with blood the next day. This discharge increases in intensity and then slowly diminishes, ending after about ten days.

During this time the bitch becomes more alert and urinates frequently, leaving signals of her impending willingness to mate. Ovulation takes place soon after the discharge has stopped. Only now will the bitch accept mating. Hormonal changes occur regardless of whether a bitch is pregnant, which is why there are no simple blood or urine tests to confirm impending motherhood.

CHECKLIST FOR MATING

Mating guidelines

1 Have the bitch examined by a vet and certified as healthy and not carrying inherited diseases.
2 Plan how you will find homes for the coming litter of puppies.
3 Check that a purebred dog is registered with the kennel club.
4 Arrange with a reputable breeder to use his stud dog.
5 If brucellosis is a problem in your area, make sure that the stud dog is routinely checked for sexually transmitted disease.
6 Exercise your bitch only on a leash while she is in season.
7 Take the bitch to the stud dog, rather than vice versa.
8 Make arrangements for two matings, two days apart.
9 If necessary, calm the bitch during mating and ensure a "tie" that lasts ten minutes.
10 Take the bitch to a vet three weeks after mating to confirm the pregnancy.

The tie
Dogs may need to be held together while they are "tied" by the swelling of the male's penis to ensure that they do not hurt each other.

TAIL DOCKING AND EAR CROPPING

A dog's ears and tail are not only for hearing and balance, they are also vital for effective body language. In the past, ears were cropped to make the dog look more fierce. The tails of working dogs were often amputated to reduce injuries, while others were docked according to the breed standard. Such mutilations are now banned in many countries. Inhumane amputations like these are cosmetic fashions, surviving from an age when humans had less understanding of animal pain.

NEUTERING PROCEDURES

Neutering
Advances in veterinary technique make it possible to neuter puppies as young as three months. Under a general anesthetic, a small incision is made in the scrotum through which both the testicles are removed. The dog appears normal the next day, and the stitches come out ten days later. Neutering may help to curb undesirable types of behavior such as straying from home and hypersexuality.

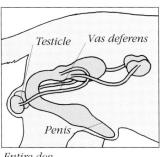
Entire dog

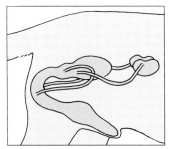
Neutered dog

Spaying
This operation is best carried out before puberty but when the bitch is physically mature. Both the ovaries and uterus are removed under anesthetic through an incision in the abdomen. Removal eliminates the likelihood of later development of mammary tumors, and ensures that the bitch's personality is unchanged. Surgery may, however, make dominant bitches even more dominant.

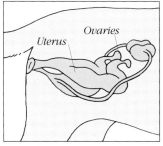
Entire bitc

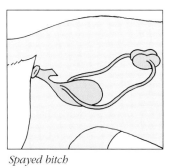
Spayed bitch

PREGNANCY AND PRENATAL CARE

There are always hormonal changes in a bitch after each biannual ovulation that cause identical signs to those that occur during pregnancy *(see page 264)*. This makes it difficult to determine whether a dog is really pregnant until she shows physical changes, such as an enlarged abdomen. When you see these changes, usually about two-thirds of the way through her nine-week pregnancy, it is time to reduce her activities and increase her food.

SIGNS OF PREGNANCY

Nipples become prominent

Mammary glands are enlarged

Conserving strength
For a few days before giving birth, the bitch spends a lot of time relaxing. You should not force her to exercise now.

CARING FOR A PREGNANT BITCH

Feeding (left)
Midway through pregnancy, gradually increase the amount of the bitch's food by 10 percent at first, increasing to 30 percent extra by the time of the birth. Be sure to provide a nutritious diet with a proper balance of calcium and phosphorus for good bone development.

Grooming (above)
Groom the bitch regularly during pregnancy. This serves to reassure her of your involvement and makes it less likely that she will resent your help when the puppies are born. Take great care not to scratch her delicate abdominal area.

Cleaning up (right)
Just before the bitch is due to go into labor, gently clip any excess or matted hair from around her vulva and mammary glands. Clean her teats with a gentle, safe disinfectant, making sure that you leave none on her skin.

DEVELOPMENT OF THE FETUS

Length of pregnancy
Pregnancy usually lasts about 62 days. A vet can diagnose pregnancy by feeling the bitch's abdomen or using ultrasound.

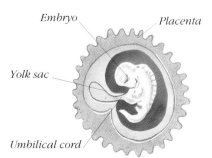

Embryo *Placenta*

Yolk sac

Umbilical cord

3 By the middle of pregnancy all internal organs have developed.

4 The skeleton has developed by six weeks.

2 By three weeks, nourishment comes from the placenta. The eyes, head, and limbs are now developing.

1 During the first weeks, the embyro obtains its nourishment from the yolk sac.

Most puppies will emerge headfirst in a diving position

5 The fetuses develop in rows in the uterus. At birth a puppy and its associated placenta are usually delivered within 15 minutes of each other. Make sure that the same number of placentas is passed as puppies produced. Prolonged pregnancies often mean large puppies and more difficult births.

WHELPING PREPARATIONS

The whelping box
Familiarize the bitch with her whelping box at least a week before she is due to give birth. Position it in a quiet and secluded place where she feels secure. The box offers security for the newborn puppies by preventing them from wandering off. Poles prevent the mother from accidentally lying on the puppies. Keep equipment, such as disinfectant, towels, and scissors, within reach, and make sure a vet is on call.

WHELPING

GIVING BIRTH

The expectant mother goes off her food between one and two days before birth. She becomes restless and seeks out her whelping box. Shortly before labor her water bag breaks, leaving a puddle of fluid that can be mistaken for urine. Initially, the contractions are simple but they soon become firm and productive. The first puppy should be delivered within two hours, then subsequent ones at intervals of between ten and eighty minutes.

1 The bitch starts to pant when the first contractions begin. Her temperature drops and she appears restless and a little tense. Watch her to make sure that she does not hide herself away.

2 The bitch stands and circles while she contracts. Other dogs prefer to lie down for the delivery. Let the dog find her own preferred position for giving birth.

3 Although this is her first litter, the mother instinctively examines her newborn puppy. She has already licked the enveloping membrane off its body. Now she chews off the umbilical cord separating the puppy from the placenta, which she later consumes.

Licking removes all delivery liquids

4 The newborn puppy is licked vigorously by its mother. This dries and warms the puppy, clears away any mucus from its mouth and nose, and stimulates it to breathe.

5 After the work and discomfort of delivery the mother rests. This gives time for her muscles to become resilient again, ready for further contractions.

Newborn puppy rests near the warmth of its mother

WHEN TO CALL A VET

You should let the vet know when a delivery is under way in case of any emergencies *(see page 294)*. Get medical advice if contractions have not begun within two hours of the water breaking, or if a puppy has not emerged after 15 minutes. Nonproductive labor may mean a breech birth or large puppies. Cesarean delivery is common for breeds of dog with large heads and in small breeds with small litters of puppies.

6 Now more relaxed, this mother lies down and prepares to deliver more puppies. Most mothers do not start feeding their litter until after the last delivery. Make sure that there is one placenta delivered for each puppy.

7 Hearing a puppy cry, the mother retrieves it from where it has wandered and carries it back to the litter. Mothers will only respond to crying. If a youngster wanders off and does not cry, the mother may abandon it.

Puppy is held firmly but gently in mouth

Newborn puppy has been completely cleaned and dried

8 All the puppies have now been delivered. The mother settles down and allows the litter to suckle together for the first time. Contact a vet if the mother cannot produce sufficient milk.

9 As the bitch feeds her litter, she licks one of her puppies. She will lick each puppy's anogenital region to stimulate it to empty its bowels and bladder, and will consume all the puppies' body wastes for the next three weeks. In the wild, eliminating all signs of the litter would protect the puppies from predators.

POSTNATAL CARE

For the first three weeks of life the newborn puppies are totally dependent upon their mother for food and security. You can help by ensuring that they are kept warm and that their mother is well nourished, healthy, and producing sufficient milk. Sometimes, with very large litters, a mother's milk must be supplemented with special canine milk formula.

MATERNAL CARE

The new pack
In the absence of their mother the puppies huddle together for warmth. Pack behavior has begun even at this age.

Puppies huddle together for warmth and security

Bonding with mother
Because it is enjoyable for her, the mother sits contentedly while her litter suckles. The puppies bond to her, and at the same time her maternal feelings for them become firmly cemented. In the next few weeks she will feed, protect, and, if necessary, defend them.

REARING PUPPIES BY HAND

Bottle feeding *(above)*

Feed milk formula initially every two hours if the mother has died, rejected her litter, or does not have enough milk. Ask a vet for guidance on the exact amounts to feed.

Stimulating body functions *(above)*

After feeding, wipe away any spilled milk, and clean each puppy's anogenital region with damp cotton. This mimics maternal licking, stimulating it to urinate and defecate.

Puppy is yawning

Cleaning up

Handle all the puppies frequently, but take care not to upset their mother. Each puppy's eyes, ears, and mouth should be cleaned daily with cotton moistened in warm water.

Nail trimming

A puppy's nails may have to be trimmed to prevent them from scratching the mother *(see page 185).*

Monitoring weight gain

Keep track of the puppies' weight gain by carefully weighing each member of the litter daily. Weak puppies and those that are not sufficiently pushy get relegated to less productive teats. Lack of weight gain means you might have to help them gain access to the most productive teats.

EARLY PUPPY CARE

FOUR WEEKS OF AGE

Just as with humans, the environment in which a puppy is raised influences its behavior in adult life. This early socialization period is very short, lasting for only a few months. During this time, puppies learn how to behave with other dogs and humans.

Lessons should start as soon as puppies are old enough to try to wander away from the mother dog. They should be routinely handled, groomed regularly, and exposed to the sights and sounds that will be part of their adult lives.

Puppies should eat and play with other puppies, so that they understand the nuances of pack hierarchy and body language. By providing a puppy with this early socialization, you will make it an ideal companion for life.

Socialization *(left)*
At four weeks of age the senses are developed. Puppies should receive mental stimulation and learn how to behave with other dogs through regular play activity. They may be kept in a pen so that they can become adjusted to their surroundings without being frightened.

Eating together *(right)*
Feed puppies together rather than separately. This will teach them not to be possessive over their food.

Early grooming *(left)*
A longhaired puppy, such as this Cocker Spaniel, needs daily grooming. This helps to keep the puppy's coat clean and satisfies its need for mothering.

Daily handling *(left)*
Handle a puppy several times daily from four weeks of age. Early socialization and handling will lead to good habits in later life. Talk to your dog frequently when you handle it so it will associate your voice with this pleasant activity.

EIGHT WEEKS OF AGE

Puppy's coat has darkened

Family mealtime (below)
Be sure to provide growing puppies with frequent, nutritious meals, necessary for both growth and the maintenance of their bodies *(see below)*.

Willing obedience (above)
At eight weeks old the puppy is used to being handled and stands quietly alert when held. The puppy's coat has now changed to its adult color pattern.

Brush and comb (left)
When acquiring a new puppy, start routine grooming immediately. Grooming and stroking are dominant gestures. The puppy will interpret this as a sign of dominance and will grow up to be an obedient dog.

Leaving home (left)
At eight weeks old the puppy is ready to leave its mother and move to its new home. It must be vaccinated against infectious diseases such as parvovirus and distemper. Early mental and physical stimulation help it to become a confident young dog, able to cope with its exciting new world.

WEANING PUPPIES

Age	Type of food	Comments
Birth	Mother's milk and water.	Puppies are dependent on mother's milk.
Three weeks	Mother's milk and water. Feed mother dry puppy food so puppies get used to the taste in her milk.	Dry puppy food and water should be left out at all times.
Five weeks	Mother's milk and water; moistened puppy food; dry puppy food.	Give moistened puppy food 3–4 times daily. Remove uneaten food after one half-hour. Keep dry food and water always available.
Six weeks	Mother's milk and water. Mother's milk will start to dry up. Dry puppy food; moistened puppy food.	Give moistened puppy food 3–4 times daily. Remove uneaten food after one half-hour. Keep dry food and water always available.
Seven weeks	Increase the amounts of dry puppy food. Water should be available at all times.	Give moistened puppy food 3–4 times daily. Remove uneaten food after one half-hour. Keep dry food and water always available.
Eight weeks	Increase the amounts of dry puppy food. Water should be available at all times.	Keep dry food available for small to medium dogs, with controlled portions for large dogs.

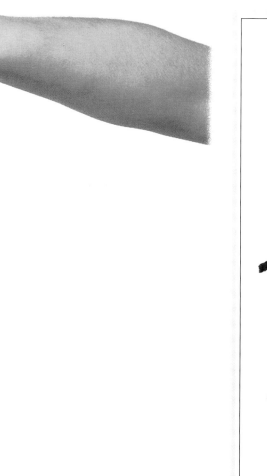

Chapter 9

FIRST AID

Even though serious accidents and emergencies do occasionally happen, you can reduce a dog's immediate pain and distress – or even save its life – with prompt action. Trauma from accidents, falls, or dogfights; chemical injuries from poisons; bites or stings; lacerations, fractures, choking, heatstroke, and hypothermia; and whelping disorders all require urgent veterinary attention. But by rendering immediate first aid, you can prevent further body damage, restore vital functions, reduce discomfort, and stabilize a dog's condition until professional veterinary assistance is available. Even if you never have to use these skills, it is best to be prepared in case of an emergency.

PRINCIPLES OF FIRST AID

Serious injuries always call for urgent, professional veterinary attention, but before an injured dog can be moved, the degree of injury should be assessed and life-supporting first aid administered. First aid involves removing a dog from the source of harm, preventing its condition from worsening, restoring vital bodily functions, alleviating pain and distress, and helping recovery to begin.

Overenthusiastic first aid can do more harm than good. First determine the seriousness of the dog's condition, provide essential treatment, and then get immediate veterinary help.

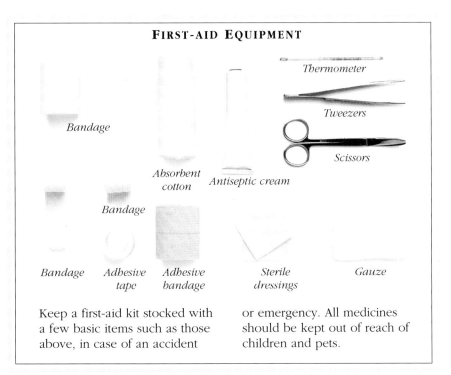

FIRST-AID EQUIPMENT

Bandage

Absorbent cotton

Antiseptic cream

Thermometer

Tweezers

Scissors

Bandage

Bandage *Adhesive tape* *Adhesive bandage* *Sterile dressings* *Gauze*

Keep a first-aid kit stocked with a few basic items such as those above, in case of an accident or emergency. All medicines should be kept out of reach of children and pets.

ASSESSING AN INJURED DOG

Clear the airway (right)
If the dog is unconscious, straighten its neck, open its mouth and remove any debris, and gently pull the tongue forward. This is most important in breeds with flat faces, in which the tongue can obstruct the dog's breathing.

Keep tongue from blocking the throat

Check breathing (above)
Watch the dog's chest movements to see if it is breathing. Normally, there will be 20–30 breaths per minute. This rate often increases after an accident. A short intake of air followed by forced breathing out may mean that the dog has an injured diaphragm.

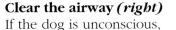

Feeling the heartbeat

Feeling the pulse

Check circulation
Feel the dog's pulse on the inside of the hind leg. The heartbeat is felt by pressing a hand firmly on the chest behind the elbow. Large dogs have heart rates between 50 and 90 beats per second, while small dogs have rates of up to 150 beats.

CHECKING REFLEXES

Touch eyelid to make dog blink

Light reflex (below)
Shine a light into the dog's eye. The pupil will constrict. If it does not, this may mean the heart has failed. If the pupil is already constricted, this may indicate brain damage.

Light makes pupil constrict

Corneal reflex (above)
To test the corneal reflex, gently touch the junction of the eyelids by the nose. If the dog is conscious it will automatically blink.

FIRST-AID WARNING

An injured dog may suddenly regain consciousness and become hysterical because of pain or shock. Take care that it does not injure itself further by trying to get up, and also be very careful that it does not bite you. If the dog is in shock, keep it quiet and warm.

Pedal reflex (left)
Pinch a toe or the web of skin between the toes. If there is no response, this can mean the dog is deeply unconscious, or that its heart has stopped. If it is only lightly unconscious, it will retract its foot.

COLLAPSE AND SHOCK

Recognizing shock (below)
Shock occurs when the body's circulation fails. The dog becomes weak, its breathing and pulse are rapid, it is cold to the touch, and its gums are pale. Make sure its airway is clear.

Treating shock (right)
Unless shock is the result of heatstroke, wrap the dog loosely in a blanket to keep it warm. Make sure it can breathe easily, and get medical advice at once.

Blanket retains dog's body heat

TRAFFIC ACCIDENTS

Prevention is always better than cure. Many traffic accidents could be prevented by proper obedience training. Make sure that your dog is well trained and always under the control of a responsible person when walking outside, especially near a busy road.

If an accident occurs, do not panic; use common sense. If a dog has been injured in a traffic accident or has fallen and is still at risk from further injury, carefully remove it from the source of danger.

A badly injured dog might bite if it is shocked or in pain, so before assessing the dog's injuries, muzzle it with a scarf, rope, or tie. Examine the dog for signs of injury and get immediate medical attention.

PREVENTING ACCIDENTS

Walking to heel
Even dogs that are superbly trained may rush across a road without looking if they see something interesting on the other side. Your dog should therefore always wear a leash when walking near traffic. In rural areas, keep it on its leash when walking it in risky terrain or around other animals.

MOVING AN INJURED DOG

1 Whether a dog is conscious or unconscious, it must be moved if it is at risk. First check for obvious injuries such as bleeding or distorted limbs. Have someone watch for oncoming traffic while you administer first aid to stabilize the dog's condition.

Start cardiac massage if the heart has stopped (see page 281)

Perform artificial respiration if the dog is not breathing (see page 280)

Do not handle a fractured limb (see page 219)

Control severe bleeding by bandaging wounds (see page 288)

EMERGENCY ACTION
If an injured dog is unconscious but breathing normally, press a finger on the gums to see if blood instantly returns when you remove your finger. If it does not, this may be due to severe hemorrhaging. Stop the flow of blood from external lacerations by holding an absorbent pad or bandage to the wound with firm pressure.

2 If another person is available to help, support the dog's body and lift it onto a blanket or coat. If you are by yourself, place the blanket along the dog's back, firmly grasp the skin over the neck and hips, and drag the dog onto the blanket. Then pull the blanket and dog out of harm's way. Avoid touching any obvious injuries.

Lift injured dog in a blanket and get it to a vet as quickly as possible

3 A dog involved in a traffic accident may have internal injuries that require immediate veterinary attention. Do not move the dog more than necessary. Using the blanket as a stretcher, carry the dog to a vehicle and get it to a vet as quickly as possible. Make sure that its neck is extended so that breathing is not obstructed.

4 If the dog is obviously in shock or in pain, make an improvised muzzle before attempting to move it. Wrap a rope or scarf around the dog's nose, knot it once under the jaws and then again behind the neck.

FIRST-AID WARNING

Some dogs have stoic personalities and may conceal their injuries. However, they are just as much at risk from complications such as postaccident concussion as more sensitive dogs. Internal bleeding may produce no visible sign until the dog goes into shock. All dogs should be examined by a vet after an accident, and be kept under observation for 24 hours.

Examine the eyes for signs of shock

5 Even if a dog appears to be normal, it may have damage to internal organs. With the dog removed from further risk, examine it thoroughly. Any dog that has been involved in a road accident should also be taken for a veterinary examination as soon as possible.

6 Gently feel each limb for broken or dislocated bones. If the dog has a suspected fracture, the limb should be moved as little as possible. A dog with spinal injuries should be lifted on a flat board.

RESUSCITATION

ARTIFICIAL RESPIRATION

Prompt cardiac massage and artificial respiration may occasionally be necessary to save a dog's life. A dog's breathing and heartbeat can fail following a traffic accident, electric shock, poisoning, drowning, or shock. If a dog's heart has failed, or if it has stopped breathing, get someone to telephone a vet for advice while you attempt to resuscitate the dog. It is crucial to get oxygen-rich blood to the brain as soon as possible to prevent brain damage. If the dog is to survive, its heart must be restarted within minutes.

1 If you cannot see the dog breathing, press your ear firmly on the chest to listen for a heartbeat. If the dog's heart is still beating, start to give mouth-to-nose resuscitation *(see below)*. If you cannot hear the heart, start cardiac massage at once *(see opposite)*.

Listen for a heartbeat

Clear any saliva or debris from the mouth

2 With the dog lying on its side, make sure the neck is stretched forward. Remove any obstructions from the mouth and pull the tongue forward. If there is damage to the nose, an unconscious dog will breathe through the mouth, and the tongue may obstruct its breathing.

3 Keeping the dog's neck as straight as possible, cup the nose with your hands and breathe into the nostrils for about three seconds to inflate the lungs. The chest should expand. Pause for two seconds, then repeat.

4 Make sure that the heart is still beating by feeling behind the dog's elbow with your hand or by placing your ear on the dog's chest. As long as the heart is beating, continue mouth-to-nose resuscitation until the dog breathes on its own. If the dog's heart should stop, you must start cardiac massage immediately *(see opposite)*.

Keep checking for a heartbeat

5 The procedure for cardiac massage is as follows. Place the heel of your hand just behind the elbow on the left side of the chest. Place your other hand on top, then firmly press both hands down and forward toward the brain. This squeezes blood out of the heart to the brain. Repeat six times at one-second intervals.

6 After six cardiac massages, give one breath of mouth-to-nose resuscitation. Continue alternating until the heart beats, then start resuscitation.

DROWNING

1 Because dogs enjoy swimming, they may sometimes enter pools of water from which they cannot get out. When weakened, they swallow water and sometimes debris, too. Drain water from the mouth and clear the airway before starting artificial respiration.

2 Hold a small dog just above the hocks on the hind legs to allow as much water as possible to drain from the lungs. The unconscious dog can be shaken moderately, but not vigorously. If it is still not breathing, lay it on its side and give artificial respiration *(see opposite)*.

EMERGENCY ACTION

You must get the heart started before attempting mouth-to-nose resuscitation. Do not worry about bruising a rib or applying too much pressure when giving cardiac massage. This is a life-or-death situation. Large dogs in particular need very forceful external pressure to squeeze blood out of the heart. Cardiac massage should be kept up for at least ten minutes. Do not give up trying to resuscitate a dog while there is still a faint heartbeat. Artificial respiration can keep an injured dog alive long enough for veterinary help to be obtained.

3 Lay a large dog on its side with its head at the lowest possible position. Lift the hind legs as high as possible to help drain water from the lungs. Allow 30 seconds for drainage, then start mouth-to-nose resuscitation until the dog starts to gasp.

SAFETY ADVICE

Garden ponds and swimming pools should be covered or fenced off to prevent accidents. Take special care when walking your dog near water. You should prevent your dog from entering a turbulent sea, swiftly flowing rivers, or water with strong undercurrents.

CHOKING AND FOREIGN BODIES

With its inquisitive nature, scavenging habits, and enjoyment in chewing, every dog, at one time or another, is likely to get something stuck in its mouth, or to have a foreign object embedded in its skin. Choking on bone splinters or twigs often occurs. A dog should be trained not to chew dangerous objects.

Small balls and toys can also be swallowed and become stuck in a dog's throat. These should be dislodged using the Heimlich maneuver *(see page 305)* as soon as possible to allow the dog to breathe. You should not allow a dog to play with balls that are small enough to be swallowed.

Thorns, glass, needles, and plant seeds can all become embedded in a dog's skin. You should examine your dog's coat and skin for foreign bodies after each walk.

CHOKING

1 Twigs and bone splinters often become lodged between the large upper teeth, or in the back of the throat. To remove them, get a helper to restrain the dog firmly, and open its mouth wide.

2 Holding the mouth open, carefully remove the object with round-ended tweezers or a pair of pliers. Do not risk putting your fingers in the dog's mouth. You are likely to get bitten.

FISHHOOK IN THE MOUTH

1 Fishhooks sometimes get caught in a dog's lips. If the hook has gone right through the skin, restrain the dog and use wire cutters to cut off the barbed end of the hook. Never pull on a fishing line protruding from a dog's mouth if you cannot see the hook. Take the dog to a vet for an X-ray.

2 Gently ease out the straight part of the hook and clean the wound with a mild antiseptic. If the hook is embedded in the skin, take the dog to a vet.

FOREIGN BODY IN THE EAR

1 During dry weather, check a dog's body and ears for plant seeds after each walk. Visible seeds can be removed with tweezers. If the dog shakes its head, this may mean the seed is lodged deeper in the ear canal.

2 Deep seeds should always be removed by a vet. To soothe the dog temporarily, fill the affected ear with olive or mineral oil. Sometimes this will float the seed up so that it can be easily removed.

FOREIGN BODY IN THE EYE

Floating out objects

If a dog is pawing at its eye or rubbing its head on the ground, hold open the eyelid and look for grit or grass seeds. Try floating out loose debris with eyedrops or olive oil. Do not attempt to remove foreign objects that have penetrated the eyeball, but seek veterinary assistance without delay.

FOREIGN BODIES

Foreign bodies such as grass seeds often enter the ears, nose, eyes, vulva, or skin, and especially the area between the toes. The dog then shakes its head, sneezes, paws at the wound, or licks it vigorously. The body tries to eliminate the object by creating a local bursting abscess, but objects such as grass seeds can migrate throughout the body.

FOREIGN BODY IN THE PAW

Removing an object

Thorns, needles, and shards of glass can penetrate a dog's paw pads, while grass seeds can enter the webs of skin between the toes. If the dog is limping, examine the paw and remove any visible object with tweezers.

Bathe minor wounds with salt water

Bathing the paw

If the object is not visible, bathe the foot several times daily in tepid salt water (a teaspoon to a cup) until the object comes to the surface of the skin and can be easily removed.

POISONING

Poisons can enter the body through the skin, by being inhaled, or by being eaten. Because of their inquisitive natures, dogs are poisoned most commonly by ingestion. Do not leave toxic substances in places where a dog can find them. Avoid keeping poisonous plants in your yard *(see page 165)*, especially if you have a young puppy. Do not allow a dog to touch the carcasses of animals such as rodents and birds that may have been poisoned.

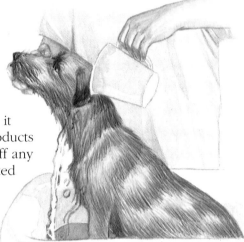

COAT CONTAMINATION

Removing paint
Never use solvent, paint stripper, concentrated detergent, or fabric softener on a dog's coat. These substances are all highly toxic if ingested. To remove paint or tar, soften it with petroleum jelly or products safe for human skin. Cut off any heavily contaminated, matted fur. Then wash the area with canine or baby shampoo, and rinse it thoroughly.

FIRST-AID WARNING

Only induce vomiting if the poison has been swallowed within the last hour, and if the dog is conscious and alert and you are certain that it has not consumed a caustic or irritating substance. Administer hydrogen peroxide or a concentrated solution of tepid salt water (one teaspoon to a cup). Get immediate veterinary attention, and take a sample of the vomit with you for analysis.

ACCIDENTAL POISONING

1 Puppies, playful adults, and bored dogs are most at risk from accidental poisoning. Common household substances such as aspirin might taste unpleasant but are still eaten by some dogs. Keep all potentially toxic substances out of reach of your dog. Signs of poisoning include severe vomiting, diarrhea, collapse, seizures, and coma.

Dog may chew at plastic container holding pills

2 If the poison has already taken effect and the dog has collapsed, take it immediately to a vet, along with a sample of the substance it has eaten. Treatment will be most effective if the vet can quickly identify the type of poison ingested and administer the appropriate antidote.

3 If you catch the dog eating something potentially toxic, restrain it and examine the package carefully for instructions. Contact a vet or your local poison control center for advice.

Restrain the dog and stop it from eating toxic substance

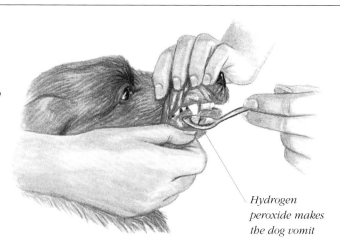

Hydrogen peroxide makes the dog vomit

4 While a helper restrains the dog, administer an emetic, if this is appropriate *(see below)*. Hydrogen peroxide is usually effective, given in small amounts by tablespoon until the dog vomits.

COMMON HOUSEHOLD POISONS

Poison	Source	Signs	Action
Alkaline household cleaners (solvent, paint stripper)	Dog walks in spilled fluid, or owner uses it to clean paint from fur.	Inflamed skin, vomiting, diarrhea, possible convulsions, ulcers on the tongue.	Do not induce vomiting. Thoroughly wash the coat and skin with soap and water. Contact a vet immediately.
Chlorinated hydrocarbon insecticide	Concentrated insecticide rinses, and flea collars.	Agitation, restlessness, twitching, salivation, convulsions, coma. Potentially fatal.	If poisoning is through skin contact, wash the coat thoroughly with soap and water. Take the dog to a vet immediately.
Organophosphate insecticide	Insecticidal sprays, shampoos, and flea collars.	Muscle tremors, drooling, breathing difficulties, frequent urinating and defecating.	Thoroughly wash the coat with soap and water. Take the dog to a vet immediately.
Warfarin rodenticide	Dog eats poison itself or poisoned rodent.	Bleeding gums and bruising to the skin. Can be fatal, especially in smaller dogs.	If recently ingested, induce vomiting with hydrogen peroxide. Get veterinary treatment at once.
Strychnine rodenticide	Rodent bait, sometimes used in malicious poisoning.	Initial stiffness, progressing to convulsions. Can be fatal within an hour.	Induce vomiting and get the dog to a vet as quickly as possible.
Slug and snail bait (metaldehyde)	Dogs like the taste of it and sometimes deliberately eat it.	Tremors, salivation, convulsions, coma. Can be fatal.	If recently ingested, induce vomiting with hydrogen peroxide. Contact a vet immediately.
Antifreeze	Sometimes leaks from car radiators. Dogs like the taste of it.	Wobbling, convulsions, vomiting, collapse, coma. Can be fatal.	If recently ingested, induce vomiting with hydrogen peroxide. Get veterinary attention immediately.
Aspirin	Wrongly given by owners to alleviate pain.	Appetite loss, depression, vomiting with or without blood.	Contact a vet for advice.
Lead	Chewing old paint, lead fishing weights, old pipes, or batteries.	Vomiting, diarrhea, and abdominal pain, followed by staggering and paralysis.	Induce vomiting if lead has just been eaten. Contact a vet, who will take blood tests and start immediate treatment.
Illegal drugs	Either discovered by or given to the dog.	Incoordination, agitation, fear biting, dilated pupils.	Get veterinary treatment immediately. Veterinary sedatives relax the dog.
Sedatives and antidepressants	Either discovered by or given to the dog.	Depression, staggering, coma.	Induce vomiting with hydrogen peroxide Contact a vet at once.

BITES AND STINGS

Dog bites most frequently occur around the neck, face, ears, and chest. Skin punctures from canine teeth look simple and clean, but there is often considerable soft-tissue damage under the skin. Bites, stings, and injuries from insects and venomous animals are often difficult to find and require symptomatic treatment. Contact a vet if a dog shows any agitation.

DOG BITES

1 Be careful not to get injured when trying to separate two dogs or stop a dogfight. Cold water from a hose or bucket may be effective in separating them. Allow a dog time to calm down before examining it. Check to see whether the skin is lacerated or punctured. If the skin is punctured, clip hair away from the wound.

Cut away fur surrounding the wound

2 Remove all clipped hair, then carefully bathe the region with warm water and a gentle disinfectant. Apply petroleum jelly around the site of the wound to prevent hair from getting inside and causing irritation.

3 If the skin is punctured, take the dog to a vet for antibiotic treatment. If it is lacerated, apply antiseptic cream to the area. Expect bruising to occur. A deep, penetrating wound may need stitching.

INSECT STINGS

Wasp stings
Wasp and hornet stings cause pain and swelling. Some dogs are allergic to stings and can react badly. Immediate veterinary care is essential if there is acute swelling to the mouth or throat.

The mouth and face are usual sites of wasp stings

Bee stings
Bees leave an embedded stinger in the skin. With a magnifying glass, remove the stinger with tweezers. An icepack may reduce the swelling.

Try to draw out the stinger with tweezers

SNAKEBITES

Treating a snakebite
If you know where a dog has been bitten, try to keep it calm and apply an icepack to the wound to slow down the flow of blood. If the dog's limb is affected, do not apply a tourniquet. Instead, apply ice, and wrap the leg tightly in a bandage. Contact a vet at once. He may be able to give it antivenin.

EMERGENCY ACTION

Snakebites are rarely observed as they occur. Suspect a poisonous snakebite if the dog is trembling, excited, drooling, vomiting, has dilated pupils, or has collapsed. There will also be considerable swelling. Venomous snakes may leave two puncture marks at the site of the bite, most often on the head or legs. Do not cut into the wound and attempt to suck out the venom. This only increases the blood flow to the region and speeds the spread of poison. Carry the dog to a vet.

TOAD AND CATERPILLAR POISONING

Poisonous toads and caterpillars
Some species of toads secrete a toxic substance on their skin. This passes into the mouth of any dog that picks up the toad to play with it. Certain types of longhaired caterpillar can also produce similar irritants.

Treating poisoning
Itchiness, redness, and swelling can be reduced by bathing the mouth with cold water. A water spray is ideal for flushing out the mouth but do not let the dog swallow any water. Contact a vet if the dog is in discomfort; it may need antihistamines to reduce swelling.

BITES AND STINGS

Poisonous spiders rarely bite dogs because their mouthparts cannot penetrate the coat. However, dogs can be bitten or stung by other animals. Puppies are very susceptible to bites and stings, especially between the toes. Apply a cold compress and take the dog to a vet. If a dog is in pain after swimming in the sea, it may have been stung by a jellyfish or anemone. Apply ammonia diluted one to ten with water and consult a vet.

PORCUPINES AND SKUNKS

Meeting other animals
Curiosity often gets the better of dogs. Porcupine quills are quite painful when caught in a dog's flesh. They can be removed with pliers, but they are best removed by a vet, with the dog sedated or anesthetized. Skunk odor can be eliminated using special products or by dousing the dog with tomato juice or mouthwash and then bathing it thoroughly with canine shampoo.

BANDAGING WOUNDS

Traffic accidents, dogfights, and unexpected traumatic injuries are the most common causes of bleeding wounds. If a dog is bleeding, remove it from risk of further injury, and clean and bandage the wound to prevent any additional damage until you can get the dog to a vet. Bandaging will prevent further blood loss and shock. Spurting blood denotes a severed artery. Apply firm, constant pressure until you reach a vet. Slower bleeding means that veins and smaller vessels are damaged. Firm pressure with an absorbent gauze pad and bandaging will stop minor bleeding.

STOPPING BLEEDING

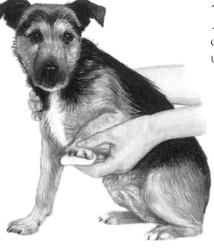

1 While someone contacts a vet, apply a gauze pad soaked in cold water to the wound. Do not use absorbent cotton because it will adhere, leaving fibers in the wound.

2 If bleeding does not stop, or to prevent it from starting again, cover the area with a nonsticking absorbent pad and secure it with a bandage.

BANDAGING AN EAR WOUND

Clean wound and apply absorbent pad

Wrap bandage around ear and head

Head bandage keeps ear from further damage

1 Ears are most frequently torn in dogfights, and bleed profusely. First calm the dog, then clean the wound. Apply an absorbent pad to the wound.

2 Wrap the ear in a bandage, winding the bandage around the head to keep it secure and prevent the ear from bleeding when the dog shakes its head.

3 Continue bandaging the ear to the head until it is held securely. Avoid putting pressure on the windpipe. If necessary, use an Elizabethan collar.

BANDAGING A TAIL WOUND

1 Dogs' tails are most frequently damaged by being caught in closing doors. They bleed profusely, especially if the tail is wagged a lot. Disinfect the wound and apply a nonsticking absorbent pad to it.

Wrap the tail in the bandage

3 Vigorous tail wagging may remove lightly applied bandaging. It also prolongs bleeding. If the dog's tail is long enough, bandage the tail to the body, but not too tightly.

Bandage tail to body to prevent wagging

2 Starting at the tip, bandage up the tail toward the body. Cover the absorbent pad, making sure that you catch all hair in the bandage.

BANDAGING A TORSO WOUND

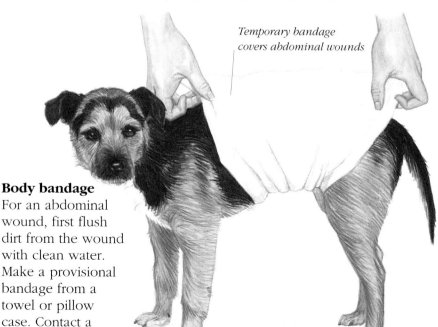

Temporary bandage covers abdominal wounds

Body bandage
For an abdominal wound, first flush dirt from the wound with clean water. Make a provisional bandage from a towel or pillow case. Contact a vet at once.

FIRST-AID WARNING

External bleeding is obvious, but internal bleeding can be more dangerous because it cannot be seen. If a dog has had a·serious fall, has been in a traffic accident, has had other traumatic injuries, or suddenly becomes pale and lethargic, suspect internal bleeding, even if there are no outward signs of damage. The spleen and liver are particularly prone to crush injuries. Keep the dog quiet if you suspect internal bleeding and get veterinary attention at once. Internal bleeding often requires immediate surgery. Blood can be replaced by transfusion from a donor, or by replacement fluids.

TEMPERATURE-RELATED INJURIES

HEATSTROKE

Dog breeds that evolved in the north of Eurasia and North America, and those with double coats of downy underhair and long outer hair, are well-equipped for the freezing weather of extreme northern or southern regions. However, they do not cope very well with heat.

Dogs cannot lose heat by sweating, since they have no sweat glands. All they can do is pant. Heatstroke is one of the commonest causes of avoidable death in dogs. Remember, in the presence of heat and without ventilation, a dog's temperature rapidly rises to 110°F (43.3°C). If left in that condition, it will die. A hot car is a deathtrap for dogs. Single-coated breeds are more prone to frostbite and hypothermia than breeds with thicker coats.

Heatstroke prevention
Do not leave a dog in a car in warm, sunny weather. Even parking in the shade and leaving a window partly open is not safe. Never leave a dog alone in a car with the heater on in cold weather. In both circumstances, a dog overheats and is unable to cool itself down.

1 The first sign of heatstroke is rapid, heavy panting, often with salivation. After a few minutes the dog becomes weak and collapses, still panting.

Panting and salivation indicate dog is overheated

2 Remove the dog from the hot environment as quickly as possible. Clear the mouth of saliva to ease breathing, and sponge its face with cool water. Contact a vet at once.

3 If possible, immerse the dog's body in cool water. Do not use ice-cold water. Alternatively, wrap it in towels soaked in cold water. Pour cold water over the towels to prevent them from getting warm. Let the dog drink if it wishes.

HYPOTHERMIA

1 Hypothermia is most likely to occur in dogs that have been in freezing water even for a few minutes, especially those without thick fur. Dry the dog by rubbing it vigorously with a towel.

Dry the dog if it has been swimming in cold water

2 Wrap a warm blanket around the dog and take its rectal temperature *(see page 252).* If this is below 98.5°F (37°C), get immediate veterinary assistance. Keep the dog warm but avoid overheating.

FROSTBITE

1 Frostbite is most likely to occur to the extremities after exposure to below-freezing temperatures, especially when it is windy. Examine the feet, ears, and tail, which may appear pale or be cold and insensitive. Massage them gently with a towel.

Immerse paws in a bowl of tepid water

Rub feet with a dry towel to warm them

2 Warm the frozen parts with tepid water heated to 90°F (32.2°C). Thawing should occur within ten minutes, and the skin may appear reddened. Keep the dog warm until veterinary assistance is available.

OTHER EMERGENCIES

You should always be prepared for potential canine emergencies, such as burns, seizures, and gastric torsion. A dog's coat insulates and protects the skin, but hot water or oil, and irritating chemicals can seep through the hair, causing skin damage. Chewing on an electrical cord can burn a dog's mouth or cause unconsciousness and cardiac arrest. When suffering a seizure, a dog will convulse and may pass out *(see page 241)*. Another emergency occurs when a dog's stomach twists on itself (gastric torsion), causing bloat. This condition is fatal without immediate veterinary attention.

CHEMICAL BURNS

Treating burns
Wash off any caustic chemicals from the coat with warm, soapy water. Contact a vet for advice. Never apply anything to a dog's coat that you would not use on your own skin.

Wash the coat to prevent the dog from ingesting chemicals

ELECTRICAL BURNS

Chewing an electrical cord is potentially fatal

If the gums look pale or bluish, the dog may be in shock

1 Hide and secure all electrical cords, especially from puppies, and unplug electrical appliances when not in use. If you see the dog chewing an electrical cord, command, "Drop it!" and pull out the plug.

2 If a dog gets a minor electric shock, examine the inside of its mouth and lips for burns. If you see any, flush them with cool water. Take the dog to a vet. Switch off the electricity before touching a dog that has suffered a major electric shock. Contact a vet at once.

GASTRIC TORSION

Gas builds up in stomach and cannot escape

Recognizing bloat
Deep-chested dogs risk twisting their stomachs if they play immediately after eating a large meal. The dog is lethargic and pants heavily. Bloat leads to collapse and fatal shock.

EMERGENCY ACTION

Gastric torsion is a critical condition that requires immediate veterinary treatment. This is a situation where a few minutes can make the difference between life and death. If action is not taken immediately the dog will die. There is little that can be done in the way of first aid. Telephone a vet immediately or even leave at once while someone telephones the clinic to alert the staff that you are on your way. A vet may be able to correct the gastric torsion by immediate surgery.

SEIZURES

Treating a seizure
Seizures vary from mild behavioral quirks such as a dog snapping at nonexistent flies, to dramatic convulsions with back arching and salivation. Make the dog comfortable. Eliminate noise and reduce lighting. Clear the dog's airway and make sure the tongue is not blocking the throat, but take care that you are not bitten. Contact a vet at once.

SCALDS AND BURNS

1 Most burns are caused by boiling water or oil. Treat minor burns by applying cold water immediately to the affected area. Follow it with an icepack.

2 Once the affected area has been cooled, apply antiseptic skin cream and contact a vet. Try to keep the wound clean. Do not apply ointment to serious burns.

WHELPING PROBLEMS

Big breeds, such as the Labrador Retriever, which produce large litters of quite small puppies, have fewer whelping problems than small breeds such as terriers, which have small litters or quite large puppies. Large-headed breeds such as bulldogs often have more difficulty giving birth than do other breeds.

To prepare for labor, gather a supply of towels, thread for tying off umbilical cords, and a safe disinfectant for your hands. When your dog goes into labor, contact a vet so that he is prepared for possible problems. Try not to interfere with whelping unless it is absolutely necessary. In some circumstances, however, you may have to assist with the birth, or even hand-rear a puppy *(see page 271).*

LABOR PROBLEMS

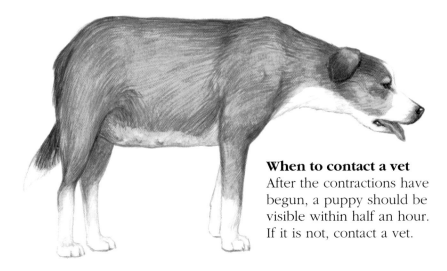

When to contact a vet
After the contractions have begun, a puppy should be visible within half an hour. If it is not, contact a vet.

EMERGENCY ACTION

A bitch should produce a puppy within two hours of the water bag breaking. The next puppies may arrive at intervals ranging from several minutes to two hours in length. Contact a vet if the bitch has been straining unproductively for more than half an hour, since the puppies may be too large for the mother to deliver. The vet may recommend a Cesarean section, in which an incision is made in the abdomen and the puppies removed by hand.

ASSISTING WITH THE BIRTH

1 Puppies are usually born headfirst in a diving position, or tail and hind legs first. If the mother is having difficulty, you can gently pull out the exposed puppy as the mother strains. If only the legs appear, call the vet.

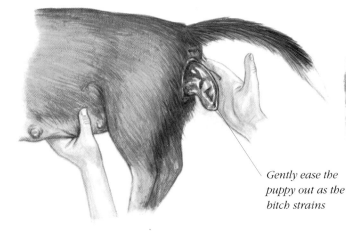

Gently ease the puppy out as the bitch strains

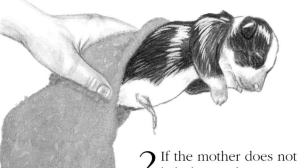

2 If the mother does not lick the newborn puppy clean, remove the membrane from its face and clear fluid from its nose and mouth. Rub it vigorously with a towel to stimulate its first breath. Do not handle the newborn puppy more than is necessary.

HELPING A WEAK PUPPY

2 If, after rubbing the puppy with a towel, it is still not breathing, suspend it by its hind legs for a few seconds to allow fluids to drain from the air passages. Keeping a secure grip on the puppy's hind legs, shake it gently. This should stimulate it to start breathing.

1 If a puppy looks normal but appears weak or lifeless, massage it with a towel, especially around the head and chest. Prolonged time in the birth canal results in a lack of oxygen to the brain.

Suspend puppy by hind legs

4 When whelping has finished, show the weak puppy to its mother and make sure it finds a productive teat. Watch it for a few days to ensure it is not bullied by stronger puppies.

3 Once the puppy is breathing, keep it warm by wrapping it in a towel until the mother has finished giving birth.

3 The mother should chew through the umbilical cord. If she does not, tie off the cord with thread about 2 in (5 cm) from the puppy's belly, then cut it on the opposite side of the knot, away from the puppy. Do not pull on the umbilical cord.

4 The mother may reject the puppy if it is taken away, so allow her to lick the puppy. Place it where it can suckle.

Chapter 10

SHOWING

DOG SHOWS are not simply for professional breeders. Anyone who enjoys the company of canines can find a suitable show. At formal conformation shows, purebred dogs are compared to a breed standard, which is a list of ideal characteristics for a perfect specimen of each breed. Only registered pedigree dogs may be entered at this type of show. In other competitions, both mixed breeds and purebreds compete in agility, retrieval work, obedience, or simply for the waggiest tail. There are even ball-catching and frisbee championships. The competition is always intense and it requires a lot of training and preparation to produce a prizewinning dog. Although the material rewards are few, the dogs seem to have as much fun as their human owners.

DOG SHOWS AND COMPETITIONS

In the 1830s and 1840s, when dogfighting and bull-baiting became illegal, dog shows developed because owners still wanted to display their dogs. Small, local events held in public houses soon caught on, and the first organized show was held in 1859 at Newcastle-upon-Tyne in England. The earliest North American show took place in the city of Québec, in 1867.

At first, with no breed standards, there was much controversy, since dogs were judged according to different rules at each show. Gradually, local breed societies were set up to oversee shows, and breeders began producing dogs that conformed to specific standards of size, shape, and bone structure.

EARLY DOG SHOWS

19th-century show
Early shows had few rules, and the dogs did not even have to be properly trained in obedience and ringcraft. The result was often a melée of excited and uncontrollable dogs. This sketch by Louis Wain shows one of the earliest competitions to be organized by the British Kennel Club, held in London in 1890.

KENNEL CLUBS

The Kennel Club of Great Britain was set up in 1873 to register the standards of each breed and to oversee dog shows. In 1884, the American Kennel Club was formed to register purebred dogs and to set the rules for dog shows and other forms of competition. The Canadian Kennel Club was set up in 1888.

International show *(left)*
Before pedigree breed standards and classes were established by a recognized organization, dogs of all kinds could compete against each other. In this print, dogs from all over the world compete in a show held at the Agricultural Hall, Islington, London in 1865

MODERN COMPETITIONS

Herding trials *(left)*

In these popular competitions, working sheepdogs compete against each other to herd and pen a flock of sheep in the shortest possible time. The dogs are controlled by a handler using a whistle or hand signals and voice commands. The sheepdogs are penalized for disobeying any command or not performing a maneuver cleanly.

Field trials *(right)*

Field trials give sporting dogs a chance to show off their skills. They compete under normal field conditions to scent, locate, or retrieve dummies on land and in water, according to the type of work for which they were bred.

Agilty competitions *(left)*

In agility competitions, dogs negotiate an obstacle course to show their fitness, speed, and training. All kinds of dogs can compete in these events. Tunnels, inclines, seesaws, and hurdles are all used to test the dog's physical and mental agility.

Obedience contests *(right)*

Different breeds and mixed breeds can all compete in obedience competitions. The dogs are required to perform basic obedience tests, such as sitting, lying down, and coming when called. You may need to do some research to determine the correct type and level of competition for you and your dog.

JUDGING SHOW DOGS

HOW DOGS ARE JUDGED

Show dogs are judged against a breed standard, which is a list of features maintained by the kennel club of each country, specifying the attributes of a perfect dog of each breed. No dog can match all these characteristics, but judges look for the dogs that come as close as possible to the breed standard.

A dog is judged on its body shape, general appearance, coat color, temperament, and the way it stands and moves in the show ring.

Smooth-haired Dachshund

Originally bred for hunting small mammals, this dog has a long body and very short legs.

Head
Long and conical, with tapering nose. Ears touch cheeks.

Body
Long and muscular, with straight back. Body should clear ground.

Coat
Short and dense, with supple skin and no wrinkles. Colors vary.

Legs and feet
Set well-apart, straight and parallel, with hard muscles on forelegs.

Tail
Without pronounced curves or kinks. Should not touch ground when at rest.

Body
Deep chest, straight back, and sloping hindquarters. Body length should be greater than shoulder height.

German Shepherd Dog

This intelligent and lively breed has a powerful body, and the ability to scent and chase for long distances.

Tail
Long and bushy. Hangs when the dog is at rest, but should be carried slightly raised when moving.

Head
Wedge-shaped, straight muzzle should be about half total length of skull.

Coat
Thick undercoat covered with dense, straight hair. Longer hair on backs of legs. Color can be black, black and tan, gray, or sable. White markings permissible in Canada.

Legs and feet
Forelegs should be longer than chest depth. Well-muscled hind legs and compact feet.

Samoyed

This hardy working dog is descended from northern European spitz breeds. It was originally bred for working in inhospitable, cold climates.

Tail
Long with profuse hair. It should be carried over the back or on one side when the dog is alert, and lower when it is resting.

Head
Broad skull, with medium-length muzzle. Erect ears are set wide and well haired. Mouth has characteristic "smile."

Body
Deep, fairly broad chest. Back should be muscular and straight. Strong, powerful loins.

Legs and feet
Straight, muscular legs. Well-feathered feet.

Coat
Thick, short undercoat. Weather-resistant outer coat should be straight and harsh, but not wiry. Color can be white, biscuit, or cream.

Miniature Schnauzer

The Miniature Schnauzer was bred in southern Germany as a barnyard ratter.

Fault
The back should be straight and the tail carried high. A curved back is a serious fault.

Coat
Dense undercoat and harsh, wiry outer coat. Short hair on shoulders and neck, and longer hair on legs. Color can be salt-and-pepper or black.

Head
Muzzle should taper to blunt, black nose with wide nostrils. Prominent mustache and eyebrows. Dark eyes set forward. High, V-shaped ears when uncropped.

Tail
High tail historically docked. In many countries, tail docking is now banned.

Body
Deep, broad chest with strong breastbone. Strong back should be straight, rising slightly higher at shoulders than at hindquarters. Length of body should be same as height at top of withers.

Legs and feet
Strong and straight, with muscular, slanting thighs. Compact feet, arched toes, and dark nails.

TAKING PART IN A SHOW

There are many types of dog shows, each with its own rules, but the basic procedure for entering a show is the same whether it is a championship, open, exemption, or local event.

There are several important things to remember before entering any show. Your dog must be in excellent health, with all its vaccinations up to date, since it may be exposed to contagious diseases at a show or pass on ailments to the other dogs. It must also have an immaculate general appearance, resulting from grooming all year long. No artificial cosmetic aids, such as coat dye, are allowed.

Your dog must also be well trained in ringcraft so that it does not disrupt the other entrants, and so that you can concentrate on showing it to its full advantage without worrying about controlling bad behavior.

ARRIVING AT THE SHOW

Settling in (above)
When you arrive at the show, both you and your dog will probably be excited. Be sure to check on when your class will compete and where. Find some place to wait with your dog. Your dog can remain in its travel kennel. You and your dog will do best if you can relax before going into the ring.

Grooming (above)
Grooming paraphernalia can range from a nail trimmer and brush for shorthaired breeds to dry shampoo, clippers, comb, anti-tangle conditioner, and grooming table for those dogs with a more demanding coat.

SHOW EQUIPMENT

Benching chain

Number clip

Collar and name tag

You will need a show leash, a kennel crate, and food and water bowls. A dog's collar will normally be removed during a show. In some countries, a benching chain is used to secure the dog when it is not in the ring.

THE JUDGING PROCEDURE

Standing (right)

Be ready to enter the ring when your number is called. Once in the ring, set your dog in its stance on a level piece of ground for the judge to make an assessment. Adjust the dog's legs and tail with as little interference as possible.

Judging (left)

A dog should stand still and remain calm when the judge examines it. Keep the dog still with its head held up to present it correctly. The judge is looking for a healthy, good-tempered dog that matches the official breed standard.

Gaiting (below)

The judge will want to see the dog's "gait" or movement. You may be asked to trot the dog in a triangle so that the judge can watch how it moves from the side, in front, and behind. An experienced show dog should move smoothly and in a straight line. Depending on the size of the dog, you may need to move at a fast walk or run.

Show classes (above)

Dogs of each breed compete in one of five different classes at a dog show: puppy, novice, bred-by-exhibitor, American-bred, and open.

Best of breed (right)

The winners of each class compete for the best-of-breed title. At an all-breed show, winners go on to compete for best in group, and then best in show.

GLOSSARY

Abscess Collection of pus forming painful swelling.
Acquired disorder Condition or illness that develops after birth.
Action Way in which a dog moves.
Acute Condition occurring suddenly and rapidly. *See also* Chronic.
Albino Lack of pigment melanin, causing white fur and pink eyes.
Alopecia Baldness.
Anestrus Not in estrus.
Anorexia Loss of appetite.
Anuria Passing no urine.
Anus Outlet of the rectum.
Ascariasis Infestation of worms.
Aural Pertaining to the ear.
Autoimmune disease Condition in which body destroys its own tissues.

Balanitis Infection of the penis.
Bay Characteristic bark of a hound.
Best in show Top award at show.
Best of breed Award given to best specimen of each breed at show.
Bitch Female dog.
Blue eye Clouding of the eye, caused by inflammation of the cornea.
Boarding kennel Establishment that boards dogs while owners are away.
Brachycephalic Dogs with short noses and pushed-in faces, such as the Pekingese and Pug.
Breed Type of pedigree dog whose characteristics are transmitted from generation to generation.
Breed standard Description of ideal characteristics against which dogs are judged at shows. Determined by national dog society of each country.
Breeding kennel Place where purebred dogs are mated to preserve the breed.

Carcinoma Malignant cancer in the skin or internal organs of the body.
Cardiac Pertaining to the heart.
Castrate To surgically remove male dog's testicles to prevent reproduction.
Chromosomes Tiny strands of DNA and protein that store genetic information.
Chronic Condition that continues or recurs over a period of time, rather than developing suddenly. *See also* Acute.
Cleft palate Deformity of puppies, in which two sides of the skull do not join together properly.
Clinical signs Symptoms or signs that are visible to the naked eye.
Coat Hair that covers a dog's body.
Collie eye anomaly Inherited disease of retina, found in collie breeds.
Conformation Structure and form of the framework of a dog.
Congenital disorder Condition that is present at birth, not necessarily inherited.

Conjunctivitis Inflammation of the thin outer layer of the eye and the lining of eyelids, causing watering and soreness.
Cropping Trimming ears for medical or cosmetic reasons. Cropping for cosmetic reasons is illegal in many countries.
Crossbreed A first-generation cross between two different pedigree breeds.
Cryptorchid Male with neither testicle descended.
Cyst Liquid-filled sac that arises through disease or infection.
Cystitis Bladder infection.

Dam Mother of a litter of puppies.
Dermatitis An inflammation of the skin.
Dermatology Study of diseases of the skin and their treatment.
Dewclaw Extra toe on inside of the legs above paw. Often removed by surgery when a puppy is a few days old.
Dewlap Flap of skin that hangs beneath the throat of some breeds.
Diabetes insipidus Disease of the pituitary gland in which the body cannot concentrate urine properly.
Diabetes mellitus Excess sugar in the blood due to malfunctioning pancreas.
Distemper Contagious viral disease, fatal if left untreated.
Distichiasis Ingrown eyelashes.
DNA Deoxyribonucleic acid, the substance that makes up genes. *See also* Chromosomes *and* Gene
Docking Cutting the tail for medical or cosmetic reasons when a puppy is a few days old. Docking for cosmetic reasons is illegal in many countries.
Dog show Exhibition of dogs in which animals are judged against a recognized breed standard.
Dominant gene The gene that overrides a recessive gene so that its characteristics are evident in the offspring.
Double coat Undercoat plus longer outer coat.
Dry eye Lack of lubrication in the eye, leading to infection and inflammation.

Ear mites Tiny parasites that live in the ear canal, causing irritation.
Eclampsia Calcium deficiency, often suffered by lactating bitches.
Ectropion Condition resulting from outward-turning eyelids.
Elizabethan collar Cardboard or plastic funnel fitted over the head to keep a dog from interfering with stitches or wounds.
Entropion Condition resulting in inward-turning eyelids. The eyelashes irritate the eyeball.
Epiphora Watery eyes.

Estrus Periods during which female dog is sexually responsive to males, commonly known as heat or season.
Even bite When upper and lower teeth meet without any overlap.

Feathering Long, fine fringe of hair on ears, legs, tail, and body.
Feral Domestic animals that have reverted to a wild state.
Field trial Outdoor competition in which dogs are judged for their tracking, pointing, or retrieving abilities.
Flank Side of a dog's body between last rib and hip.
Flea collar Special collar impregnated with chemicals to kill fleas.
Fleas The most common external parasite living on a dog's skin and feeding on its blood. Dogs are sometimes sensitive to flea bites or droppings.
Flukes Parasites found in intestines and liver, causing diarrhea and anemia.
Fringe *See* Feathering.

Gait Style of a dog's movement.
Gastritis Inflammation of stomach walls, causing vomiting and reluctance to eat.
Gastroenteritis Infection causing vomiting and diarrhea.
Gene Segment of DNA on chromosomes that carries information on physical characteristics, such as coat color and eye color.
Gingivitis Inflammation of gums at edge of teeth, caused by tartar buildup.
Glaucoma Enlargement of eyeball caused by increased pressure.
Groom To brush and comb a dog's coat.
Guard hairs Long, stiff hairs that extend beyond the undercoat.

Halitosis Bad breath.
Harvest mites Parasites that appear in the autumn and cause skin irritation.
Heartworms Parasites living in the heart. Larvae are transmitted by mosquitoes.
Heat *See* Estrus.

Heimlich maneuver The manual application of sudden upward pressure on the upper abdomen of a choking victim to force a foreign object from the windpipe.
Hematoma Blood blister, often in ear flap, where it is caused by head shaking.
Hereditary disorder Condition passed down through generations, via genetic information on chromosomes.
Hip dysplasia Hereditary condition of certain breeds causing lameness.
Hock Central, back joint on hind leg.
Hookworms Blood-sucking worms that live in the small intestine.
House breaking Training a dog not to soil the house.

Inbreeding Breeding of dogs that are closely related.
Incisors Upper and lower front teeth.
Interbreeding Crossbreeding of different varieties of dog.

Jaundice In dogs, yellow color of gums, caused by liver disease.
Jowls Fleshy parts of mouth.

Kennel cough Infectious disorder of respiratory system.
Keratitis Clouding of the eye, caused by inflammation of the cornea.

Lens luxation Condition in which lens drops out of normal position in eye.
Lice Parasites that suck blood, causing anemia in a severe infestation.
Litter Puppies born in a single whelping. Size of litter varies according to breed.
Lyme disease Transmitted to humans by ticks. Causes swollen lymph glands, fever, and joint inflammation.

Malocclusion Misaligned bite.
Mange mites Minute parasites that burrow into a dog's skin, causing chronic hair loss, irritation, and inflammation.
Mastitis Inflammation of milk glands.

Melanoma Dark, pigmented tumor.
Milk fever *See* Eclampsia.
Milk teeth First teeth. Puppies usually lose them between the ages of four and six months.
Mixed breed Dog of unknown parentage.
Monorchid Male with only one testicle descended.
Muzzle Front part of the head.

Neuter To castrate males or spay females to prevent reproduction and unwanted sexual behavior.
Nictitating membrane *See* Third eyelid.

Otitis externa Inflammation of the outer ear, caused by mites, bacteria, or foreign bodies. Also known as canker.
Otitis interna Infection of the inner ear.
Otitis media Infection of the middle ear.
Outcross Use of a totally unrelated pedigree dog for breeding purposes.
Overshot Jaw where the upper incisors extend past the lower ones.

Paraphimosis Condition in which the penis cannot be withdrawn into sheath.
Pedigree A record of ancestry, showing a family tree over several generations.
Poodle eye Condition in breeds such as poodles, in which tears stain the face.
Progressive retinal atrophy Inherited disorder causing loss of sight.
Prolapse Condition in which an internal organ is pushed through to the outside.
Prostatitis Condition in which a male's prostate gland is enlarged, causing constipation or urinary problems.
Pruritus Itchiness.
Purebred Dog whose parents are of the same breed and of unmixed descent.
Pyometra Pus in the womb.

Quarantine Period of time for which animals entering certain countries, such as Great Britain and Australia, must be isolated to prevent the spread of rabies.

Rabies Fatal viral disease affecting nervous system. Usually transmitted through a bite from an infected animal.
Recessive gene One whose characteristics are overridden by a dominant gene in each pairing of chromosomes, so that it is not evident in the features of the resulting offspring.
Register List of pedigree dogs. In order to enter shows, purebred dogs must be registered upon birth with the national dog authority.
Ringworm Form of fungal infection that causes scaly skin and mild irritation.

Roundworms Parasites that live in a dog's digestive tract, feeding on digesting food. Can cause diarrhea.

Scent marking A dog marks its territory with urine or with scent from special glands in the face and paws, sending a clear message to other dogs.
Season *See* Estrus.
Selective breeding Breeding of pedigree dogs by planned matings to enhance certain physical characteristics, such as coat color and body shape.
Spay To surgically remove bitch's ovaries and uterus to prevent estrus and unwanted pregnancy.
Sporting dogs Breeds of dog that were traditionally used to find live game and retrieve shot game.
Stifle Hind leg above the hock.
Strip To remove hair on a wire-coated dog with a stripping knife.
Stud Pedigree male dog used for breeding. Owner usually charges fee.

Tapeworms Intestinal parasites that feed on a dog's partly digested food.
Terrier Small dog traditionally bred to go to ground after small game.
Territory Area considered by a dog to be its own, usually garden or house. A dog may defend its territory against intruders.
Third eyelid Filmy lid that is sometimes visible at the corner of a dog's eye.
Ticks Parasites that bury their heads in a dog's skin to feed on its blood. Some types of tick can transmit diseases.
Trauma Shock, injury, or wound.
Tumor Abnormal growth of tissue. Can be benign (local) or malignant (having the ability to spread elsewhere).

Undercoat Dense second coat that is hidden by the topcoat.
Undershot Jaw where the lower incisors overlap the upper incisors.

Weaning Gradual change in a puppy's diet from its mother's milk to solid food.
Whelping Act of giving birth.
Whiskers Long hair on muzzle and jaw.
Wire-haired Rough-coated dog.
Withers Highest point of the shoulders, from where a dog's height is measured.
Wobbler syndrome Nervous disorder caused by a neck vertebra rotating. Results in partial paralysis.

X-chromosome Chromosome responsible for development of female characteristics.

Y-chromosome Chromosome responsible for development of male characteristics.

Zoonoses Diseases that can be passed between vertebrate species, including humans. Rabies is by far the most dangerous. *See also* Rabies.

Additional Information

USEFUL ADDRESSES

American Boarding Kennels Association
4575 Galley Road,
Suite 400A,
Colorado Springs,
Colorado 80915

American Humane Society
P.O. Box 3597,
Englewood,
Colorado 80155

The American Kennel Club (AKC)
51 Madison Avenue,
New York,
New York 10010

American Society for the Prevention of Cruelty to Animals (ASPCA)
424 East 92nd. Street,
New York,
New York 10128

American Veterinary Medical Association
1931 North Meacham Road,
Schaumberg,
Illinois 60173

Assistance Dog Institute
421 East Cotati Avenue
Cotati, CA 94931-4000

Delta Society
P.O. Box 1080,
Renton,
Washington 98057

Humane Society of the United States
2100 L Street, NW,
Washington,
DC 20037

United Kennel Club
100 East Kilgore Road,
Kalamazoo,
Michigan 49001

FURTHER READING

Periodicals

Dog Fancy
P.O. Box 53264,
Boulder,
Colorado 80322

Dog World
29 North Wacker Drive,
Chicago,
Illinois 60606

Groom and Board
207 S. Wabash Avenue,
Suite 504,
Chicago,
Illinois 60604

Purebred Dogs/American Kennel Gazette
American Kennel Club,
51 Madison Avenue,
New York,
New York 10010

FURTHER READING

American Kennel Club Staff, *The Complete Dog* Howell Book, 1992
Benjamin, Carol, *Secondhand Dog,* Howell Book, 1988
Caras, Roger, *A Dog is Listening,* Summit Books, 1992
Caras, Roger, *The Roger Caras Dog Book,* 2nd. Edition, Marboro Books, 1992
Evans, Job Michael, *The Evans Guide for Housetraining Your Dog,* Howell Book, 1987
Fogle, Bruce, *The Dog's Mind,* Pelham Books, 1990
Kay, William, & Randolph, Elizabeth, *The Complete Book of Dog Health,* Macmillan, 1985
Milani, Myrna M., D.V.M., *The Invisible Leash,* Signet, 1985
Monks of New Skete, *The Art of Raising a Puppy,* Little, Brown, and Company, 1991
The Reader's Digest Illustrated Book of Dogs, 1988
Taylor, David, *The Ultimate Dog,* Dorling Kindersley Ltd., 1990
Taylor, David, *You & Your Dog,* Alfred A. Knopf, Inc., 1991
Tortora, Daniel, *The Right Dog for You,* Fireside Books, 1980
Volhard & Bartlett, *What All Good Dogs Should Know,* Howell Book, 1991

Index

ACKNOWLEDGMENTS

SECTION ONE

Author's acknowledgments

Now that you've read the book, you'll understand how much fun it was to produce. Imagine working with the variety of dogs in these pictures! I feel more proprietorial about this book than any other. I've known David Ward, the photographer, for 12 years. He's my head nurse's husband. I know almost every dog in the book, because they're patients, and I know several especially well. Edwin, the Boxer, comes to work with her owner, Amanda Topp, one of my veterinary nurses. The Italian Spinones, Badger and Hattie, also live their days at my veterinary clinic. They belong to my other nurse, Jenny Berry. And you might notice a couple of Golden Retrievers appearing here and there with their female owner. They're all mine! Thanks to all of them, and to Ashley McManus, another nurse who worked so willingly on the book.

If you think we enjoyed the photo sessions, the dogs loved them even more. We made sure that nothing unpleasant happened. All the dogs showing aggression were chosen because they would turn it on and off at their owners' commands. And for all the sequences on dominance and submission we had a superb dog handler and trainer, Colin Tennant, present.

Editorial teams can sometimes be dispassionate about assignments. Not so this team. Krystyna Mayer brought her best friend's Akita to a shoot and willingly got slobbered on. Roger Smoothy was there each week, graciously allowing dogs to fantasize that he was a fire hydrant, and Candida Ross-Macdonald whizzed in when Roger was called off to another assignment. All the while, Nigel Hazle told us about the joys of parenthood and drolly commented that we, and he, were all nuts. Thanks to all of them for their enjoyable company, and to Derek Coombes for saying "yes" whenever we asked questions. Finally, I hope my parents enjoy showing this one, too, to their friends.

Dorling Kindersley would like to thank

Roger Smoothy for planning and attending photographic sessions, and initial editorial work; Vanessa Hamilton for design assistance; Mary Ann Lynch for Americanization; Janos Marffy for airbrushing; Nylabone Ltd. for plastic chews and toys; The Company of Animals Ltd. for toys; Jenny Berry for help with dogs and photography, and all the owners who brought their dogs along – there are far too many to name individually, but our thanks go out to all.

KEY: l = left, r = right, t = top, b = bottom, c = center
Illustrations
Rowan Clifford p.12-13 wolves
Janos Marffy p.12-13 map

Photographic credits

All photography by David Ward except for:
Jane Burton p.22 tl, p.71 br, p.94-119; Bruce Coleman Ltd. p.12 cl, c, p.13 cb, tr, p.17 ct, p.23 br, p.45 tr, p. 55 tr, p.69 tr, p.115 ct; Dave King p.115 b; Lynn Rogers p.35 br, p.39 c, p.47 br, p.51 tr, p.59 br, p.60 cb, p.75 tr, p.80 bl, p.107 tr; Steve Shott p.16 t; Jerry Young p.13 ct.

SECTION TWO

Author's acknowledgments

This might look like a book to you, but it is really a jigsaw puzzle in which a team of people work together, neatly and efficiently, to finish the puzzle. Thanks to Alison Melvin, Nigel Hazle, Lynn Parr, and Hazel Taylor for their day-to-day planning, and to the photographers, Tim Ridley, Andy Crawford, and Steve Gorton for their superb work. Like parents not wanting to interfere with the developing child, but all the while keeping a close eye on what we were doing, were Krystyna Mayer, the Managing Editor, and Derek Coombes, the Managing Art Editor. Like a grandparent, David Lamb, the Editorial Director, organized lunches and made sure everyone was happy. And like Banquo's ghost, Peter Kindersley, the Chairman, kept a hawk's eye on everyone. Thanks to them all. The system works.

My gratitude also to my clients who offered their model dogs; to my nurses Jenny Berry, Amanda Topp, and Ashley McManus for finding some of the models (including their own – Winnie the Boxer puppy living permanently under my receptionist's desk); and to Dr. Ivan Burger at the Waltham Centre for Pet Nutrition, who cheerfully faxed me answers to any questions I asked of him. And, finally, special thanks to Andrew Edney, who, by writing the *ASPCA Complete Cat Care Manual*, saved us all from walking down many dead ends.

Publisher's acknowledgments

Dorling Kindersley would like to thank the following:
Atalanta De Bendern (Semi Soul Dancing); Rosemary Baker (Ben); Jenny Berry (Mr. Badger and Hattie); Rowan Clifford (William); Sandra Dunne (Tanya); Kate Forey (Daisy); Bruce Fogle (Lexington); Maggi Fox (Archie and Angus); Mrs. Guy (Buster); Fil Manning (Scampy); Danuta Mayer (Gip and Bilbo); Anita McCarthy (Gunner); Mrs. Murkett (Luke, Sam, and Nike); Loretta Nobes (Dawn and puppies); Christina Oates (Cloud the Burmese cat); Peter's Posh Pets (Dizzy, Fifi, Beryl, Dilly, and Chippie); Paolo Pimental (Islay); Angela Ratner (Lizzie); June Raymond (Rocky); Colin Tennant (Spike, Huxley, Nelson, Holly, Claude, and Rufus); Amanda Topp (Edwin and Winnie); Hazel Taylor (Maisey and Zak); Samantha Ware (Jaffa, Flynn, Jace, Percy, Ginnie, and Jessie); Mrs Williams (Genghis); Andrew Woodhead (Rex). Kate Forey, Barnabas Kindersley, Nina Fortnam, Rachel Simm, and Colin Tennant for modeling and dog handling. Animal Fair, Kensington; Jennifer Corker; and The Company of Animals for supplying equipment and materials. Diana Morris for picture research. Colette Cheng for design assistance.
Dorling Kindersley also wish to thank Terence C. Bate BVSc, LLB, MRCVS of the RSPCA for his advice on the text.

ASPCA acknowledgments

Numerous staff and friends provided special assistance, helping to research and review material for this publication. Most especially: Gordon Robinson, VMD; Jane Bicks, DVM; Mickey Niego, Jacque Schultz, and Liz Teal.

KEY: t *top*, b *bottom*, c *center*, l *left*, r *right*
Illustrations
Rowan Clifford: pp 185cr, 232t, 244, 265b, 275t, 276–277, 278–279, 280–281, 284–285, 286–287, 288–289, 292–293, 294–295
Angelica Elsebach: pp 275cr, 275b, 282–283, 290–291
Chris Forsey: pp 134–135, 164bl, 218, 220, 222, 224, 226, 228, 230, 232b, 234, 236, 238, 240, 242, 246, 267
Jane Pickering: pp 164–165
Photography
All photography by Tim Ridley, Andy Crawford, and Steve Gorton except for: Animal Photography: Sally Ann Thompson 167cl, 299cl, 303bl; R. Wilibie 302br; Animals Unlimited: 297br, 303t; Sarah Ashun: 302t, 303cl, 303br; Jane Burton: 236t, 246t; Bruce Coleman Ltd.: Peter F.R. Jackson 135cr; Johnny Johnson 134bc; Hans Reinhard 135tl; Hazel Edington: 164t; E.T. Archive: 133tl, 133tr, 133b; Mary Evans Picture Library: 298t, 298bl; Guide Dogs for the Blind Assoc.: 143tr; Marc Henrie: 299t, 299b, 303cr; Michael Holford: 132bl, 132br; Images Colour Library: 132t; Dave King: 124–5, 131t, 131b, 134, 135, 136t, 136br, 137bl, 138t, 139b, 141b, 143tl, 143br, 144br, 145, 147b, 148t, 149tl, 149cr, 182, 183t, 183bl, 211t, 211cr, 214–215, 218b, 236b, 296–297, 297cr, 300, 301; Natural History Photographic Agency: David Tomlinson 299cr; David Ward: 130–131, 136bl, 137t, 138b, 140t, 140cl, 141t, 141c, 142t, 143bl, 144t, 144cl, 147t, 148bl, 149tr, 160t, 162t, 162c, 162bl, 163t, 163c, 167br, 168b, 169tl, 169bl, 170–71, 171b, 174, 175b, 178bl, 216bl, 220t, 228b, 230, 232b, 238, 240b, 242b, 258t, 304–305, 307b; Wood Green Animal Shelters: 149bl; Jerry Young: 134bl, 137c, 137br, 140b, 143cl, 149br, 171c

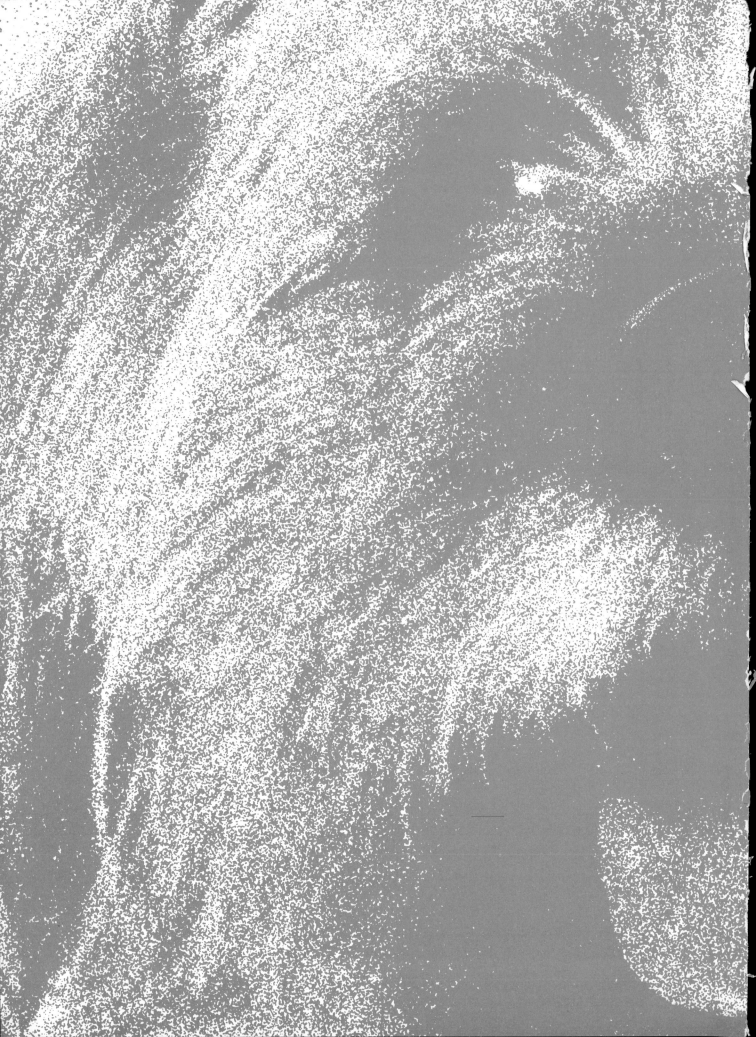